Annett Gräfe-Geusch
Aiming for Diversity

Research in Social Difference,
Education, and Culture

Edited by
Jürgen Budde

Volume 20

Studien zu Differenz, Bildung und Kultur

herausgegeben von
Jürgen Budde

Band 20

Annett Gräfe-Geusch

Aiming for Diversity
Inclusive and Exclusive Logics on Ethno-Religious Diversity in Berlin's Secondary Schools

Verlag Barbara Budrich
Opladen • Berlin • Toronto 2025

All rights reserved. No part of this publication may be reproduced, stored in or introduced into a retrieval system, or transmitted, in any form, or by any means (electronic, mechanical, photocopying, recording or otherwise) without the prior written permission of Verlag Barbara Budrich. Any person who does any unauthorized act in relation to this publication may be liable to criminal prosecution and civil claims for damages.

You must not circulate this book in any other binding or cover and you must impose this same condition on any acquirer.

A CIP catalogue record for this book is available from
Die Deutsche Nationalbibliothek (The German National Library):
https://portal.dnb.de.

Carbon compensated production

© 2025 by Verlag Barbara Budrich GmbH, Opladen, Berlin & Toronto

    ISBN   978-3-8474-3143-5 (Paperback)
    eISBN   978-3-8474-3280-7 (PDF)
    DOI   10.3224/84743143

Verlag Barbara Budrich GmbH
Stauffenbergstr. 7. D-51379 Leverkusen Opladen, Germany | info@budrich.de |
www.budrich.de

86 Delma Drive. Toronto, ON M8W 4P6 Canada | info@budrich.de | www.budrich.eu

Cover design by Bettina Lehfeldt, Kleinmachnow – www.lehfeldtgraphic.de
Typographic editing by Anja Borkam, Langenhagen – kontakt@lektorat-borkam.de
Printed in Europe on FSC®-certified paper by Libri Plureos, Hamburg

Acknowledgments

This project would not have been possible without the support of many individuals. First, I have to thank my family for their support in this endeavor. My husband, Steffen, was my rock, my unwavering support system throughout data collection and writing. He cheered me on when I felt like giving up. He gave me a sounding board for ideas and problems I encountered. And most importantly he believed in me. I am equally thankful to have my daughter, Emma, who in her own way helped me to write this book. She brought joy, laughter, and an unending optimism and quizzicality into my life, making even the most frustrating setbacks and writing days worth the while. I love you both and am eternally grateful to have you in my life. I also have to thank, Reni and Manfred Geusch for being amazing grandparents to Emma, providing childcare, and making it possible for me to present my findings at conferences around the world.

I also must thank my fantastic committee Dana Burde, Cynthia Miller-Idriss and James Fraser for their support and patience. I thank Dana Burde for taking me on, affording me the opportunity to work with her, and for reminding me to streamline my arguments and chapters, and for providing amazingly detailed feedback. I thank Cynthia for her great big picture lens on my work which helped me to refocus and reshape the overall arguments in this study. I also thank her for cheering on my progress and being a source of motivation and positivity throughout. Jim's history and religion lens, his critical comments and intriguing questions pushed this work forward and made its analysis and conclusions more detailed and nuanced. Each of them read many drafts and sections, provided valuable feedback and asked questions that made me think even harder about my analysis and findings. All of them dedicated many hours of their time to my work and each of them shaped this research in their own ways and without them this would not have been possible.

The NYU community and especially the ASH doctoral students with whom I shared this journey were tremendously important in my life and my work. I have to thank Grace Pai and Ozen Guven for being my first friends at NYU and supporting me through course work and conferences. Equally important are Jo Kelcey and Heddy Lahmann, who read every bit of this work in multiple drafts sometimes the same day and provided amazing comments, feedback, and edits. The International Ed Doctoral Student Seminar and Dr. Elisabeth Kind read tons of drafts, chapters, and journal articles and made this study much better through their feedback. I also must thank Jon Friedman, Noah Kippley-Ogman, Ali Wood, Naomi Moland and the many others with whom I shared conversations, concerns and laughs. Beyond NYU, I have to thank Stefan Beljean for his feedback on early drafts, and the participants of the 2019 Georg Arnhold Summer School for their comments and feedback on my work especially Simona Szakács-Behling, the Humboldt University Comparative and International Education Research Colloquium for reading and providing feedback on chapter five, and the Consensus and conflict department at the German Center for Integration and Migration Research (DeZIM) and especially Sabrina Zajak for providing a rich environment for thought.

For financial support I must thank the Shearwater foundation for various research and conference travel grants. I also must thank NYU's global Research Initiative Fellowship for its generous support and the fantastic office space in Berlin. This project was also supported by the Steinhardt Doctoral Student Fellowship and Scholarship. I also must thank the Georg Eckert Institute for their support and the time and space to finish writing. Finally, I have to thank the teachers that opened their classrooms to me and shared their perspectives. Without them this study would not have been possible.

Table of Contents

Acknowledgments 5

List of Figures and Tables 11

1 Toward a Post-migrant Society? German Political Actors between Inclusion and Exclusion 13
   1.1 Integrating Diversity? The Importance of Political Actors' Negotiations 13
   1.2 Diversity, Belonging, and Violence: Situating Ethics within the larger Socio-Cultural Context 20
   1.3 The Case of Berlin 22
   1.4 Inclusion and Exclusion of Diversity in Education Policy and Practice 23
      1.4.1 Education Policy: Including Diversity in the Political Imagination 23
      1.4.2 Minority Group Academic Achievement and Teaching in Ethnically and Religiously Diverse Classrooms 25
      1.4.3 Incorporating Diversity into Teaching, Curricula, and Textbooks 26
   1.5 Diversity in German Policy and Public Opinion 27
      1.5.1 Between Inclusion and Exclusion: Immigration, Integration, and Failed Multiculturalism in Germany 28
      1.5.2 Negative Public Perception of Diversity and Growing Diverse Populations in Germany 32
   1.6 Understanding and Negotiating Logics of Diversity in Context: Research Question and Significance of the Study 33
   1.7 Overview of the Study 34

2 Teachers als Political Actors, Diversity, and Institutional Logics 38
   2.1 Understanding and Negotiating Diversity at Various Levels of Society 38
   2.2 Neo-Institutional Explanations of the Divergence between Policy and Practice 39
      2.2.1 Institutional Logics: A Way to Account for Heterogeneity and Bringing Micro and Macro Levels Together 42
      2.2.2 Conceptualizing Diversity and Power Relations within Institutional Logics 44

		2.2.3 Situating Diversity within Institutional Logics Theory: The Institutional Order of Community	47
	2.3	Teachers as Single-Level Actors: Advocating for a Multilevel Account	48
		2.3.1 Conceptualizing Teachers Liminal Position	50
	2.4	Bringing it all together: Constructing Diversity in Berlin's Mandatory Ethics Instruction	51
3	Methodology		53
	3.1	A Comparative Case Study of Diversity in Schools	53
	3.2	The Vertical Case Study Approach	54
	3.3	Sampling Strategy and Overall Sample Description	57
		3.3.1 Interview Data	60
		3.3.2 Observation Data	63
		3.3.4 Document Data	64
	3.4	Access and the Influence of the Socio-Political Context	66
	3.5	Data Analysis, Triangulation, and Validity	67
	3.6	Role of the Researcher	69
	3.7	Conclusion	69
4	Ethics and the Question of Diversity: Berlin's Quest for Value Education		71
	4.1	Value education in Berlin: A Contested Field	71
	4.2	Losing Faith: Putting Value Education on the Political Agenda	74
	4.3	Diversity Matters: The Speedy Introduction of Ethics Instruction	78
	4.4	The Last Rebellion in a Lost Culture War? The Referendum for Mandatory Religious Education	83
	4.5	Productive and Destructive Diversity	86
	4.6	Arriving at Diversity	89
5	Logics of Diversity in Ethics Teaching: Between Inclusion and Exclusion		91
	5.1	Striving for Integration	91
	5.2	Heterogeneity of Practice and Teachers as State Agents	93
	5.3	Teaching about Diversity: Exclusive and Inclusive Logics in Diverse and Non-Diverse Classrooms	95
		5.3.1 Assimilationist Teaching: Exclusion in Diverse School Contexts	96

		5.3.2 Philosophical Teaching: Exclusion in Non-Diverse School Context	99
		5.3.3 Intercultural Teaching: Inclusion in Diverse School Contexts	101
		5.3.4 Critical Teaching: Inclusion in Non-Diverse School Contexts	104
		5.3.5 Muddying the Waters: Heterogeneity and Crossing Logics within Teachers' Sense-making	107
	5.4	Creating a Peaceful Pluralistic Society: Teaching Approaches and Their Underlying Logics	108
	5.5	Political Actors and Diversity: Teaching Diversity in Ethics	110
6	The Struggle for Legitimacy: Removing the Stigma of Diversity from Classroom Teaching		111
	6.1	Reforming Berlin's Schools to Include Diversity?	111
	6.2	Legitimacy, Diversity, and Change	113
	6.3	The Challenge to Ethics' Legitimacy: Not just a Waste of Time ("Laberfach")	114
	6.4	Invoking Elements of Professional Logics for Improvement: Teaching Degrees and the Disciplinary Grounding	116
		6.4.1 Guarding the Entrance into the Profession: The Importance of the Right Degree	117
		6.4.2 Linking a Strong Disciplinary Grounding	120
		6.4.3 Linking Professional and Community Logics: The Stigma of Teaching about Diversity	122
	6.5	Changing the Idea of Ethics Instruction: From Multidisciplinary to Philosophy Instruction	125
	6.6	Finding Legitimacy and Losing Diversity?	126
7	Beyond Ethics Instruction: School Reform and Diversity Inclusion in Education		128
	7.1	Oscillating between Inclusion and Exclusion	128
	7.2	A German Identity Crisis: Continuity in Diversity Constructions between Inclusive and Exclusive Logics	130
		7.2.1 The Construction of Diversity within an Exclusive Logic	132
		7.2.2 The Construction of Diversity within an Inclusive Logic	133
	7.3	Discontinuities Between Political and Classroom Level: The Question of Gaining Legitimacy	135

7.4	The Implications of Logic Continuity and Discontinuity between Policy and Practice	137
7.5	Teaching Diversity: Towards a new Pedagogy?	139
7.6	Beyond Ethics Instruction	142

References 145

Appendix 169

Index 175

List of Figures and Tables

Figure 1:	Participation in Christian Religious Education in Percent ...	75
Figure 2:	Results of Referendum Election in Percentage by District Group	85
Table 1:	Overview of Schools in the Sample	169
Table 2:	Overview of Participants	170
Table 3:	Comprehensive Chronological Order of Events Leading to the Introduction of Ethics Education in Berlin	172

1 Toward a Post-migrant Society? German Political Actors between Inclusion and Exclusion

"Education policies must raise the value placed on intercultural skills. Our youth must learn that people with values, religions, cultural backgrounds, and ethnicities different from their own do not pose a threat to their identities."
Rita Süssmuth (2007, pp. 201–202) – Former German Federal Minister of Family Affairs, Senior Citizens, Women and Youth

1.1 Integrating Diversity? The Importance of Political Actors' Negotiations

In early September 2015, I was invited to present my research and seek participants at a teachers' conference for ethics and social sciences at a low track school in highly diverse central Berlin. The school is located on a busy street in a small cul-de-sac surrounded by apartment buildings. When I entered through the school gates the school yard was quiet compared to the busy street a few meters behind me. It was after school hours, but some students were still hanging out on school grounds, talking, playing soccer, and getting ready to go home. I entered the main building, following the signs to the main office, to meet the school's principal and walk with her to the meeting.

I knocked and entered. Only one secretary, the principal and a few teachers were present. Yet the office was buzzing with activity. Despite the low number of people and the fact that the school year had just started, the atmosphere in the office felt hectic to me, hurried, as if too many things still needed to be accomplished with no time left to actually complete them. It was quite a contrast to the calm and tranquility of the surrounding school building and school yard. The principal greeted me quickly and asked me to take a seat while she finished a few things. "There is a lot going on at the moment" she said to me. I sat down and watched her make phone calls and sign paperwork.

A few minutes later the vice principal entered and was quickly introduced to me. Both principal and vice-principal grabbed a few notepads and indicated to me that we were now leaving. Just outside the office, another administrator ran up to the vice-principal holding up paperwork. "And what should we do about him?" she asked, continuing a previous conversation I had not witnessed. We did not stop as we were already running late for the meeting. Instead, the administrator walked with us. The vice-principal replied: "Who knows if he should even be here. He looks too old to be 14, I mean he already has a beard." The administrator nodded in agreement and replied "Yes, it is hard to tell with some of them." The vice-principal elaborated, "Well, if he does not stop harassing the girls, he cannot be here." The administrator was satisfied with this answer, nodded and walked away as we continued our way to the meeting.

Guessing my puzzlement about this exchange the vice principal turned to me and explained that some of the newly arrived male refugees they had at the school were causing problems. He continued to explain that it was hard since refugees rarely had paperwork and no one knew anything about them. For all intents and purposes these youth could make things up to be counted as minors and attend school, he explained. The suspicion both the administrator and vice-principal based their conversation on was that the male student in question had lied about his age and was already beyond the law-mandated required school age of 16. The vice-principal concluded this exchange by saying, "And we have to suffer the consequences" (field notes, 9/8/2015).

This brief episode was one of my first encounters with the ramifications of the large influx of refugees that had arrived in Germany, and Berlin in particular, during the summer and fall of 2015. According to the national government (BMI and BAMF, 2016) about 890,000 new refugees came in 2015 alone. The number of asylum applications for 2015 showed an increase of 135 percent compared to the previous year (ibid, p. 9). Media coverage was dominated by images of overcrowded and underfunded refugee camps at the EU's southern borders, children that drowned during attempted crossings of the Mediterranean Sea, and large groups making their way north. Across Europe anti-refugee sentiments flared, borders were closed and policed again. Politicians negotiated new contracts to move the problem beyond Europe's borders. Later researchers would call this period the long summer of migration; to reframe the name media and politics had given it: the European migration crisis.

In Berlin, local media publications were filled with the catastrophic conditions around Berlin's registration administration. The city struggled greatly with registering, housing, and generally accommodating new arrivals to the point of a complete breakdown of administrative structures (cf. Kögel, 2015; Müchler, 2015; Pearson, 2015). What went unpublished was the profound uncertainty that arrived in Berlin's schools. They now had to accommodate and provide room for *Welcome Classes* that were to teach refugee students German and prepare them to enter regular classes and school activities (for an overview of inclusion practices in Germany see Massumi et al., 2015; for a discussion of them see Gräfe-Geusch and Okroi, 2024). During this time, teachers also had to confront their ideas of diversity as they now needed to engage with students in discussions about what was happening in their city, Germany, and Europe. During my fieldwork many of the schools I visited had student-designed poster presentations about refugees in entrance areas and hallways showing that thinking about refugees with students was common in classrooms around Berlin at the time.

The influx of refugees changed the narrative that schools related to me in response to my inquiry about study participation. When I initially started to procure possible participants for my study in January of 2015 the topic of how to accommodate religious and cultural diversity was ever present in media and public conception but not many schools felt it actually applied to them. Schools had cited a lack of (immigrant and Muslim) diversity at their schools when asked about participation, although my recruitment letter never mentioned that I was interested in Muslim students in particular or students with migration biographies more generally. However, these were the two categories that teachers assumed were important for my inquiry. During early stages of communication with schools, even schools that were willing to participate would point to a lack of diversity. One example of this would be the following passage from an Email I received from school 12: "… the students at this school are to be sure heterogeneous but the number of Muslim students is relatively low." (Personal Email communication, January 21, 2015).

Suddenly, however, during the summer of 2015 diversity, immigration, and especially refugee movements came to be front and center of communications about my research.[1] Now schools would not reference a lack of diversity but instead would claim to be overwhelmed with the amount of diversity they had to deal with. This is the response of one principal who had initially agreed to participate in January of 2015, but had changed their mind by early 2016. It is representative of many other conversations I had with school leaders:

> Yes, your topic is indeed very fascinating and interesting. I hope you understand that we too are currently grappling with this demanding situation of dealing with migration and refugees every day. In this position we are currently not able to exert additional energy and dedication for your undertaking. We work and act, to cope with, reflect upon, and process these daily challenges." (Personal Email communication, 2/8/2016).

This communication shows the desperation and powerlessness with which the topic of diversity and immigration was now viewed by schools. The strain put on schools by the sudden influx of new students, the lack of structures that provided schools with simple information, such as when and how many new students would join them, was palpable throughout many of the schools I communicated with and visited.

The uncertainties that these events placed on schools was also echoed in the ways that teachers discussed refugees and the new diversity they were faced with. This description by Herr Stade is a good example of just how pertinent this topic was:

---

[1] In fact, all participating teachers stated during our conversations that the topic of the refugee movement was hugely important in their lessons during the 2015/2016 school year. Every single one had covered it in one way or another in their classes. For a discussion of my data related to teaching refugees please see Gräfe-Geusch (2020).

> Well, you never know... if there are people arriving here who are, I would say, strongly traumatized. Without being able to tell immediately what their background is and if they may, as a result have strange modes of behavior [...] Because especially now, in the face of these new refugee streams, I would not like to make a prediction. [...] I mean, we have already shown our goodwill in taking two such classes [welcome classes]. However, what are two classes in comparison to what is coming. Well, you have to look at it unemotionally. I have...I don't quite know what to do about it honestly. Like, no one here really does, it hits us more or less unprepared... Well, I am also really skeptical about how we can deal with this. We don't have a solution for it [...] Well, so there are quite a few people, that... I would say, were indeed psychologically traumatized and they were exposed to hardships, grew up with violence, know the language of violence better than the other language [...] Well, if you are used to solving conflicts with violence, then you cannot just get rid of it just because you are somewhere different. This is how I.... just see it. [...] Then you add cultural destabilizers to it...Because they come from different countries, that are often shaped by Islam and if you then see from the outside what Berlin looks like... it doesn't necessarily fit together with a conservative Muslim attitude. Well, I am openly skeptical [laughs]. (Herr Stade, Interview on 9/1/2015)[2]

The fear of these uncertainties, produced by the influx of refugees and the sheer chaos it caused in Berlin's bureaucracy, can be felt in these words. They echo public and political discourse of the time.

Researchers have pointed out that "forced migration is a study about *us*" (Pinson et al., 2010, p. 1, emphasis in original). The strains put on societies by large refugee streams and the logics they expose "requires us [...] to ask what our responsibility is and what our moral commitments are to the strangers on our doorstep" (Pinson et al., 2010, p. 1). Further, the question of refugees also "importantly illuminates remaining and ongoing challenges in meeting the right to education for the most marginalized national children" (Dryden-Peterson et al., 2018, p. 7). It is therefore not surprising that these events prompted the teachers in my study to carefully consider the categories of diversity and belonging they espoused in their conversations with me, as well as in their teaching.

While my study focused on ethics instruction in typical Berlin classrooms, my data captures a moment when categories of diversity and national identity were actively negotiated and re-evaluated by teachers, policy makers, and the German public. This period marks a profound shift in Germany's attitude towards (ethnic and religious) diversity. These events strengthened the street mobilization of the *Patriotic Europeans against the Islamization of the Occident* (PEGIDA, cf. Herold and Schäller, 2023) and prepared the electoral success of

---

[2] Herr Stade speaks of the psychological traumas that children in conflict affected areas would be exposed to, not to mention the possible traumas endured along the way to their country of refuge. We also know little about the educational experience of refugee children prior to resettlement in Europe, the US, Australia or elsewhere; (cf. Dryden-Peterson, 2016).

the Alternative for Germany (AfD; cf. Gessler and Hunger, 2023). They are best described within what Foroutan (2019) termed a post-migrant society. This conceptual framework pays close attention to the ways that migration in its myriad forms transforms and reshapes societies (Yurdakul, 2024). That is, within it the analysis seeks to correlate "societal transformation moments" beyond the act of migration with each other (Foroutan 2019: 60; original in German translation by the author). For education this means that schools are not just places of diversity integration, but rather exist within the tension of the „negotiation and acceptance of equality as central promise of a modern democracy" (Foroutan, 2019, p. 13).

To understand how Germany would manage the transformation moment created by the influx of people in the summer and fall of 2015, it is essential to examine the structures and logics regarding diversity that were already in place as well as those that were being created during this time. The questions of how to deal with diversity in education and how to create inclusive school environments would and will be one of the most pressing challenges for Germany, and the rest of Europe more generally, in the past and coming decades.[3] Thus, Berlin is not alone in its quest to include minoritized and racialized group identities in its society. Over the past two and a half decades, Germany and many Western European societies have vastly extended their education policy frameworks with regard to minority populations (cf. Jackson, 2008). In Germany, these policy frameworks are inclusive of minority populations, calling for more attention and integration in curricula and practice (Kultusministerkonferenz, 1996/2013, 2003, 2015). Yet, research has also shown that there is a stark division between inclusive and diversity-oriented policy frameworks and the reality and practice in public schools (Abu El-Haj, 2010; Abu El-Haj et al., 2017; Bowen, Bertossi, Duyvendak, Krook, 2013; Jaffe-Walter, 2013; Niehaus, 2017, 2018; Ríos-Rojas, 2014; Schiffauer, 2015; Simel, 1996; Štimac, 2014; Sunier, 2013). This study examines how inclusive education policies can become exclusive and discriminatory practices.

Historically, sociologists have understood this divergence between policy and practice as a natural division of policy ideals and practical reality (Edelman, 1990, 1992; Meyer and Rowan, 1977; Nonet and Selznick, 1978). In other words, diversity-friendly policies are mere window-dressing that do not impact educational practice. More recently, others have theorized a lack of knowledge at the policy level regarding what works, which may ultimately lead to divergence in practice (Dobbin and Kalev, 2017). Policy makers are thus assumed not to know enough about teaching practice to propose laws or measures that promote a diversity-friendly school environment. A third expla-

---

3 The issue of diversity integration becomes even more pressing if we consider research on refugees which has pointed to the fact that most refugee situations are protracted and refugees need to be provided with ways to permanently integrate and settle in their country of asylum (Dryden-Peterson, 2017; Loescher, et al. 2008).

nation stipulates that individualistic factors which cannot be systematically captured are the reason why diversity-friendly policy may fail in practice (Ortloff, 2009; Sunier, 2013). It may be a teacher's previous interaction with students, their personal history or other specific factors. Anthropologists often interpret minority youth discrimination in school through a framework of deterministic governmentality that does not allow for individual actors' agency (Jaffe-Walter, 2013; Ríos-Rojas, 2014). These arguments assume state interests of minority group surveillance and control to be uncritically carried out by teachers in schools. German education scholars rather point to structural discrimination immanently anchored in schools' organizational logics and frameworks (Gomolla, 2020; Gomolla and Radtke, 2009). However, these theories generally focus on either the level of policy formation *or* the ways in which policies are enacted at the school level (cf. Levin, 2009; for a critique of this division see also Ball, 1993, 2015). By examining how diversity is understood and negotiated within and across these levels drawing on the vertical case study approach (Vavrus and Bartlett, 2006, 2009), this study offers rich insights into the complexities of the policy process and sheds light on how and why certain outcomes are more or less likely to emerge.

Further, research is often limited to ethnic and religiously highly diverse contexts, thus ignoring the possible ways in which hegemonic logics and structures may be reproduced within majority populations. Through an in-depth comparison of ethnic and religiously diverse and non-diverse school environments, I seek to offer an account that transverses this singular focus on highly diverse classrooms. I thus ask:

1. How do political actors (in government and public education) understand and negotiate diversity and diversity's place in society?
2. How do these negotiations vary across different school and individual contexts?

These questions allow me to trace the negotiation of logics of diversity in multiple contexts to expose the ways in which they might differ across and within them.

In this study, I choose the term diversity rather than immigrant population specifically for three reasons. First, while much of Germany's ethnic and religious diversity has roots in international migration processes, it is not the sole source of diversity. Many of those that are perceived to be ethnically and religiously diverse were in fact born in Germany and are German citizens. In Germany these populations are commonly referred to and statistically researched as people "with migration background" (Menschen mit Migrationshintergrund). However, there is much critical debate about this category and its potential for prolonged othering and exclusion from the national imagination (Elrick and Farah Schwartzman, 2015; Will, 2019). Second, a focus on migration exclusively also obscures other sources of religious diversity like religious conversion (cf. Bendixsen, 2013) or mixed marriages as well as other dimensions of diversity that may produce exclusion like those protected by German Anti-Discrimination Law. Third, rather than focus on pre-determined dimensions of difference, my analysis seeks to highlight the construction and negotiation of them. I therefore chose the much more encompassing term of diversity to highlight that migration is only one driver of the demographic and social differences salient for this discussion (cf. chapter 2).

Teachers are conceptualized as political actors (Guven, 2018; Riggan, 2016) in this study, who act as state agents transmitting state sanctioned knowledge, on the one hand, and as citizens and possible forces for resistance against state policy, on the other. Employing institutional logics theory, I pay particular attention to how teachers and politicians negotiate logics of diversity through the case of Berlin's mandatory ethics instruction. While my attention to policy stakeholders provides the macro context of this study, I privilege the role that teachers play in negotiating societal diversification in their classrooms as they are in many cases the first state agents that youth engage with. Thus, they play a crucial role in socializing them into the national community (Burde, 2014; Lipsky, 2010, p. 4; Luykx, 1999; Riggan, 2016; F. Wilson, 2001). Throughout this study I show that there are two main logics of diversity that significantly shape the ways in which political actors imagine a pluralistic society: one inclusive of ethnic and religious diversity and one that excludes diversity.

In practice, my research shows that the existence of multiple conflicting logics about diversity moderated by school environments drives heterogeneity across and within various school contexts. This indicates an unstable institutional environment open to challenge. Hence, when it comes to imagining the future of ethics instruction in Berlin, teachers unlike politicians do not rely on diversity-friendly international discourses and logics as a source of mobilization and legitimacy. Rather, they employ traditional, national logics of the teaching profession to achieve their goals. Through these logics teachers stigmatize and remove teaching about diversity from their understandings of ethics instruction. In the end, this study thus speaks to the much larger question of whether and how global logics and policy frameworks about diversity – such as those encompassed by Human Rights Law and specifically the principle of equality and nondiscrimination (United Nations, n. d.) – can drive truly transformative and sustainable social change.

I continue this chapter by first situating ethics instruction in a larger sociocultural context and briefly discuss my case selection. To draw out the division between diversity-oriented policy and discriminatory practice I review the ways in which education policies have engaged the topic of diversity internationally and within Germany. Then, I turn my discussion to the issue of diversity in schooling by situating this discussion in the larger context and history of diversity in German national policy. I argue that there is a struggle between an inclusive and exclusive logic of diversity at the national level. To highlight the urgency of understanding how diversity is negotiated by political actors, I discuss the mainstreaming of right-wing attitudes within the public sphere and the simultaneously occurring growth predicted for diverse populations in Germany and Europe. The chapter ends with a summary of the overall significance of this study and a review of my research questions before providing an overview of the book and each chapter's main argument.

1.2 Diversity, Belonging, and Violence: Situating Ethics within the larger Socio-Cultural Context

This research engages with a political and social debate deeply rooted within German society. Namely, it touches on the question of what it means to be German, who is included in the national imagination and who is excluded. This debate, for obvious historical reasons, is a challenging topic in the German context (cf. Miller-Idriss, 2009). It concerns the meaning of diversity, and more specifically, the role that religious and ethnic diversity (and indeed immigration more generally) has (and ultimately should have) in German society. Thus, through a focused examination of one core policy issue, this study examines the negotiation process that is taking place around whether and how to diversify German society and ultimately arrive at a post-migrant society that takes the promise of equality made by modern democracies serious.

The question of inclusion and exclusion of diverse social groups is pressing not only because of the large influx of refugees in recent years but also because it extends beyond the German case. Similar to other nations in Western Europe and North America, the beginning of the 21st century in Germany has been marked by increasing international, national, and local tensions over diversity. These tensions have culminated in a renewed rise of nationalist populism, anti-immigrant and anti-minority sentiments, and right-wing violence, on the one hand, and minority group resistance and violence, on the other hand. Events such as the attacks and killing of the far-right National Socialist Underground (NSU) in Germany discovered in 2011, or in Oslo and Utøya, Norway in July of the same year, are but a few examples of growing violence against minorities from right wing and conservative groups. This list can be continued by shootings at a Wisconsin Sikh temple in August 2012 and at a South Carolina Methodist church in June 2015. The list also includes the attacks on Mosques in Christ Church, New Zealand in March 2019, the attempted attack on a Synagogue in Halle, Germany on Yom Kippur 2019, and the racist murders in Hanau, Germany in 2020. They all show the violent backlash against the inclusion of diverse social groups by far-right actors. On the other hand, one could list the riots in Paris' banlieue in 2005, where disenfranchised racialized youth voiced their frustration with Franc's politics. In addition, attacks such as the one at Charlie Hebdo's Paris office in January 2015, following an outcry about a caricature depicting the prophet Mohammed, killings in crowded cafés and restaurants as well as the mass shooting and taking of hostages at the Bataclan theater in Paris by Islamist terrorists on November 13th, 2015. Beyond France, there were attacks in Orlando, Florida, USA in June 2016, Nice, Italy in July 2016, and Berlin, Germany in December 2016. They all gained media attention as examples of Islamic terror and growing minority group frustration and resistance. Despite this increased threat of violence and intergroup tension, Western European societies also desperately need migration fueled diversity in order to ensure economic stability due to demographic changes (Fuchs et al., 2019) and to secure a stable workforce (Bundesministerium für Arbeit und Soziales, 2022).

Governments and civil societies the world over are thus attempting to find peaceful ways of integrating diversity into the national fabric. Diversity and minority populations challenge the taken for granted assumption of cultural homogeneity of the nation state and the conventional role that education systems play in shaping this homogeneity. Throughout social science literature, education systems have been implicated as strong agents of producing homogeneity (cf. Bendix, 2017; Foucault, 1995; Weber, 1976) and a sense of national unity (Anderson, 2016). Diversity prompts state officials, policy makers, and teachers to reconsider the very idea of co-existence and co-habitation within the boundaries of these political constructs and actively negotiate the notions of diversity and its place within society.

As one of the first areas for politicians to address any form of societal struggle or change, schools are an important area focus in order to study the process of diversity integration. In fact, Labaree (2009) commenting on the US context suggests that governments routinely ask schools to take on tasks they are not set up to succeed in as they are contradictions inherent in liberal democracies overall. As he states: "The apparently dysfunctional outcomes of the educational system, therefore, are not necessarily the result of bad planning, deception, or political cynicism; they are an institutional expression of the contradictions in the liberal democratic mind." (Labaree, 2009, p. 17). Schools thus provide essential knowledge of how societal transformation processes are negotiated. In addition, given the relative youthfulness of diverse populations, schools, especially in urban centers, are also the places where changes in ethnic population composition are visible first. To illustrate this, in 2011 research found that 43,8 percent of all children in Berlin under the age of six had a migrant background (Foroutan, 2015, p. 3). In 2023, 43 percent of all children in Germany under the age of six and 51,7 percent of children between six and 17 in Berlin had a migration background (Sachverständigenrat für Integration und Migration, 2025). Migration-driven diversity should thus be considered normality in German and especially Berlin's schools.

In policy conceptualizations, schools have thus become a "crucial key" to successful diversity integration (Die Bundesregierung, 2007, p. 3; original in German, translation by the author). Researchers even hypothesize that finding ways to integrate the growing urban diversity into school curricula and practice will be achieved and innovated in major cities first (Crul et al., 2013, p. 20). Others find that urban areas are much more likely to implement diversity friendly policies (Martínez-Ariño et al., 2019). There is thus an assumed correlation between diversity-oriented policies and urban areas. Therefore, this study is well placed to contribute empirical evidence regarding this assumption.

1.3 The Case of Berlin

As a city state Berlin is able to respond directly to the diversity in its public school system since it is able to produce its own education policy.[4] Moreover, Berlin is one of the most progressive federal states regarding its education reforms and was the first federal state to have produced a modernized school system (Helbig and Nikolai, 2015).[5] Education policy in Berlin is thus highly innovative and open to reform. Further, Berlin is the only federal state in Germany that combines both former East and West German parts. In terms of its population, it thus represents a micro-cosmos of Germany. As such, Berlin is an ideal setting for a study aimed at understanding the way that societal diversification processes are negotiated in everyday schooling.

Berlin's ethics instruction is a prime example of how the tensions between logics of diversity inclusion and exclusion were (and are) negotiated in a local setting. After intense political debate driven by the issue of diversity, manda-

---

4   In Germany education policy is the right and obligation of federal states rather than a national endeavor. This means that each federal state produces slightly different regulations for its schools. Berlin is one of three city states in Germany - the others being Bremen and Hamburg. While there are cities in Germany that are ethnically more diverse than Berlin - Frankfurt Main for example (cf. statistic on ethnic minority children under age six in 2011 in Foroutan (2015, p. 3)) - these cities generally do not have the legal power to determine education policy based on their urban populations alone but rather also need to consider rural areas. City states are thus much faster at responding to demographic change and fit better into the theorization of urban education laboratories.

5   Helbig and Nikolai (2015) consider school systems that have ten years of compulsory schooling, six years of primary school or some kind of orientation phase following primary school. Further, they consider integrative schools (schools that combine the three traditional academic tracks of German schooling) as regular, and less than 80 percent of schools where students can gain an Abitur (high school degree enabling university attendance) are Gymnasium (high academic track schools) (cf. p. 258).

tory ethics instruction was established as Berlin's way to create a peaceful pluralistic society. This solution is unique among federal states in Germany. Berlin's ethics instruction is imagined to be deeply shaped by the engagement "with the fundamental cultural and ethical problems of individual life and societal cohabitation as well as different moral and spiritual explanations" (Schulgesetz für das Land Berlin/vom 26. Januar 2004, Section 12, Paragraph 6). It is thus in myriad ways a refractor of the much larger societal contest over diversity in Germany and the ways that the state and citizens engage with it. Teachers were (and are) at the center of the negotiations in Berlin and this study highlights their role within these processes.

1.4 Inclusion and Exclusion of Diversity in Education Policy and Practice

Accounting for the growing diversity within school environments, neighborhoods, cities and nations has become a clear focus of educational research especially in terms of policy, teaching practices, and teacher attitudes. The research in this area can be classified into three different areas: 1) diversity inclusion in education policy, 2) teaching diverse student populations, and 3) teaching about diversity in different contexts. The following sections show that while educational policy espouses diversity inclusive frameworks, in educational practice minorities often experience discrimination and attain lower academic outcomes than their majority group peers.

1.4.1 Education Policy: Including Diversity in the Political Imagination

Scholars have argued that teaching about religions and developing intercultural skills in public schools is essential to help integrate migrant students (Banks, 2009; Collet, 2018; Süssmuth, 2007). Additionally, they attribute great importance to diversity conscious teachers to facilitate integration (Suárez-Orozco and Suárez-Orozco, 2009). Researchers have also argued that teaching inter-religious and intercultural skills can counter religious extremism (Gosh and Chan, 2018) and abate inter-ethnic and inter-religious tensions (Barnes, 2018; Katz, 2018) reinforcing policy attention to this skill set. However, some researchers also caution that under certain circumstances education may contribute to conflict (Bentrovato, 2015; Burde, 2014; Bush and Saltarelli, 2000; King, 2013).

Accordingly, national and international educational policy frameworks have increasingly turned to the issue of diversity. In order to counter violent extremism, prevent radicalization and ideological indoctrination, and foster peaceful conviviality, international and national policy frameworks often focus on religions, ethnicity, and culture as markers of difference to be addressed. UNESCO, the European Union, the Council of Europe, and the Organization for Security and Co-operation in Europe (OSCE) respectively[6] developed frameworks to address the study of religions, ethnic, and cultural difference in public education. Analysis of these frameworks shows a focus specifically on Human Rights education, tolerance, respect for difference, critical thinking skills, and an emphasis on social cohesion, highlighting the importance of developing intercultural skills in public education around the world (cf. Christodoulou and Szakács-Behling, 2018, p. 44; Jackson, 2008, p. 152).

In Germany, policy directives in this area have been exceedingly pro-diversity as compared to immigration and integration policy directives (see Krüger-Potratz, 2005 for an analysis). While education policy decisions are the responsibility of the federal states, there is one important national advisory board. The Standing Conference of the Ministers of Education and Cultural Affairs (Kultusministerkonferenz - KMK) is composed of all federal state ministers for education. It publishes guidelines on education policy at the national level in Germany. The KMK first published a resolution to improve intercultural competences in German public education in 1996 and substantially revised it in 2013. It justified the importance of intercultural competences with the increasing diversification of society, on the one hand, and the rise in racist sentiments, on the other. Intercultural competences are labeled as a key competence in public education (Kultusministerkonferenz, 1996/2013). In addition, the KMK published the so-called Weimar Appeal (Kultusministerkonferenz, 2003) highlighting the urgency of including Islam and Muslim minority students in education. Furthermore, a resolution on the "Depiction of Cultural Diversity, Integration and Migration in Educational Media" (Kultusministerkonferenz, 2015) raised the importance of diversity conscious education media and practice in Germany. More recently, the national government published its Strategy to Prevent Extremism and Promote Democracy (Die Bundesregierung, 2016) focusing on strengthening democracy and Human Rights education (cf. Christodoulou and Szakács-Behling, 2018). At the national (and international) policy level we thus see great attention and commitment to the issue of including diversity in public schooling by emphasizing the inclusion of minorities in curricula and practice, while highlighting the importance of intercultural skills.

---

6   See Jackson (2008); UNESCO (2017), and Christodoulou and Szakács-Behling (2018) for a list and discussion of relevant policy documents. As Christodoulou and Szakács-Behling 2018 (p. 27) point out most of these efforts are in the global north, specifically in Europe and the United States.

1.4.2 Minority Group Academic Achievement and Teaching in Ethnically and Religiously Diverse Classrooms

In contrast to inclusive policy frameworks, research focused on teaching (ethnically and religiously) diverse student populations shows that in Germany minority students often lag behind their ethnic German peers. In addition, there are reports that teachers have troubled relationships with their students, and that teachers' preparation for working in diverse classrooms is often ineffective or lacking altogether. Children with migrant backgrounds in Germany achieve lower academic outcomes overall (Lelie et al., 2012), are less likely to find apprenticeships and enter the labor market (Baethge et al., 2007; BiBB, 2021; Boss-Nünning, 2006; Seibert et al., 2009). Further, they are more likely to be referred to special education tracks (Kottmann, 2006). Historians of education argue that the German school system has not changed in spite of the recognition of ethno-religious diversity (Castles, 2000; Geiger, 2003; Luchtenberg, 2009). In fact, they go as far as diagnosing the German education system as "dysfunctional" for an immigrant society (Auernheimer, 2005; Bade, 2011). Teaching philosophy in Germany assumes and aims to achieve homogeneity of students conceptualizing heterogeneity as deviance and a problem to be addressed (cf. Clycq, 2017; Geiger, 2003; Weber, 1976). This is detrimental to minority student achievement (Gogolin, 2008; Gogolin and Neumann, 1997).

Furthermore, research on German teacher education has shown that teachers are ill-prepared to handle diverse student bodies (Bender-Szymanski, 2000; Weber, 2003) mirroring concerns about teacher education for diverse populations across the globe (Cardona et al., 2018; Jafralie and Zaver, 2019; Szelei and Alves, 2018; Yuan, 2017, 2018). The interaction of teachers with their minority students while deemed essential for students' academic success is also often found to be problematic (cf. Banks, 2009; Cherng and Davis, 2019; Georgi et al., 2011; Luchtenberg, 2009; Suárez-Orozco et al., 2008; Suárez-Orozco, 2007). The 2015 Migrant Integration Policy Index (MIPEX) ranked Germany at number 16 out of 38 countries (with Sweden, Australia, and New Zealand at the top and Hungary, Turkey, and Bulgaria at the bottom) in terms of educational outcomes for immigrant students. Thus, classifying Germany as only half-way favorable (MIPEX, 2015). This position changed only slightly to rank number 15 in 2020 (MIPEX, 2020). Research has also shown that school practices discriminate against ethno-religious minority students in various contexts, for example, Jews in Bavarian schools (Simel, 1996) and Muslim students in Germany (Schiffauer, 2015; Sunier, 2013). This mirrors research findings across Europe and the US (Abu El-Haj, 2010; Abu El-Haj et al., 2017; Bowen, 2013; Jaffe-Walter, 2013; Ríos-Rojas, 2014).

While this study does not discuss the academic outcomes of students, the link that this line of research establishes about the academic failure of ethno-religious minority students (globally and in the German context) and the potential role that public schooling and especially teachers play in this failure is important to consider. This research shows that culture matters in schooling. The way in which teachers construct minority status in their classrooms and negotiate diversity across student groups, has far reaching impact on students' educational attainment and future prospects. As a result, this deserves ample research attention.

1.4.3 Incorporating Diversity into Teaching, Curricula, and Textbooks

Across the globe, teaching about diversity is generally subsumed under the concepts of multicultural education, intercultural education, and sometimes anti-racist education.[7] Recently scholars have focused on diversity education, and inclusion of diversity (see Niehaus, 2018; Schmidtke, 2005). However, these terms are frequently used interchangeable (cf. Niehaus, 2018, p. 329; Shiao, 2005). Each of them falls within the broader concept of diversity management in schools.

Incorporating positive lessons about diversity in educational practice has been shown to be problematic around the globe as well as in Germany. To illustrate, Moland (2015) based on her ethnographic study in Nigeria reveals that the success of multicultural education may largely depend on the sociopolitical context. Her study concludes that multiculturalism might best work in settings that already have some kind of social cohesion. In her evaluation of social studies teachers, Ortloff (2009) finds that German teachers' perceptions of the effectiveness of multicultural education are subject to state logics about citizenship. An exclusive logic of citizenship defined in ethno-cultural terms is detrimental to teachers' positive engagement with diversity. Reviews of German textbooks and curricula show that the integration of diversity friendly content and education to counter violent extremism is still lackluster or missing altogether (Christodoulou and Szakács-Behling, 2018; Niehaus, 2018; Štimac, 2014, 2015; Štimac and Spielhaus, 2018).

In the available research on Germany, multicultural, intercultural, and diversity education are predominantly the subject of studies on foreign language teaching (e.g. Euler, 2017) or associated directly with the education of minority students (cf. Kiel et al., 2017). These topics are thus rarely considered within non-diverse settings. Research that does explore teaching diversity specifically beyond foreign language classrooms focuses on history and social studies (Sozialkunde; cf. Ortloff, 2009). Based on an evaluation of multiple state ethics curricula, Rösch (2018) concludes that curricula assume a diverse group of learners in ethics classrooms in terms of "origin, language, culture, religion,

---

7 See Allemann-Ghionda (2009) for an overview of these terms in Europe and Schmidtke (2005) for a discussion of the historical developments of these concepts in Germany.

and world view" (p. 88). Curricula also emphasize "dialogue and debate about attitudes and traditions operating in our society" (Rösch, 2018, p. 81). Research on ethics instruction in Berlin specifically is concerned with the historical and political process of its inception (Beschorner, 2006; Gräb and Thieme, 2011), uses it as a case study for direct democracy (Jung, 2011), or discusses ethics with the goal to affirm the importance of religious instruction (Gräb and Thieme, 2011; Häusler, 2007; Schluß, 2010). Even though ethics instruction and its goals are thus predominantly concerned with teaching about diversity (cf. Rösch, 2018; Štimac, 2014, 2015), I could not identify any research that has evaluated this component of ethics instruction in practice.

To summarize, research assumes positive outcomes when students are engaged in intergroup dialogue, develop intercultural skills or are exposed to content about diversity. However, research engaged with practical implementation of pro-diversity content often finds severe shortcomings in terms of textbook content and teaching practice. In addition, research on teaching about diversity in Germany, in general terms, has received limited attention beyond foreign language instruction or hyper-diverse classroom environments. To date, ethics as a subject deeply engaged in teaching about diversity, has received little research attention evaluating its practice in real world contexts. Thus, by encompassing diverse and non-diverse school environments and analyzing contexts traditionally not included in studies of teaching diversity, this study fills relevant gaps in the literature.

1.5 Diversity in German Policy and Public Opinion

Public education and the ways in which diverse students are managed through policies and classroom practices are embedded in larger debates surrounding immigration and diversity. Over the past two decades, Germany has gone through a major political transformation by reluctantly accepting the status of a country of immigration. This has been marked by the reform of its citizenship laws and immigration laws. In her thesis about achieving a post-migrant society in Germany,[8] Foroutan (2015) criticizes how "[p]olitics missed its chance to give this heterogeneous new Germany a narrative that could produce action" (p. 2). Indeed, as I will show in the following section, German national policy

---

8   Foroutan (2015) and other researchers engaged with immigrant integration postulate that Germany should move towards a conception of post-migration, accepting that society is heterogeneous, migration is a significant force shaping society, and structures need to be inclusive of diverse populations (cf. p. 2). These researchers aim to change political and social discourses towards a narrative that accepts diversity as part of society rather than the sole result of (foreign) immigration (cf. Foroutan (2019) for an expansion of the concept of post-migration).

on diversity has mainly espoused an exclusive attitude towards minority populations. However, around the turn of the 21st century the country began to oscillate between inclusion and exclusion. Further, I show below that after the initial push for more inclusive policy and political discourse around diversity, prominent German politicians have pushed back towards more exclusive ideas.

While diversity and immigration are not exclusively 20th century phenomena, political attention in recent decades has largely focused on ethnic and religious minority groups. These groups saw their largest increase in Germany in the second half of the 20th century, specifically after the guest worker contracts were introduced in the 1960s. I therefore focus my discussion predominantly on diversity politics of the second half of the 20th century and the first decades of the 21st century. Subsequently, I provide a discussion of public attitudes and demographic trends. In addition, I show that mainstream public attitudes have increasingly espoused anti-diversity sentiments, despite or maybe because of an increasing demographic diversification.

1.5.1 Between Inclusion and Exclusion: Immigration, Integration, and Failed Multiculturalism in Germany

In general, German immigrants can be divided into three different groups (cf. Geiger, 2003), the largest of which were ethnic German refugees and expellees (a result of geopolitical changes and new borders after World War II). This group was expected to fit into the German nation without specific political attention. While some of these expellees (Aussiedler) came immediately after the end of the war from eastern territories that had been lost, many others (Spätaussiedler) came only after the fall of the Iron Curtain in the 1990s. The second largest group of immigrants are economic immigrants or so-called guest workers. They arrived in Germany throughout the 1960s and were thought of as short-term inhabitants. The intention was that these people would return to their country of origin when their contracts ended. This group is largely comprised of Italians and Turks.[9] A third group of immigrants came as refugees from for example Turkey, the former Yugoslavia (Geiger, 2003, pp. 144–146) and the Middle East and Syria (BMI and BAMF, 2016, p. 9).

---

[9] The first bilateral contract to recruit foreign labor in order to boost the West German economy came in 1955 in a contract between Germany and Italy. Spain and Greece followed in 1960, Turkey in 1961, Portugal in 1964, Tunisia and Morocco in 1965 and Yugoslavia in 1968. Recruitment stopped in 1973 following a recession. Overall, about three million guest workers permanently settled in Germany (cf. Bade, 2011, p. 160).

Although Germany's status as a country of immigration[10] and the need for political attention to immigrant integration was already acknowledged in 1979 by first director of the newly established office for the integration of foreigners (Kühn, 1979), politicians denied this status until the early 2000s (Geddes, 2010; Geiger, 2003). German political attitudes towards immigrant populations were shaped by the belief that Germany was not a country of immigration (Schönwälder, 2010) and thus only allowed ethnic Germans to permanently resettle. This attitude was based on a conception of ethno-cultural homogeneity which was reflected in German citizenship law derived from jus sanguinis (literally translated to "right of blood"). This only allowed those with ethnic-German parents to gain citizenship rights. Thus, the immigration of minority groups was predominantly considered temporary with the expectation that ethnic minority workers and refugees would soon to return home. As Bade (2011) shows, however, German economic stakeholders actively boycotted the return of their foreign workers as they did not wish to train new foreign workers every few years. The reluctance to reform political attitudes about immigration thus ran counter to economic reality.

Yet, policymaking was dominated by financially supporting and promoting return migration and ignoring structural reforms to promote integration or ease requirements for attaining citizenship (Bade, 2011, p. 162; Schönwälder, 2010). This four-decade long denial to acknowledge the permanent settlement of ethnic minorities led to hardened structural divisions between ethnic Germans and ethnic minorities (cf. Bade, 2011)[11]: "a country of immigration without immigration policy" (Bade, 2011, p. 163). This promoted a state where, as Panayi (2004) argues, a physical alteration of the national space occurred but hegemonic power structures remained unchanged (p. 476). This also had structural implications for schools. Most importantly, these unequal power relationships and opportunities to participate are still reflected in the silences visible in the political conceptions of diversity's place within society (cf. chapter 4). In addition, the ethno-religious diversity of the teaching force employed in schools is estimated to range from one to six percent of the national teaching force (Georgi et al., 2011, p. 18) severely underrepresenting minority populations.

---

10 In immigration theory this is referred to as settler society. For a long time the USA and Canada were seen as settler societies rather than European countries. These differences are assumed to be disappearing as many European countries (among them Germany) have become de facto settler societies (cf. Alba and Foner, 2015; Crul, 2016). German scholars, however, use the direct translation of country of immigration from German Einwanderungsland.

11 Local governments, NGOs, and immigrant organization during this time did promote social and political integration. However, there was no national political effort to integrate Germany's diverse populations (cf. Bade, 2011; Yurdakul, 2006).

German reunification in 1990 did not impact immigration reform or political attitudes significantly. However, the structural and economic changes that re-unification brought impacted public attitudes. In particular, this was the case in the former East where high rates of unemployment, under-developed infrastructure, and a lack of employment opportunities sparked the rise of the German skinhead and neo-Nazi culture and violence.[12] For ethnic minorities in Germany the fall of the Berlin Wall exaggerated the perception of being an outsider in German society eroding their spaces of belonging (Çil, 2007; Thomsen Vierra, 2018).

The late 1990s and early 2000s saw a significant change when a leftist national government reformed the citizenship law (1999) and Germany's immigration laws (2005). Germany opened avenues for its ethnic minority inhabitants to obtain citizenship by espousing a *jus soli* model that allowed citizenship based on place of birth. The first decade of the 21st century also saw many other reforms intended to facilitate the inclusion and integration of diverse populations. Among them, the German anti-discrimination law (2006), the creation of the German Islam Conference (2006), the Federal Office for Migration and Refugees (2004), the annual integration summit (2006), the national integration plan (2007), and an integration program (2010).

The early 2000s were also marked by a change of narrative from Germany's conservative politicians. After decades of reiterating that Germany was not a country of immigration – stated as late as November 6th, 2000, in a CDU position paper on immigration (CDU, 2000) – and thus did not need to pay attention to foreign nationals' long-term resettlement, Christian Democrats emphasized their attention to the issue of integration. An example of this is Angela Merkel's statement: "If we are honest, we have to say that we have shelved the topic of [diversity] integration in our country for too long" (Meier-Braun, 2014, paragraph six). This showed a newly found conscience within German political discourse that actively sought to find ways of diversity inclusion and politically directed national diversity management in Germany.

However, Germany has since struggled with this newly formed identity, culminating in a speech given by chancellor Merkel in October 2010. In it she declared that German multiculturalism had 'utterly failed' (Weaver, 2010).[13]

---

12 Right-wing violence, however, was not strictly limited to East Germany. Attacks in the 1990s, for example, took place in Hoyerswerda (1991, East), Rostock (1992, East), Moelln (1992, West), and Solingen (1993, West).

13 Officially Germany never followed a multicultural policy. Merkel echoed sentiments voiced all over Northern Europe that grew increasingly weary of the political acceptance of diversity based on multicultural ideals. David Cameron respectively called for a muscular liberalism in response to growing anxiety over ethnic diversity in the UK (BBC, 2011). Political philosophers have called this assertive liberalism connected to civic integration regimes that try to coerce migrant populations to adopt the political values and identities of host nations (Hansen, 2011; Joppke, 2007a). It has been criti-

Instead of a multicultural agenda which has been criticized as producing parallel societies (cf. Vertovec and Wessendorf, 2010) the country has since emphasized integration following the mantra of "To Demand and To Support" ("Fordern und Fördern"). Thus, integration is seen as a closely monitored process that first demands certain achievements from minority populations (the acquisition of language skills, for example) and then tries to support and foster further movement towards a German ideal (cf. Schönwälder, 2010).

The meaning of integration is vague, however. The sociological literature defines it broadly as "the process of settlement, interaction with the host society, and social change that follows immigration" (Favell, 2014, p. 63). In German policy documents, integration by minority populations is seen as the achievement of economic self-reliance, language acquisition, and adherence to the German liberal-democratic values (cf. BAMF, 2010). Despite the introductory declaration that integration has to be achieved through the efforts and engagement of both majority, ethnic minority, and immigrant population (BAMF, 2010, p. 10), suggestions from the National Integration Program mainly targeted ethnic minority and immigrant populations and their deficiencies (cf. Terkessidis, 2010, p. 9). Integration in German policy documents may thus be a thinly veiled demand for assimilation (asserting the values of the dominant (ethnic-German) group and its hegemonic position within society). Critiques point to international comparisons such as the Multiculturalism Policy Index (MCP) and Migrant Integration Policy Index (MIPEX) respectively, to attest that much work remains to be done in order to achieve a diversity inclusive environment in German society and policy frameworks (Kober and Süssmuth, 2012).

The so-called long summer of migration of the fall of 2015 and spring of 2016 further highlighted the various inclusive and exclusive tendencies toward minorities within the German political class. The topic of diversity became nothing short of an open battle within the government. Of particular note was Angela Merkel's explicit decision to allow refugees who were stranded on the Eastern European borders to enter Germany. Not only did her decision stand in stark contrast to the policies being pursued in neighboring countries such as Austria, but Merkel was vigorously criticized for this decision within her own party and government. Politicians such as former German Minister of the Interior Horst Seehofer even called immigration the "mother of all problems" in September 2018 (cf. Roßmann, 2018). He happily boasted that on his 69th birthday 69 Afghan asylum seekers were deported (cf. Vu, 2018).

Germany's national policy and treatment of diversity has thus oscillated between tendencies towards inclusion and exclusion. After decades of ignoring the status and importance of minority population within Germany the national government went through a brief period in the early 2000s of inclusive policy-

---

cized as "repressive, "illiberal," and "Foucauldian" (cf. Joppke, 2007a, pp. 15–16), and a "liberalism of power and discipline" (Jaffe-Walter, 2013, p. 631).

making and vigorous efforts to make up for lost time. Recently, however, national political discourse about diversity and immigration has again swung towards exclusive tendencies by placing the burden of integration entirely on minority groups without serious reform in majority group cultural logics and hegemonic structures. The next section looks in more detail at German public attitudes towards diversity.

1.5.2 Negative Public Perception of Diversity and Growing Diverse Populations in Germany

Recent studies show that there is a societal mainstreaming of populist, anti-diversity ideology in Germany (cf. Miller-Idriss, 2017; Zick et al., 2019). Overall, these sentiments are widespread and increasing within majority society (see for example the difference in far-right attitudes between 2016 and 2023 (Zick et al., 2019; 2016; Zick et al., 2023). Some scholars thus go as far as calling recent developments a movement towards the "radicalized mainstream" (cf. Sponholz et al., 2025). Anti-diversity and immigrant sentiments increasingly manifest themselves in anti-diversity far-right attacks, or a major surge in the success of right-wing, anti-immigration, anti-EU, and anti-government political mobilization. In addition, these sentiments are voiced at the marches of the Patriotic Europeans Against the Islamization of the Occident (PEGIDA), during the Anti-Corona demonstrations in 2020 (cf. Virchow et al., 2020) and in the electoral success of Alternative for Germany (AFD), for example.

In addition, German fears of a violent Muslim minority were projected directly onto youth as the speech of German Minister of the Interior Thomas De Maiziere on September 12th, 2014, in connection to the outlawing of the Islamic State makes clear. He stated: "The ban [of the Islamic State] does not replace an intellectual examination of the reasons for the radicalization of young men and also women. Security services alone will not be able to win the fight against Islamic radicalization." (Bundesministerium des Innern, 2014). Muslim youth are thus the main scapegoat in Germany (and Europe more generally) and are placed under general suspicion. This mirrors a larger trend in education of projecting security discourses and concerns into multi-ethnic classrooms and unto minority youth (cf. Shamim, 2017).

These findings are problematic, if considered in conjunction with projections for the growth of minority populations in Europe and Germany. Pew Research Center (2015) projects that by 2050 Europe's Muslim population will increase by 63 percent to 71 million from 43 million in 2010. For Germany specifically, the Muslim population is projected to grow from 5.8 percent in 2010 to 10 percent of the total population by 2050 (Pew Research Center, 2015, p. 237). In addition, other religious groups such as Hindus, Buddhists and folk religions are projected to experience "large gains," with the exception of Christians and Jews who are both projected to decline (Pew Research Center, 2015, p. 147). The projected growth in Germany's Muslim and other religious minority population is going to be especially significant in urban centers (Crul et al., 2013; Vertovec, 2011), however, as demographic research from the US context suggests diversity may also spread into suburban and rural areas in the near future (cf. Frey, 2018, p. 246).

Overall, therefore we see a steady rise and the mainstreaming of populist, anti-immigrant, and right-wing attitudes in Germany in conjunction with a negative perception of Islam. At the same time minority populations are projected to grow and spread beyond urban centers. Germany is becoming more diverse while anti-diversity sentiments in the majority population are growing. Thus, creating more social cohesion in society is deeply connected to perceptions and the construction of the role of ethnic and religious diversity in society by the majority population.

1.6 Understanding and Negotiating Logics of Diversity in Context: Research Question and Significance of the Study

This study responds to pressing questions that have emerged from policy and practice and extend beyond the case study presented in the following chapters. I also address significant gaps in the research literature. The increasing diversification of societies has sparked a myriad of responses in policy, public opinion, and practice. Western European and North American societies have seen an increase in tensions between ethnic majority and minority populations, culminating in violence from the far right as well as minority groups. In Germany, public attitudes towards minority populations, and particularly Islam, are negative. Yet, research suggests that Germany needs the influx and growth of minority and immigrant populations to sustain its economic stability (Fuchs et al., 2019). Reflecting broader political trends, global and national education policies have advocated for greater attention to diversity and the inclusion of minority populations in schools. These objectives are often promoted through intergroup dialogue and the development of intercultural skills to prevent radicalization and violence. However, findings from school practice often show the inability of teachers, curricula, and textbooks to properly include minority populations and diversity. Often this leads to the academic underperformance of ethnic and religious minority students when compared to their ethnic German peers.

Sociological theory has not yet found a way to systematically explain the divergence between policies and practice (see chapter 2). In addition, research into the integration of minority populations has not looked beyond hyper-diverse classroom settings. It thus misses the chance to understand how hegemonic structures are perpetuated within non-diverse or less diverse majority population classrooms. Education about diversity is rarely considered beyond the subjects of history, social studies, and foreign language instruction in Germany. Research has thus artificially limited our knowledge of the possible scope and place of teaching about diversity within public education to but a few subject areas. While teachers are arguably some of the most important political actors, functioning as some of the first state agents that youth encounter and play a substantial role in their socialization into the national community, we know little about how they understand and negotiate issues of diversity within their classrooms and beyond.

How do societies, and especially public schools, respond to migration driven diversification processes? How are taken-for-granted understandings of diversity negotiated by various actors? How may this vary across levels and school contexts? This study will analyze the response of one German state to the demographic and social changes already in progress. Berlin's ethics instruction seeks to facilitate the creation of a peaceful pluralistic society addressing current and future social and political challenges. Examining how educators perceive their role in this subject and how they translate policy directives into their classroom environments can shed much needed light on the way the German education system is responding to increased diversity, immigration, and threats of violence. We need to know more about the taken-for-granted assumptions underlying ethics teachers' understandings of their role in this process and teaching about diversity. In addition, we need to understand how the organizational environment teachers work in, and the pressures exerted by the education system interact with teachers' conduct and understandings.

1.7 Overview of the Study

In chapter 2, I situate my study within the theoretical literature. I argue that previous accounts engaging with the divergence between policy and practice, as well as the role teachers play in this process, have four distinct shortcomings. First, they fail to account for the multiple levels at which teachers are engaged. Teachers are often assumed to be unidirectional actor who either transfer state knowledge to students or acts as agents of change against the state. Second, these studies treat diversity as a social fact rather than as the outcome of social and political negotiations. As such they de-emphasize the power relations inherent in the creation of diversity, including the labelling of some groups as majorities and others as minorities. Third, these accounts assume a single underlying dominant logic, attributing deviations either to individual factors or failing to account for them altogether. Fourth, research designs generally privilege one level of the policymaking and implementation process, rarely integrating multiple levels of negotiation involving different education actors who shape both policy and practice. To address these shortcomings, I argue that it is essential to understand how logics of diversity are negotiated both in policymaking and everyday classroom interactions. I propose a theoretical framework that conceptualizes teachers as political actors in two ways: 1) in relation to the citizenry, represented by their students, and 2) in relation to the state, as representatives of their profession. Additionally, I adopt the perspective of diversity as "social organization of difference" (Vertovec, 2019) to emphasize the importance of political actors' understanding and negotiation of diversity. To integrate the idea of teachers as political agents with my conception of diversity into a single analytical framework, I draw on institutional logics as an overarching theory, as it focuses on the negotiation of heterogeneity within taken-for-granted frameworks.

Chapter 3 focuses on my methodology. I outline the rational for designing a vertical case study to better understand societal diversification processes and their negotiation in education. Furthermore, I explain my approach to sampling, data collection, and data analysis. I show that the teachers in my sample are predominantly interested in teaching about different cultures and intercultural skills, making them a best-case-scenario in this regard. This renders some of the findings (cf. chapter 5 and 6) even more significant. I argue that my sample allows me to move beyond the narrow focus on high-diversity contexts, which dominates previous research on integration processes, by enabling a comparison between high- and low-diversity school settings. Additionally, I describe the social and political context surrounding my data collection and reflect on its potential impact on the data gathered, before addressing possible limitations of my approach. Overall, I argue that a qualitative vertical case study – drawing on document analysis, semi-structured interviews, and participant observations – is best suited to answer the research questions posed in this study.

Chapter 4 discusses the historical background and the political negotiations surrounding ethics education. It demonstrates that Berlin's approach to value education – what would later become mandatory ethics – was closely tied to contentious debates about the concept of diversity. Political action was specifically triggered by concerns over honor-related violence in ethnic minority communities in Berlin. I argue that these negotiations were shaped by two distinct logics of diversity: productive diversity and destructive diversity. While the productive diversity argument emerged as the dominant policy logic, the destructive diversity argument served as the foundation for challenges to the legitimacy of ethics education. Both logics played a crucial role in shaping Berlin's approach to diversity management through mandatory ethics instruction.

In Chapter 5, I examine how teachers make sense of diversity in their teaching across different school contexts. To compare diverse and non-diverse school settings, I focus on how teachers teach about diversity and how they conceptualize their approaches. As in chapter 4, I show that teachers' approaches are shaped by two overarching logics of diversity: one inclusive and the other exclusive. However, depending on the school context, different elements of these logics are mobilized, resulting in four distinct ideal-type approaches. I argue that an exclusive view of diversity is adopted in what I call the assimilationist approach in diverse school contexts and the philosophical approach in non-diverse school contexts. Conversely, an inclusive logic of diversity gives rise to an intercultural approach to teaching diversity in diverse school settings and a critical approach in non-diverse school settings. I further argue that the heterogeneity of these approaches, along with the coexistence of two competing logics institutionalized in practice, highlights the instability of Berlin's ethics instruction. This unstable institutional environment allows for ongoing challenges and competition over the very conception of what ethics instruction in Berlin ought to be.

Chapter 6 moves beyond the individual school context to examine how teachers respond to the significant challenges to the legitimacy of ethics as a subject. In contrast to Berlin's politicians, who used diversity as a mobilizing element in policymaking, teachers perceive teaching about diversity as a factor that de-legitimizes mandatory ethics. They struggle with the low standing of their subject and put forward two interlinked arguments, rooted in professional teaching logics, to enhance its legitimacy. First, they emphasize the need for the "appropriate" type of accreditation for ethics teachers – specifically, a university degree in philosophy. They argue that teachers without such a qualification fail in their teaching by focusing on intercultural skill development and dialogue, which they dismiss as a waste of time. Second, they advocate for a curriculum shift towards a stronger focus on philosophy, excluding the study of religions as external to the disciplinary scope of ethics. Both strategies serve to justify the removal of diversity-related content from the curriculum. By doing so, these teachers reaffirm a long-standing monocultural and monolingual habitus (Gogolin, 2008; Gogolin and Neumann, 1997) in German education, positioning themselves against the more diversity-inclusive political vision of schooling in Berlin.

The final chapter summarizes the findings and relates them to the overarching research questions posed in this study. I argue that what initially appears as a divergence between diversity-friendly policy and discriminatory educational practices in everyday schooling should instead be understood as a spectrum, with many gray areas between the two extremes of inclusion and exclusion. Teachers play a crucial role in negotiating these tensions, both in relation to their students and in response to state policy. However, given the different pressures in each of these fields of interaction, teachers and politicians relate to logics of diversity in distinct ways and draw on additional logics to support their arguments. Moreover, the way diversity logics are mobilized differs fundamentally between the domains of policy and public education examined in this study, revealing underlying and unequal power relationships within and between these domains. Overall, this study offers a novel perspective on diversity integration in education, proposing important theoretical insights for future research as well as significant recommendations for educational practice.

2 Teachers als Political Actors, Diversity, and Institutional Logics

2.1 Understanding and Negotiating Diversity at Various Levels of Society

This chapter builds a theoretical framework to answer the question why policy and practice might diverge in Berlin's public schools. I argue that only through an in-depth analysis of the negotiations of diversity logics in policymaking and public school practice can we understand this divergence. I situate my study in broader scholarly debates around education, integration, and diversity. To facilitate the discussion, I consider both the macro context (the policymaking environment regarding diversity) and the micro classroom context that shapes how diversity policies are actually implemented. Methodologically, I draw on the vertical case study approach proposed by Vavrus and Bartlett (2006). This allows me to compare "knowledge claims among actors with different social locations in a vertically bounded analysis. [...] It strives to situate local action and interpretation within a broader cultural, historical, and political investigation" (Vavrus and Bartlett, 2006, p. 96). I argue that to explain the divergence between diversity-friendly policy, on the one hand, and exclusionary practices on the other, it is essential to engage in a multi-level analysis that examines how political actors (in policy and public education) understand and negotiate multiple competing logics of diversity. I also argue that teachers play a crucial role in this process. Teachers are among the first agents of the state that young people encounter and thus significantly shape their socialization into the political community (Burde, 2014; Lipsky, 2010, p. 4; Luykx, 1999; Riggan, 2016; Wilson, 2001). However, teachers are also crucial agents in determining the success or failure of education policy in practice (cf. Gardinier, 2012; Worden, 2011).

Previous theories on diversity integration in education and policy implementation exhibit four distinctive weaknesses: 1) they do not account for the possibility that different logics of diversity may co-exist and influence teachers' actions. 2) They often posit a clear separation between policy and practice in their research. 3) They tend to overlook the power relations that are inherent in negotiations of diversity. 4) And they cannot account for teachers' multiple levels of action. These shortcomings leave ample room for new ways to conceptualize the topic of diversity integration through education. Specifically, I argue institutional logics as an overarching-theory is best suited to conceptualize the negotiation and construction of diversity within policymaking and teaching processes while also paying close attention to levels on which teachers interact (vis-à-vis the citizenry and vis-à-vis the state). This theory thus provides an often overlooked but empirically productive way to analyze education policy aimed to integrate minority populations.

Conceptualizing the analysis in this way offers three distinctive advantages. 1) It allows me to bridge gaps between institutional logics theory, diversity and teacher practice and thus combine them in analysis. 2) It provides a way to compare actors at different societal levels, i.e. the politicians that made the decision to introduce mandatory ethics and the teachers who are engaged in everyday (classroom) negotiations about the subject's content. And 3) it allows me to contribute to theory building within the area of neo-institutional organization theory which has so far under-theorized power (Friedland and Arjaliès, 2019; Lawrence and Buchanan, 2008) and diversity (Rojas, 2017).

I structure this chapter around the four shortcomings in the literature listed above. First, I look at neo-institutional organization theory theories that seek to explain the divergence between diversity-inclusive policy and exclusive practice, before introducing institutional logics as an overarching theoretical framework that brings together micro and macro level analysis and allows for the heterogeneity of underlying cultural logics as a way to explain the gap between diversity-inclusive policy and discriminatory education practice. I then outline my conception of diversity and its relationship to power and institutional logics theory. Last, I examine the literature on the role of teachers in policy institutionalization. I show how a notion of teachers as political actors brings together two distinct levels of policy engagement that may provide a more nuanced view on existing research narratives that view teachers' role in a more one-dimensional capacity - either as agents of change or of stasis.

2.2 Neo-Institutional Explanations of the Divergence between Policy and Practice

The sociological literature and more specifically neo-institutional organization studies that examine the taken-for-granted ideational principles underlying social arrangements theorize discrepancies between policy and practice in three main ways: 1) As a natural division of policy ideals and practical reality (Edelman, 1990, 1992; Meyer and Rowan, 1977; Nonet and Selznick, 1978), 2) as a lack of knowledge regarding what works at the policy level which may ultimately lead to divergence in practice (Dobbin and Kalev, 2017), or 3) they assume individualistic factors that cannot systematically capture why diversity friendly policy may fail in practice (Ortloff, 2009; Sunier, 2013). In this theory institutions are conceptualized as the "taken-for-granted" scripts, rules, and classifications that structure behaviors and "both constrain the inclination and capacity of actors to optimize as well as privilege some groups whose interests are secured" (DiMaggio and Powell, 1991, p. 11; see also Meyer and Rowan, 1977). Organizations are "generally understood to be systems of coordinated and controlled activities that arise when work is embedded in complex networks of technical relations and boundary-spanning exchanges." (Meyer and Rowan, 1977, p. 340).

Specifically, in their seminal study of organizations and institutions, John W. Meyer and Rowan (1977) argue that organizations are embedded in highly institutionalized settings. They are subject to pressures that will drive incorporation of institutionalized practices and structures regardless of their efficacy in order to increase organizational legitimacy. The adoption of organizational policies and structures that conform to institutional pressures – new legal frameworks, changing cultural ideals – are thus often theorized as ceremonial rather than producing change within practice (Meyer and Rowan, 1977; see also the "symbolic compliance" hypothesis, Edelman, 1990, 1992). In other words, this theory poses that, for example, structures within U.S. companies that complied with Equal Employment Opportunity and Affirmative Action laws (EEO/AA) did nothing to improve the economic situation of minority groups within these companies (U.S. context: Berrey, 2014; Edelman, 1990, 1992; Kelly and Dobbin, 1998; Shen et al., 2010; international: Boxenbaum, 2006; Stringfellow, 2012). Institutions are seen as myths (or symbolic expressions) that grant legitimacy but may be unrelated to concerns about efficiency, technical activity, and productivity (also called loose coupling; cf. March and Olsen, 1976). Research finds that compliance with laws in companies seeks to adopt new legal mandates "in a manner that is minimally disruptive to the status quo" (Edelman, 1992, p. 1535).

Rather than focus on micro level interactions however, these studies generally rely on macro level policy analysis and assume the homogeneity of institutional pressures (Meyer et al., 1992). This is mainly due to neo-institutional theory's concern for isomorphism and macro-structural processes. Often this assumes the homogeneity of prevalent logics – arguing, for example, for the convergence of education policy on a world level (Meyer et al., 1992). If practice is of concern, it is conceptualized as loosely coupled with policy and institutional logic. That is to say that practice may diverge from policy. Policy implementation thus becomes a case of symbolic compliance. The policymaking process thus is assumed to provide only one dominant logic that needs to be institutionalized in practice. Hence, this theory would predict that while schools officially have ethics instruction, providing a timeslot in the schedule, room, electricity, and a staff member in attendance, whether or not this instruction actually focuses on diversity and creating a peaceful pluralistic society is questionable. There may be a heterogeneity of practical response to the law, but this is divorced from lawmaking.

A critique of the symbolic compliance literature argues for a focus on managerial level negotiation of the compliance process. The argument focuses not on the diffusion of symbolic structures across different fields and types of organizations but rather looks at the relationship between intentions and effects (cf. Dobbin and Kalev, 2017). The analysis thus shifts to a negotiation process within the managerial staff. Dobbin and Kalev (2017) suggest that structural compliance is often based on a lack of evidence for what would actually work in practice. This hypothesis thus would explain the divergence between inclusive education policy and discriminatory education practice as the result of a lack of practical knowledge at the stage of policymaking. However, it does not account for the fact that some teachers do comply with the law and others do not (cf. chapter 5). As a theory closely settled within the managerial research literature, this argument does not explain variation and consistency across different school contexts. Nor does it allow for the possibility of teachers actively challenging the policy framework in their work beyond the school level (cf. chapter 6). By examining managerial responses to written law and failing to account for the contested nature of policymaking this line of argument does not allow for the influence of multiple logics of diversity.

Yet other research acknowledges the embeddedness of teachers' actions within culture and accounts agency to them but also treats the cultural construct they rely on as a homogeneous entity. Variation in teacher behavior is accounted for by citing individual influences on teachers' actions:

> Students, and also staff, may opt in or out of these principles in ways that depend on particular characteristics of schools, and of each set of local histories [...] and are in no way simple reflections of national ideologies (Sunier, 2013, p. 71).

Since variation in this theory is explained as individualistic factors it cannot be systematized or further elaborated. Other studies explain the exclusions and othering of ethno-religious minorities in German schools (Bender-Szymanski, 2000; Luchtenberg, 2009; Ortloff, 2009; Ortloff and Frey, 2007) with an emphasis on nation and national belonging due to the "monocultural and monolingual identity of German schools" (Auernheimer, 2005, p. 76; Gogolin, 2008). Teachers either opt in or out of this logic based on individual factors. To understand the ways diversification processes are enacted in everyday life, however, it is important to grasp how different logics of diversity might interact with school environments and teachers' beliefs.

All three of these lines of explanation assume an underlying single logic that actors either comply with or not. The symbolic compliance literature is mostly focused on the macro-structural diffusion rather than micro level negotiation processes. Theory positing a lack of knowledge as the main driver of what works is concerned with managerial level negotiations, in public education this would be the policy level, but not with those implementing the actual reforms. The last line of explanation relies on micro process analysis but posits convergence or divergence also on the existence of one uncontested cultural logic. The individual factors cited as explaining divergence are not systematically explained or theorized. I thus argue that to overcome these weaknesses and fully account for the divergence of policy and practice theoretical models need to allow for the heterogeneity of underlying cultural logics and bring together macro and micro level negotiations in one study. Below I will show how employing institutional logics theory achieves this goal.

2.2.1 Institutional Logics: A Way to Account for Heterogeneity and Bringing Micro and Macro Levels Together

Institutional logics are defined as:

> ... the socially constructed, historical patterns of cultural symbols and material practices, assumptions, values, and beliefs by which individuals produce and reproduce their material subsistence, organize time and space, and provide meaning to their daily activity (Thornton and Ocasio, 1999, p. 804).

They are organized in an inter-institutional system made up of institutional orders and elemental categories. This system is configured as ideal type categories (cf. Thornton et al., 2012, pp. 52–53). Core to the conceptualization are seven cornerstone institutional orders: profession, market, state, family, religion, corporation, and community. Each can be broken down into specific building blocks or elemental categories "which represent the cultural symbols and material practices particular to that order" (Thornton et al., 2012, p. 54). Culture thus is broken down into larger ordering categories (i.e. that of profession, market, state, family, religion, corporation and community) and smaller assembling blocks that organizations and individuals may combine and negotiate.

This theory relies on the assumption that negotiation of logics into practice is central to understanding social organization. In other words, what is important and highlighted are "conceptual understandings, cognitive frames and rules that constituted the very nature of the doing, that were part of the production function of rationality itself" (cf. Friedland and Arjaliès, 2019, p. 7). This theory assumes cultural understandings, taken-for-granted ideas to be underlying practice and shaping organizational structures. These ideas and understandings are negotiated on a daily basis by politicians, teachers, students, parents, news media outlets and citizens to name just a few. That is culture, the way it is practiced and the structures that it produces, are operational at different levels of society and get negotiated within but also between these levels. There is thus an interplay between individuals, organizations, and institutions (Thornton and Ocasio, 2008, p. 120). Teachers may negotiate their specific understandings vis-à-vis their students, but they may also engage elements from other institutional orders to promote a different imaginary of their subject vis-à-vis a political imagination.

Inherent in this theory is also the idea of change and instability. Overall, this theory asks, "how institutions through their underlying logics of action, shape heterogeneity, stability and change in individuals and organizations?" (Thornton and Ocasio, 2008, p. 103). Lounsbury (2008) stipulates that heterogeneity of practice may be created by a heterogeneity of underlying logics. This allows for variation within actors' cognitive sense-making and debate over the legitimacy of various practices. The theory's idea of change is thus built on an assumption of the existence of heterogeneity and conflict within and between institutional orders and their elements. This is in contrast to the assumptions espoused by Meyer et al. (1992) and DiMaggio and Powell (1991) which are focused on homogeneity (world culture system) and isomorphism respectively. Alternative institutional logics may serve as toolkits for action (Swidler, 1986). Rather than relying on those logics that are most accessible, social actors may invoke and activate other available logics drawn from other situational contexts" (Thornton et al., 2012, pp. 100–101). This theory thus disassembles culture and provides a way for individual or organizational action upon institutions and culture (cf. Friedland and Alford, 1991; Thornton and Ocasio, 2008). Not all of these combinations need to make rational sense either. As Skrentny (2004) states: "our perception of a thing or person need not be related to other things in any coherent way and may appear illogical if subjected to close scrutiny" (p. 10). That is, there may be inherent disjoints and areas for contesting within each process of meaning-making. For example, it may not make much sense to link so called honor killings with marriage laws leading to the restriction of immigration rights, however, that is exactly what happened in German national political discourse and policymaking. This betrays an underlying logic that is more interested in removing the perceived source of violence, i.e. minority populations, than targeting violence against women (Korteweg and Yurdakul, 2010).

Approaching the question of divergence between policy and practice in this way, allows me to highlight the impacts that multiple logics and their negotiations at the micro and macro level produce. In addition, this aids an analysis of instability, change, and continuities between the imaginations of the subject at different levels. It also allows for systematic explanation of the heterogeneity of practice that can be found within ethics classrooms, where some teachers espouse the imaginary of the subject put forth by the law and others directly oppose it (cf. chapter 5).

It is worth mentioning that I distinguish the concept of imagination from the analytical concepts of narrative, frame, and theory as proposed by Thornton et al. (2012, pp. 152–154). Thornton et al. (2012) define theories, frames and narratives as symbolic constructions. "Theories provide general guiding principles and explanations for why and how institutional structures and practices should operate" (p. 152). Using Goffman, they define frames as "schema[s] of interpretation" that allow individuals "to locate, perceive, identify, and label" events within their life space and their world at large" (p. 154). And finally, "a narrative is a story or account that organizes events and human actions into a whole, thereby attributing significance to individual actions and events according to their effect on the story or account" (p. 155).

I use imagination to speak about the products of sense-making by policymakers and teachers. The concept of imagination I propose combines elements of a theory and narrative to emphasis an aspiration, or as Appadurai (2010) put it, carries "the sense of being a prelude to some sort of expression" and "fuel for action" (p. 7). In other words, an imagination represents the aspiration for material manifestation by its collective creators. Imagination rather than narrative or theory thus highlights the aspect of hope on the level of its creators but also the possibility for change and resistance at the level of those asked to implement it. With this terminology I hope to emphasize the process of negotiation at all levels of education. That is underlying political conceptions of ethics instruction were specific ways of imagining a community in Berlin and beyond. Within the context of this study, the target of the imaginations connected to ethics instruction, I argue, is the creation of some specific form of national community with one possible way of organizing diversity within it.

2.2.2 Conceptualizing Diversity and Power Relations within Institutional Logics

Institutional logics theory and neo-institutional organization theory more generally have been criticized for undertheorizing power relationships (cf. Lawrence and Buchanan, 2008; Willmott, 2015). In addition, neo-institutional theory has been criticized for not paying enough attention to diversity (cf. Rojas, 2017). This is especially critical as the concept of diversity has in many instances replaced ideas like multiculturalism and interculturalism (cf. Çil, 2011; Niehaus, 2018). I argue below that an analysis of the negotiations of underlying logics of diversity also highlights power relationships and thus theoretically expands neo-institutional theory.

Following Vertovec (2015; Vertovec, 2019), I understand diversity as the "social organization of difference" (2019, p. 12) – to highlight the nature of production. This conception is also in line with Foucault's idea of discourse (Foucault, 2013). Michel Foucault (2013) defines discourse as speech acts "composed of signs but what they do is more than use these signs to designate things. It is this move that renders them irreducible to the language and to speech. It is this "move" that we must reveal and describe" (p. 54). Foucault's idea of discourse is essentially based in a social constructivist view of knowledge production and human beings. His goal was to "create a history of the different modes by which, in our culture, human beings are made subjects" (Foucault, 1982, p. 208). Within this view of knowledge production and negotiation Foucault heavily focused on power relationships. Foucault's perception of power is also in line with institutional logics perspective. As Friedland and Arjaliès (2019) argue:

> An institutional logic is a materially and culturally specific organization of systemic power. Power is its inside, not its outside. [...] Institutional logics, as Foucault argues, are themselves powers. The institutional logical view is, in fact, all about power, not as decision, nor structure, but as a systemic grammar of practice. It consequently poses vexing problems for how we conceptualize power" (p. 18).

That is to say, ethnicity, race, and other dimensions of diversity are constructed and in turn constitute social realities.[14] As such diversity is governed by and negotiated through institutional logics in society. This also means that categories of diversity are negotiated within several domains in society, including public education.

I further assume diversity to be context specific (geographic, historical what some have summarized as "situated diversity" (Ye, 2015, p. 173) and have a normative function - that is, its perception and the discourses used to create these categorizations (cf. Foucault, 2013) define the Other in social contexts (cf. Mecheril, 2002). As such it constitutes certain power relationships among groups. The term diversity may include many different categories that share a common core: they are only relevant if perceived to be relevant by social and political actors and must by definition include a norm that they are judged as different against. In other words, conceptions of diversity always construct an Other often with consequences for inherent power relationships.

More specifically, what is diverse depends not only on the perception of social and political actors but also on the context in which these actors are situated (cf. "situated diversity", Ye, 2015). For example, while a Muslim woman in Germany or France may be categorized as diverse or Other (cf. Shooman, 2014; Spielhaus, 2014), this would not be the case in a predominantly Muslim country like Pakistan where rather a white European Christian would be the Other. Furthermore, who is considered diverse depends on historical time (cf. Morning, 2011; Rojas, 2017). The Irish and Italian, for example, were viewed as dangerous to national cohesion at the beginning of the 20th

---

14 Within sociology especially the concept of race has produced much research, going back to the civil rights area in US history (Kelly and Dobbin, 1998) – expanding from African Americans to Hispanic, and Asian Americans and other groups (Skrentny, 2004). In more recent decades diversity has started to include categories like sexual orientation, gender, physical and mental disabilities, age and other categories of individual identity difference (cf. for example Vertovec, 2019). Citizenship and migration scholars also include categories like citizenship status, country of origin, and length of stay, migration route, whether the migration was forced or voluntary in the term (cf. Çil, 2011; Vertovec, 2007).

century in the USA and have since been subsumed under the category of white (with all its social advantages). The categories of diversity are thus inherently negotiated and contested.

Politically, dimensions of diversity may also be leveraged for power and legitimacy (cf. Bell, 2014; Shiao, 2005; Skrentny, 2004). When this is done by those in power the process may have no or negative consequences for diverse populations (see for example "symbolic compliance" literature or "pinkwashing", "whitewashing", and "Colorblind" literature). However, this may also happen by under-privileged groups as a means to increase their rights (e.g. cf. social movements literature such as Zajak et al., 2023; see also literature of the commercialization of minority culture – e.g. Comaroff and Comaroff, 2009; Miller-Idriss, 2017). Thus, diversity may be created and mobilized strategically for various purposes.

Most scholarship on the development of diversity policy sees a historical progression from discriminating laws such as Jim Crow laws to anti-discrimination and minority rights laws (Shiao, 2005; Skrentny, 2004). A liberal narrative of progress with increasingly better and more discrimination critical race-relations. Talking about power, however, Shiao (2005) complicates this linear history by allowing for the existence of heterogeneous positions toward diversity competing for political power, speaking specifically of pro diversity, diversity-queasy, and anti-diversity positions, as well as the existence of mixed sense-making: "one might be pro-diversity with respect to certain groups and issues and diversity-queasy with regard to others" (p. 14). Diversity policies he warns, may "asymmetrically target non-White acceptability while leaving White attitudes and behaviors untouched." (Shiao, 2005, p. 15). Others have also criticized that "Nation States today develop a variety of ways to translate nationalist exclusivism into inclusivist narratives of participation, integration, and identification" (Sunier, 2013, p. 54). Thus, a focus on the negotiations of logics of diversity in public education also needs to account for inherent power relationships. Teachers and their construction of categories of diversity are a pivotal yet under examined area to study this. Whether or not it matters that a student is a Christian, Muslim, Jew, second-generation immigrant, or in the German nomenclature a person with migrant background, is entirely up to the teachers' negotiation of diversity logics. As I will show below, a Vietnamese student "whose parents have lived here for decades" may be counted toward the homogeneous German student body, whereas students with "Turkish or Arabic migration background" may be always foreign (Frau Zimmermann, Interview on 3/3/2016, cf. chapter 5).

Hence, if we truly want to understand how societies plan to integrate ethnic and religious diversity, what role diversity-inclusive policies play, and why they may fail in practice we need to focus not only on contexts that are highly diverse but also on those that are dominated by the majority. In public education, it is important to understand what place the issue of diversity is given in contexts where the majority of students are not diverse. In fact, as (Crul and Lelie, 2023) show, it is especially the group without migration biography that we should pay attention to. It is important to highlight the silences that are present, the voices heard and not heard, within the negotiation of logics in policymaking and in everyday classrooms. Focusing on diversity as an area of negotiating institutional logics will highlight the way power works within these processes.

2.2.3 Situating Diversity within Institutional Logics Theory: The Institutional Order of Community

In some ways Thornton et al. (2012) recognized the importance of diversity and race relations for institutional logics theory by adding the order of community to the initial framework proposed by Friedland and Alford (1991). However, while Thornton et al. (2012) give a broad theoretical account of what this order entails, they do not focus specifically on questions of diversity management. To them the addition of the order of community generally countered a neo-institutional focus on global isomorphism (Marquis and Battilana, 2007) and promised to refocus analysis of organizational behavior on the local community (Shiao, 2005; Thornton et al., 2012, p. 70). Following Brint (2001) community is defined as:

> … aggregates of people who share common activities and/or beliefs and who are bound together principally by relations of affect, loyalty, common values, and/or personal concern. (p. 8)

As such communities may be conceptualized as any number of groups that feel a connection such as social and protest movements (Ingram and Rao, 2004; Ingram et al., 2010), academic communities (Knorr-Cetina, 2022); occupations (Bechky, 2003), communities of practice (Wenger, 1998, 2000) and many more.

Implied in this definition of community is also the question of belonging, inclusion and exclusion. What my research suggests is that within the logic of community there is an inherently antagonistic relationship between logics that seek inclusion and those that exclude outsiders. At various societal levels these are continuously negotiated by political and social actors. Paying attention to when and how these two logics are negotiated, illuminates new empirical insights into the connection of power and diversity to institutions and highlights the importance of community as an institutional order. In this way, this study also contributes to theory building within undertheorized areas of neo-institutional organization theory (Friedland and Arjaliès, 2019; Lawrence and Buchanan, 2008; Rojas, 2017).

2.3 Teachers as Single-Level Actors: Advocating for a Multilevel Account

Throughout this study, I further argue that in order to account for the divergence between policy and practice and the inherent power relationships negotiated by teachers, it is important to pay attention to the level at which teachers are active. In the research literature, teachers are either analyzed as working as transmitters of state sanctioned knowledge or as agents acting against state policy. Within both of these levels of teacher agency they may either occupy a role as agents of change (Berkovich, 2011; Bracho, 2015; Guven, 2018; Mazawi, 1994; Worden, 2011) or as agents of policy stasis (Abu El-Haj, 2010; Abu El-Haj et al., 2017; Jaffe-Walter, 2013, 2017; Ríos-Rojas, 2014; Shirazi, 2017; Simel, 1996; Slavkin, 2012). However, research rarely pays attention to both levels of teacher policy interaction in the same analysis (Riggan (2016) is an exception to this). Research conceptualizing teachers thus glosses over the heterogeneous drivers acting within the profession and the liminal position that teachers occupy. Said differently, these accounts miss the complex roles that teachers play in creating an imagination of the nation and its community (Anderson, 2016).

Research examining the interactions of teachers with students often emphasize their role as uncritical transmitters of state-sanctioned acts of discrimination. Slavkin (2012), for example, shows that German teachers during the Nazi regime were complicit in the Holocaust acting as cultural agents preparing atrocities and actively participating in discrimination by transmitting a regime sanctioned curriculum in their classrooms. They also show how this was aided by the removal of not-Arian and dissenting teachers early in the Nazi regime (Slavkin, 2012, p. 438). Research on contemporary issues surrounding ethnic and religious diversity also sees teachers' work as "an expression of national policies and political discourse" (Jaffe-Walter, 2017, p. 64). Rather than looking at the formal curriculum – that is the content of instruction – these accounts often examine an informal curriculum – that is the ways that teachers treat, and sanction students differently based on their ethnic or religious backgrounds (Abu El-Haj, 2010; Abu El-Haj et al., 2017; Ríos-Rojas, 2014; Simel, 1996). Teachers in these accounts are mere extensions of the state apparatus following a single, dominant, state sanctioned logic and acting upon a cultural, ethnic, or religious Other. Often this line of argument is interested in state-sanctioned discrimination and exclusion processes enacted in schools conducting research in highly diverse school environments.

Accounts that see teachers as agents of change on the other hand focus on teacher interaction against state policy either implicitly by changing formal curricula (Guven, 2018) or explicitly by engaging in political mobilization directly (Bracho, 2015). The social movements' literature emphasizes the role of unions and professional associations in the mobilization and political claims making process (Bracho, 2015; Chisholm, 1999; Gardinier, 2012; Hilferty, 2008; Keating, Preston, Burke, Van Heertum, and Arnove, 2013; LeTendre, 1994; McGinty, 2009). Teachers' actions, and professional behavior are seen as mediated through individual identities, life histories, and beliefs (Beauchamp and Thomas, 2009; Guven, 2018; Mazawi, 1994; Worden, 2011). Especially teachers' own minority identities may become relevant motivators for resistance and change (Mazawi, 1994). In these accounts teachers thus become quasi-rational actors, relying on self-interest and personal factors that are, for example, shaped by local traditions (Bracho, 2015). Whereas teachers in the previous line of argument were instruments of state sanctioned discrimination, in the second line of argument they are often motivated by resistance to discrimination and exclusion of their own group identities. That is, in this case teachers are part of the state-constructed Other.[15]

These theories thus either support an argument that sees discrimination and racism "as the problem of a few bad apples" (Bell, 2014, p. 7) – those that do not resist discriminatory policy due to individual factors – or as deterministic power structures that teachers inadvertently re-produce. That is, the policy practice division is either seen as the result of too much teacher agency or a complete lack thereof. These accounts, however, cannot fully explain the puzzle of the German division between policy and practice: where a low number of minority group teachers in Germany – estimates range between two and six percent of the German teaching force (Georgi et al., 2011, p. 18) – is combined with pro-diversity education policy. Resistance to state policy of inclusion is thus not based on teachers' minority status. Based on the arguments above we would either expect to see better minority group outcomes as teachers uncritically follow pro-diversity education policy inclusive of minority group identities. Alternatively, we would have to assume that a majority of teachers based on individualistic factors follow racist or discriminatory assumptions about their students exercising their own agency. Neither of these hypotheses, however, explain why teachers may on the one hand espouse teaching approaches that are diversity inclusive in the classroom, but simultaneously engage in policy interaction beyond their school context that actively seeks to eliminate the teaching of diversity, on the other hand (cf. chapter 5 and 6). There is therefore a difference in the engagement with policy based on the two separate levels of teacher interaction that may nuance and further our understanding of why diversity-friendly policy may fail in various ways in practice. Below I thus propose conceptualizing teachers' liminal position and the ways in which they act politically.

---

15 Within the sociological literature othering is referred to as communicating "perpetuating prejudice, discrimination, and injustice either through deliberate or ignorant means" (MacQuarrie, 2009, p. 635). The term *Other* is thus often used as a reference for the person or social group targeted by these prejudices, discriminations, and injustices.

2.3.1 Conceptualizing Teachers Liminal Position

Teachers occupy different roles vis-à-vis the state and civic society and as such, exert different forms of power and agency. First, teachers may act as state agents enacting education policy. Their decisions, practices and routines effectively become the policy to their students (Lipsky, 2010, p. xiii). Students also perceive schools as state agents as the Fridays for Future movement shows. In an attempt to sway national politics on climate change youth utilize schools and more precisely a refusal to attend them as a strategic means to get the states attention. Schools are thus intensely political locations.

Second, teachers act as citizens, and professionals that sometimes do not fully agree with state policy decisions and might thus resist the political imagination produced and signed into law by policy makers (cf. Guven, 2018; Riggan, 2016). As such they also actively imagine and create the state and nation, they envisage themselves to be representatives of (cf. Anderson, 2016). Recent research has shown that in fragile contexts the imagined unity between state and nation may fracture and decouple. In these cases, the state no longer represents, creates or shapes the nation (cf. Riggan, 2016). Resistance may happen violently through strikes and protest movements (cf. Bracho, 2015) or in the classroom by changing the curriculum presented to students (cf. Guven, 2018).

When we conceptualize teachers as political agents, they may thus exercise their agency at two different levels: (1) vis-à-vis the (future) citizenry represented by their students – as agents of the state – and (2) vis-à-vis the state – as part of the citizenry or semi-autonomous professional group to change policy. Teachers thus represent a middle actor (Riggan, 2016, p. 16). They are employed by the state, entrusted with state sanctioned knowledge transfer and policy enactment. At the same time, they are also subject to "the same quotidian social, political, and economic processes as the broader citizenry" (ibid.). A Foucauldian reading of teachers as subject under state control argues that new testing and evaluation regimes essential put teachers under constant surveillance (cf. Bushnell, 2003). They may thus be subject to pressures that make them leave their role as state agents.

Either of these positions is guided and motivated by a different set of cultural logics. Teachers acting as state agents may mobilize security logics (cf. Skrentny (2004) for a discussion of this in U.S. policymaking) or logics of national belonging (cf. Ortloff, 2009; Sunier, 2013) to differentiate their students or justify a specific curriculum. Teachers acting as representatives of the citizenry may mobilize professional logics against the state to justify a more conservative course that they see connected to more job security (cf. chapter 6).

In both cases, whether they act in accordance with or against state policy, teachers in public schools are often the first state agents that children and youth will encounter in their lives and thus play a crucial role in socializing students into their "place in the political community" (Burde, 2014; Lipsky, 2010, p. 4; Luykx, 1999; Riggan, 2016; Wilson, 2001) but also in how their students may imagine the state they live in and the community they are a part of (Anderson, 2016; Appadurai, 2010). As such teachers are hugely influential in the way that the next generation of citizens feels and imagines the state and the nation (Anderson, 2016; Appadurai, 2010; Bendix, 2017; Foucault, 1995; Weber, 1976). As Riggan (2016) states:

> In material terms, The State does not act on bodies; rather, individual state agents do. But through state agents' interactions with the bodies of state subjects, everyone involved - agents and subjects alike - come to imagine the state and their relationship to it. (p. 16)

Absences of representation and spaces for minority youth in schools may thus become reflective of an inaccessibility of the nation to these groups more generally. In addition, these absences may signal a false national homogeneity to majority students, symbolically removing diverse groups from the imagined national community. The same is true of the opposite scenario. That is teachers that are inclusive of diversity in their teaching signal societal openness and inclusion to their students.

The state as such does not exist but is rather constituted by the imagination of citizens (Appadurai, 2010; Riggan, 2016). Teachers thus constitute the actions and imaginations of the state (Riggan, 2016, p. 12). The state is established by policies, agencies, and political constructs that hold sovereignty over the national territory and its people and creates an imagination about the national community (Riggan, 2016, pp. 3–4). What happens in the domain of public education, thus matters immensely in terms how the state is imagined, enacted, constructed and experienced by youth. In their attempts to make sense of diversity, teachers aspire to one possible way of incorporating diversity into their local and national community. These imaginations are *political* in the sense that they provide a certain way of experiencing the state and its relationship to diversity for students. Thus, teachers are critical actors to study if we are to understand how the nation is imagined writ large and how diversity is experienced at the local level.

2.4 Bringing it all together: Constructing Diversity in Berlin's Mandatory Ethics Instruction

Throughout this chapter, I have argued that existing theories examining the division between policy and practice, diversity, and teachers' roles in this phenomenon falls short in four distinct ways: 1) They assume a homogeneity of underlying logics and 2) they divide policy and practice in their research. 3)

They don't account for the power relationships inherent in the negotiation of diversity. And 4) they don't adequately account for liminal status of teachers.

By employing institutional logics theory and methodologically structuring this study as a vertical case study (cf. chapter 3) I overcome these weaknesses. This enables me to show how similar logics are negotiated at the political and classroom level leading to an internally contested policymaking process on the one hand (cf. chapter 4) and a heterogeneity of practice and unstable institutional environment ripe for challenges from within on the other (cf. chapter 5 and 6). In other words, I offer an empirical and theoretical account of policy and practice dissonance.

In addition, by highlighting the role the negotiation of logics of diversity played my empirical account of diversity management in Berlin's public education is able to build theory along the previously undertheorized areas of power and diversity within neo-institutional organization theory. I argue that understanding these processes of negotiation can help us account for how predominantly diversity friendly education policies in Germany may turn into discriminatory and exclusionary education outcomes. I show that how logics of diversity are negotiated by political actors exposes where political imagination and practice diverge.

3 Methodology

3.1 A Comparative Case Study of Diversity in Schools

In this chapter, I discuss the methodological base for designing my investigation as an ethnographic comparative case study following Bartlett and Vavrus (2016). More precisely, most of my analysis depends on the comparison between policy actors and teachers, which incorporates the vertical axis of comparison (Bartlett and Vavrus, 2016). I thus also draw heavily on their earlier conceptions of a vertical case study (cf. Vavrus and Bartlett, 2006, 2009). Further, I argue that is the best way to answer how political actors (in government and public education) understand and negotiate diversity in their work and how this varies across different school and individual contexts. As I argue in the previous chapter, in order to fully understand the divergence between policy and practice, we need to analyze the micro level negotiations of the logics of diversity in everyday schooling and education policymaking. Thus, utilizing this design allows me to bring together an analysis of the macro policy and micro classroom context.

As I describe in the following, for my analysis I collected ethnographic data including semi-structured interviews, classroom observations, and policy, instructional, and curriculum documents. The multitude of data sources allowed me to construct an in-depth examination of both policy discourse and teachers' sense-making about diversity, and thus answer my research questions. This approach also allows for data triangulation and thus increases the study's validity.

Furthermore, I indicate the details of my sampling strategy affords maximum variation according to school location in Berlin, student body academic achievement,[16] and student body diversity. Due to self-selection bias, the teach-

---

16 Germany's school system is divided into three different tracks after primary school (in Berlin beyond 6th grade), based on student achievement. In the highest track, *Gymansium*, students graduate after grade 12 with the *Abitur* enabling them to go to university. The middle track is called *Realschule*, and students in this track graduate after 10th grade, and traditionally have embarked upon an apprenticeship. The lowest academic track, *Hauptschule*, ends after 9th or 10th grade and students on this track also go on to learn a trade, via apprenticeships. However, over the past four decades this last track has increasingly become stigmatizing and students graduating from this track have severe problems finding apprenticeships. In Berlin the lower two tracks were combined in 2010/2011 to counteract this stigmatization and enable better school-work transitions for students. Thus, Berlin offers only two tracks: *Gymnasium* and *Integrierte Sekundarschule*. In the context of this study, high track refers to *Gymnasium* while low track references the *Integrierte Sekundarschule*.

ing staff sample was, 1) overall better qualified compared to the population of ethics teachers in Berlin according to the level of qualification they had achieved for ethics,[17] and 2) they were generally interested in cultural differences, intercultural, and interreligious teaching which they told me repeatedly during and after the interviews. They thus represented a best case when it comes to the issue of diversity negotiation in Berlin's secondary schools. This is especially significant given my finding that some participating teachers are actively advocating for the removal of certain curriculum components regarding the teaching of diversity from ethics courses (see chapter 6). These teacher characteristics also contributed to a bias towards high track and popular/selective schools in the sample. The teachers in my sample worked in settings that allowed them to predominantly concentrate on the content in their ethics instruction. In addition, teachers were almost equally distributed between teaching in diverse and non-diverse school contexts.

This chapter proceeds as follows: First, I discuss my rationale for designing my investigation as a vertical comparative case study before describing my sampling strategy and overall sample. I then review each data source starting with interview data, followed by observation, and document data. Next, I explain access and the socio-political context shaping my data collection before providing a description of my data analysis and triangulation procedures. Last, I outline and my role as researcher within the process.

3.2 The Vertical Case Study Approach

Case studies have a long tradition in comparative and international education research and started as a complement to quantitative inquiry (Crossley and Vulliamy, 1984; Tight, 2017). Typically, they are a form of qualitative or mixed methods research that analyzes research questions with systems "bounded by time and place" (Bassey, 1999; Creswell, 2013, p. 97). To answer

---

17 Ethics teachers can qualify for teaching the subject in various ways in Berlin. They either have studied philosophy/ethics at university (this is considered the highest and "best" level of qualification according to ethics teachers; cf. chapter 6). They may have completed a one and a half year long training seminar and gained an additional qualification certificate (additional to the subjects they studied at university and entered the profession with). However, in some cases, they may not have any training at all in ethics but instead become certified by the individual school's principal as having an aptitude for the subject (this is called *Kompetenz* or *Neigungsfach* in German and literally means having an affinity or liking for the area). These three ways of qualifying for ethics instruction are perceived to be hierarchical by ethics teachers with university studies being the most appropriate form of qualification and no training being considered as requiring further professional development.

my research questions, I employ a specific form of case study: an ethnographic vertical case study design.

The vertical case study is one aspect of Bartlett and Vavrus's (2016) broader approach to comparative case studies. Since first publishing their methodological reflections on vertical case studies and establishing its place within comparative and international education, the authors have significantly expanded and re-conceptualized their methodological designs. In this new conceptualization they change the name to comparative case study where the vertical is one axis of comparison, along with horizontal and transversal aspects. While my study includes some aspects discussed in their design, I chose to focus on the vertical dimension predominantly as it allows me to best answer my research question. Thus, I continue to apply the term vertical case study and focus on the 2006 and 2009 concepts discussed by Vavrus and Bartlett throughout this work.

Vertical case studies specifically are geared towards "a multisited, qualitative case study that traces the linkages among local, national, and international forces and institutions that together shape and are shaped by education in a particular locale" (Vavrus and Bartlett, 2009, pp. 11–12). The goal of this approach is thus to connect macro and micro level structures with each other and "develop a thorough understanding of the particular at each level and to analyze how these understandings produce similar and different interpretations of the policy, problem, or phenomenon under study" (Vavrus and Bartlett, 2009, p. 11). The authors further argue that "vertical comparisons across levels, such as the local, the national, and the international, are essential" for three different reasons: 1) to avoid generically attributing causal effects to macro structures and thus taking the macro "for granted" (p. 9); 2) to decenter the nation state as the primary unit of analysis (p. 11); and 3) to avoid ignoring or downplaying "the role of modern schools in structuring identities and power relations" (Vavrus and Bartlett, 2009, p. 11 citing Levinson, 1999, p. 594). This approach is thus ideally suited for my investigation.

Further, I situate my case study in ethics instruction, exclusively in Berlin, to examine Germany's effort to create inclusive schools, teach students about the concept of peaceful coexistence, and facilitate cultural integration. Specifically, I examine one subject that has received scarce research attention in the published literature. The study is bounded by a specific policy issue (mandatory ethics; cf. Thomas, 2011, p. 23 for the inclusion of policy as a case), a place (Berlin), and it includes multiple sites. In addition to the geographic boundaries, the case presented in this study is also bounded by time. It spans two distinctive periods linked to the macro and micro level compared: the policymaking dimension of this study focuses predominantly on the 1990s and early 2000s, while also engaging with the history after WW2. The ethnographic data collected in schools is bounded by a period of one and a half years and includes the fall term of 2015, and spring, summer, and fall of 2016. To present an in-depth description and analysis of the case, I collected and analyzed three different types of data: 1) documents, 2) semi-structured qualitative interviews, and 3) observations. Each of these sources will be described in further detail.

This research carefully considers various levels in the policy formation around mandatory ethics in educational institutions in Berlin. This approach also fits with my overarching theoretical framework. As specified previously, institutional logics theory relies on the careful examination of multiple levels of analysis and the cross-effects between these levels (Thornton et al., 2012). The main players in this analysis are ethics teachers, at a variety of secondary schools in Berlin, and politicians in Berlin's Senate, as well as external political stakeholders such as the teachers' union and professional associations. Based on the larger research question, these individual actors can be subsumed in different levels of analysis: the federal state government (cf. chapter 4), the organizational field of secondary schools in Berlin (cf. chapter 6), and individual schools as organizations (cf. chapter 5). The input from these levels is assimilated in the final discussion of this research (chapter 7).

Employing a vertical case study in the context of Berlin's approach to diversity in education offers distinct epistemological advantages. 1) I do not consider the macro structure as a taken for granted causal force. This work highlights the contentious processes that characterized the political negotiations about the introduction of mandatory ethics in Berlin's secondary schools and its subsequent challenge in a public referendum. I thus seek to complicate the macro level and show that both political visions of value education in Berlin had effects on how the subject came to be imagined by the public and by teachers. At the level of policy negotiation within Berlin's Senate, I also consider the influences of international forces such as increasing security discourses linked to Muslim minority populations and the prevalence of Human Rights as a basis for educational interventions. 2) The nation state is not the primary unit of analysis. Rather, I consider how ideas of nation and national belonging are negotiated at the federal state level (Länder) and in classrooms in Berlin. Finally, 3) by considering how teachers negotiate and apply the logics of diversity to their classrooms and teaching, as well as how they collectively imagine the subject beyond their individual school context. In addition, I carefully take into account how identities and power relations are structured, perpetuated and challenged in public schools. Overall, this allows me to present a holistic indepth analysis of mandatory ethics instruction in Berlin's public secondary schools as a case of how societal diversification may influence education practice and policy.

3.3 Sampling Strategy and Overall Sample Description

This section focuses on my ethnographic data and how I recruited and selected participants. I base my sampling strategy on the assumption that answering the question of what institutional logics underlie the understandings and classroom behaviors of ethics teachers requires a thorough understanding of the commonalities and differences between individual teachers and different organizational (school) contexts. Thus, comparison of multiple schools with different populations was crucial to my study design. This comparison across different populations also breaks with the overwhelming focus of the current research literature on schools with predominantly ethno-religiously diverse student populations (cf. chapter 1 and 2). I also wanted to gain an understanding of ethics teachers across Berlin. Therefore, I sampled for maximum variation in terms of location and contacted all 224 high and low track public secondary schools in Berlin via email. Emails were sent either to the schools' principal or the administrative office. In general, at German schools, principles are the gate keepers to the schools' teacher and student population. They have to agree to participate and facilitate contact to specific departments. In addition, for most schools only the principals and/or administrative offices email contacts are publicly available. The overall response rate was low at just around nine percent with a total of 21 schools willing to participate initially. However, due to scheduling conflicts and various other reasons not all of them actually participated in the end. I expected a low response rate, however, the socio-political circumstances that surrounded my recruitment and study overall may have contributed to an even more guarded attitude towards a study that seeks to understand diversity in public schools (see chapter 1 and below). A few teachers and schools were also recruited through snowball sampling as teachers I had interviewed suggested and facilitated contact to other teachers that they thought were a great fit for my study. I was able to conduct research at a total of 17 different secondary schools. Schools were located in all 12 districts in Berlin. Schools differed according to their academic track level, their student body diversity, and socio-economic background.

Schools that participated usually employed ethics teachers that were highly interested in the development of ethics as a subject and in the issue of religious and ethnic diversity. In the conversations I had with them during and after the interviews they also frequently spoke about their dedication and interest in the issues focused on by my study. Teachers' dedication to the subject was also evident in the engagement of teachers beyond the individual school levels, acting for example as co-authors of state curricula, educating student teachers, chairing professional associations, and organizing and teaching continued education workshops for in-service teachers. Overall, about 20.5 percent of the teachers in my sample were engaged in some way outside of their place of employment. This could mean that they served as instructors for student teachers, taught at universities or served other functions beyond their schools. 23.1 percent of the teachers in my sample were also engaged in additional leadership functions within their schools. This usually meant that they were department heads for ethics. These numbers may include the same teacher in both counts as oftentimes department heads also served leadership and other functions beyond their schools. In terms of understanding negotiations of diversity in ethics classrooms they thus represent a best case as none of them thought teaching about diversity in public education was unnecessary. In addition, to understand how teachers imagined the subject they represented individuals that were actively engaged in shaping the future of the subject.

In terms of their qualification credentials for ethics, the teachers in my sample were highly qualified as ethics teachers.[18] They on average had higher types of qualifications than the population of ethics teachers in Berlin for the school year 2015/2016. Specifically, 53.8 percent of teachers in my sample had a university degree qualifying them to teach ethics compared to 36.6 percent in the population. 33.3 percent of my sample had completed an additional training compared to 54.9 percent in the population and 12.8 percent in my sample had no qualification for ethics compared to 8.5 percent in the sample (source: this research and Senatsverwaltung für Bildung, Jugend und Familie, n. d.–a). This can be explained by the fact that teachers who had higher qualifications were more confident in their knowledge of the subject (cf. chapter 6). For example, almost all of the student teachers (Referendare) who participated told me at the beginning of the interview that they thought they did not yet have enough teaching experience. They thus were unsure if, what they had to say, was actually going to be useful for my study. The teachers represented in this study are thus in majority confident in their abilities to teach ethics and are excellent informants on how this subject is taught in Berlin's schools.

In addition, as a result of these self-selection mechanisms the majority of schools in the sample were high academic track schools (Gymnasium). Throughout Berlin the percentage of teachers with university qualifications for

---

18 Having a well-educated ethics teaching staff is not the rule throughout Berlin. In fact, there was a general lack of trained ethics teachers. About 65.3 percent of ethics at lower track secondary schools and 35 percent at higher track secondary schools in 2013 was taught by teachers without a certification in ethics, which was widely cited in the press (cf. Anders (2013)). Compared to the statistics from 2013, not much had changed in the 2015/16 school year. There was a total of 1.025 certified ethics teachers who worked in Berlin's primary and secondary schools - 42.3 percent (434) of whom had a university education in ethics/ philosophy, 52.8 percent (541) had completed an additional certification (Zusatzqualifikation), and 7.8 percent (80) were certified by principals with a competency for ethics (Kompetenzfach) with no training at all. At lower secondary schools (ISS) about one third (32.1 percent) of ethics teachers had a university qualification, compared to 42.8 percent at higher secondary schools (cf. Senatsverwaltung für Bildung, Jugend und Familie n. d.-a).

ethics is higher at high track schools. That is the best qualified teachers in terms of their degrees also teach at high track schools. Furthermore, many of the schools in this study were performing at or above their peers' academic levels (as measured by student GPAs) and were among the most popular schools in their respective districts.[19] This resulted in those schools being selective in their student intake. Schools would, for example, have specific entry criteria, require individual interviews with prospective candidates or application material for in school specializations (i.e. arts focused etc.).

Below are detailed descriptions of the school characteristics most important to my analysis (see Table 1 in the Appendix for an overview):

1. *Track*: Of the 17 schools who participated in the study, ten were of the highest academic track (Gymnasium) while seven were lower academic track (Integrierte Sekundarschule). Of the overall sample 67.5 percent of the teachers interviewed taught at the Gymnasium while only 32.5 percent taught at Integrierte Sekundarschule. There is thus a slight bias in the sample towards high track schools.
2. *Diversity*: Measuring diversity in schools is difficult as statistical data collected may not reflect the actual diversity based on ethnicity, religion, or migration status at any given school. I used two measures to support an approximation of student body diversity at any given school in terms of its ethnic makeup (as measured by non-German home language NGHL) and students' citizenship status (as measured by students with non-German citizenship NGC).[20] I combined both of these measures here and compared them against the city-wide average for the 2015/2016 school year. Overall 34.1 percent of students in Berlins secondary schools did not speak German at home (Senatsverwaltung für Bildung, Jugend und Familie, 2015, p. 5 my calculation). Foreign students (students without German citizenship) comprised an average of 12.6 percent of Berlin's student body (Senatsverwaltung für Bildung, Jugend und Familie, 2015, p. 4, my calculation). I classified schools who fell distinctly below both measures as non-diverse while schools that were around or above these averages were classified as diverse.
3. *Socio-Economic Status*: Socio-economic status was included in my analysis as a control measure to gain more context on the characteristics

---

19 Within Berlin parents can indicate three schools that they would like their children to attend after primary school. Over-enrolled schools in Berlin are those most frequently picked as number one schools by parents, however, this does not mean that these schools enroll more students than they have capacities for. In my sample three of the seven participating lower secondary schools and three of the ten participating higher secondary schools were among the top ten schools in 2018, (cf. Senatsverwaltung für Bildung, Jugend und Familie, 2017).
20 However, at least NGHL may be highly unreliable as it is based on teachers' perception and judgement (personal communication with Riem Spielhaus, 30.7.2019).

of the student body, especially considering the highly unreliable variables available to measure diversity. I grouped schools according to students' socio-economic status (SES) as measured by teaching material subsidies (Lehrmittelzuzahlungsbefreiung) awarded to parents by Berlin's department of education. The higher the number of students with subsidies the lower the SES of the student body overall. I compared individual school data to the overall average in Berlin for secondary schools which for the school year 2015/2016 was at 20.4 percent. I classified schools with a relatively low percentage of subsidies (below 15 percent of the student body) as having a high SES. Those schools with a percentage of students with subsides around the Berlin average (between 15 and 25 percent of the student body) were classified as median SES. While those with a high percentage of students with subsidies were classified as having a low SES. Respectively the majority of schools (64.3 percent) in the sample had a student body with high SES, 29.4 percent of the schools in my sample had a student body with a median SES overall and only 17.5 percent of the schools in my sample had a student body with a low SES. Due to the unequal distribution of interviews per school this meant that 16 (42.1 percent) of the interviewees served at schools with high SES, nine teachers (23.7 percent) worked at schools with median SES, and 13 interviewees (34.2 percent) taught at schools with low SES.

School 12 and 13 represent outliers in the category of diverse student body if contextualized with socio-economic status. School 12 is marked by a comparatively low number of students who did not speak German at home but had a comparatively high number of students without German citizenship. Both measures are combined with a high level of student body socio-economic background. School 13 has high levels of non-German home language and non-German citizenship students but again this is combined with a high student body SES status. This can be explained by the schools' international focus and their rigid entry examination. The ethnic and religious diversity presented at these schools is thus different from that at the other schools classified as diverse in this sample.

3.3.1 Interview Data

Semi-structured in-depth interviews were an ideal way to explore how ethics teachers understood and negotiated logics of diversity. In addition to interviews with teachers I also spoke with political stakeholders (experts). My interview data include semi-structured interviews with 39 ethics teachers and two experts. Teacher interviews are the main corpus of data for analysis in the teacher focused chapters 5 and 6 while the expert interviews informed chapter 4.

My interview design and protocol were based on the methods of "responsive interviewing" described by Rubin and Rubin (2011). They define semi-structured interviews as "scheduled, usually extended conversation between researcher and interviewee" which the researcher prepares by having a "specific topic to learn about, [...] a limited number of questions," and "plans to ask follow-up questions" (p. 31). They lay out three characteristics of qualitative interviews: 1) the researcher seeks rich, detailed information such as examples, experiences, narratives or stories from interviewees, 2) the interviewer asks open ended questions, 3) "the questions [...] are not fixed" (Rubin and Rubin, 2011, p. 29). The overall goal of interviewing, they argue, is for the researcher to "explore in detail the experiences, motives, and opinions of others and learn to see the world from their perspective" (Rubin and Rubin, 2011, p. 3).

All interviews conducted for this study were either transcribed by me or by professional transcription agencies (identified by referral from colleagues) verbatim according to scientific standards that include utterances like "ehm", "mh" and pauses, laughs or other non-language sounds. Below I detail each type of interview data.

Teacher Interviews: Over the course of my field work, I interviewed 39 ethics teachers. Except for one interview, all interviews were conducted one-on-one usually in teachers' lounges, empty classrooms, or empty preparation rooms in free blocks of time during the school day or in some cases after the school day had ended. Interviews were audio-recorded with two devices. This served as a backup method and was explained to interview participants. It was used to ensure that even if one device failed to record properly a back-up copy of the data existed. Interviews with teachers were conducted between September 1st, 2015 and July 18th, 2016 and lasted between 25 and 98 minutes. Short interviews were usually the result of scheduling restraints that teachers communicated to me before the interview started. In these cases, I generally left out some of the questions from the interview protocol or refrained from asking too many follow up questions.

The number of teachers interviewed per school depended mostly on how supportive the ethics department head was of the study and on how big the ethics faculty was (which varied considerably across the schools). At some schools I interviewed all or the majority of the ethics teaching staff. Department heads even took it upon themselves to create an interview schedule and had signup sheets for the teachers in their department. At other schools I was invited to department meetings to introduce the study, recruit teachers, and schedule interviews myself. At yet other schools only one teacher (usually the department head) was interested in participating or the faculty decided collectively (without my presence) who the best representative for an interview would be.

All interviews followed the same pattern. I presented interviewees with the consent form and informed them of their rights as study participants. I then introduced the study and its purpose to the interviewee. The interview protocol followed four general themes, starting with questions about interviewees' personal and professional experience, followed by a general description of their school and classroom environment, specific questions about ethics instruction and its goals, and more general questions about the relationship of religion and society. In accordance with Berlin's guidelines and laws, teachers were not asked personal details like age or religion. However, over the course of the interviews some voluntarily offered this information. The question series about ethics instruction included a question that prompted teachers with a quote from Berlin's school laws about the goal of ethics instruction after teachers had already been asked about their personal objectives and goals for ethics and their students. My rationale for including this question was to prompt a direct response of teachers to the policy and political imagination of ethics and thus be able to establish the relationship of teachers to this policy directive.

I classified teachers across a variety of measures like gender, religiosity, career level, ethics education, and engagement within and outside of the school. I also recorded the other subjects that they taught at their respective schools (see Table 2 in the Appendix). In order to protect my participants' identity, however, I did not include their other subjects or level of engagement in the overview below.

Expert Interviews: These interviews were conducted with two interviewees that were and are involved in mandatory ethics political justification and conception. One of the two interviewees was highly involved as the speaker for the teacher's union and for Pro Ethics, a group established when mandatory ethics was challenged in the public referendum. He was involved and attended important political meetings and discussions and led efforts from the teacher's union to advocate for curriculum changes. He also agreed that his real name could be used in the analysis. The second expert was the national head of the teacher's association for ethics and author of ethics teaching methodology books. He was also involved albeit less visibly in the political negotiation processes around mandatory ethics introduction and the referendum serving as an adviser within the Pro Ethics.

I did not create specific interview protocols for these two interviews but rather engaged in an open non-structured discussion with them about the history of ethics in Berlin, the goals of ethics instruction as well as problems that ethics may face politically and in the classroom. Both interviews were long as a result, lasting 112 and 134 minutes respectively. The experts also provided additional historical documents, methodology books, and other material which created a rich source of background data for my analysis as well as providing documents (like the first federal state curriculum for ethics) that I could not obtain otherwise. In addition, these experts also supplied further clarifications on specific historical details via email communications. In my analysis of the material, they provided however, I also stayed aware of and considered their particular political agenda.

3.3.2 Observation Data

Creswell (2013) defines observations as "the act of noting a phenomenon in the field setting through the five senses of the observer, often with an instrument, and recording if for scientific purposes" (p. 166). My observations were modeled according to Lofland et al.'s (2006) methodology of observations. They write that "only through direct observation and/or participation can one get close to apprehending those studied and the character of their social worlds and lives" (p. 3). Further they do not see ethnographic data as being "procured" but rather as seeking to "register the events and behaviors unfolding, or the words being spoken, before them" (Lofland et al., 2006, p. 81). In order for these events, behaviors, and words to be relevant to the research, investigators specifically position themselves in what they deem to be relevant events (cf. ibid.). The fieldworker then needs to pay attention and record events, words, behaviors and impressions meticulously so that later analysis can determine what details are significant. I therefore carefully chose who to recruit for observation and deliberated with teachers, which times would best fit my research interests while at the same time also attending events that might not initially seem relevant. Observations are essential to my research design as they allowed me to check for inconsistencies between what teachers said during the interview and how they behave in the classroom. Observations at events outside of ethics classrooms also provided background knowledge for my analysis as detailed below.

Overall, I conducted 45 hours of observation over my 1.5 years in the field. The overall time spent at each school was quite different between schools and contexts of observations. At some schools I spent several months observing the teaching of entire topics or textbook chapters in addition to department meetings. At other schools I only observed individual lessons. How much access I was granted usually dependent on individual teachers and their preferences. The bulk of this time, about 35 hours which amounts to about 46 lesson units each being 45 minutes long, I spent in ethics classrooms. This time also includes ten hours of observations during a 9th grade project on world religions. During these times I generally tried to take the role of non-participant observer, however, on occasion teachers or students involved me in classroom activities by asking me questions directly, prompting me to report anecdotal evidence on certain topics, or tasking me with overseeing a work group. If teachers specifically asked me if I wanted to teach part of a lesson, I declined their offers. The remaining 10 hours of observations were spent in department conferences, continuing education workshops for in service teachers, and student teacher training sessions. This does not include the countless hours of conversations I had with ethics teachers in and around their classes, while recruiting them, or after their interviews or the events I attended in Berlin outside of schools that dealt with ethnic and religious diversity such as the Long Night of Religions (Lange Nacht der Religion). This is an annual event where different religious groups open their temples, churches, mosques and community sites to the public and organize talks about different religions. I took notes during all observations, or if it was not possible to take notes because I observed projects or field trips, I wrote detailed notes from memory after the events. These notes were written by hand and then digitized and expanded into detailed field notes that evening or the following day.

I observed events at six different schools[21] and classroom and project activities at five schools. Schools for observations were purposefully sampled along the following criteria 1) their place in Berlin's tracking hierarchy, and 2) their district within Berlin. All of the schools in the observation sample were located in a different district within Berlin, representing Kreuzberg-Friedrichshain (Central), Charlottenburg-Wilmersdorf (Center West), Steglitz-Zehlendorf (Southwest), Neukölln (South Central), and Reinickendorf (Northwest) respectively. Overall, there were slightly more low track schools in my observation sample. However, I observed a total of 18.25 hours of ethics classrooms (about 24 lesson units) at low track schools and 16.5 hours (22 units) at high track schools. In terms of track level this distribution thus represents a balanced sample. Most of the schools in the observation sample were classified as diverse, only one of these schools was classified as non-diverse. Most of the students in the classes I observed were thus ethnically and religiously diverse. This is mainly because teachers at non-diverse schools did not feel their lessons were relevant to my research topic. Overall, I spent the bulk of my time (34.75 hours) in classroom observations (teaching activities). In addition, I spent 5.25 hours observing department conferences (school organization) and 4.5 hours in teacher education.

3.3.4 Document Data

Following Wolff (2015), I understand documents as "standardized artifacts" (p. 509) that is they are material (or digital) objects that were produced for different purposes. Moreover, as Flick (2016) states documents are "not a simple depiction of facts or reality. Rather, they are always created by someone (or some kind of institution) for a specific (practical) purpose and way of usage (which also includes who has access)" (p. 324, cf. also Rubin and Rubin, 2011,

---

21 At school 17 I only observed a department meeting and student teacher instruction but no actual ethics instruction. I thus did not include this school here.

p. 27). Multiple types of documents were collected for this study and will be described below. I classify the documents I collected into three different types: 1) policy documents, 2) curriculum documents, 3) instructional documents. These documents represent a wide variety of knowledge sources about ethics and thus are ideal sources of information about the subject, its history, and content crucial to my analysis. Curriculum and instructional documents mainly provided background knowledge. The bulk of my analysis in chapter 4 focuses on the policy documents.

Policy Documents: The policy documents I collected were produced and published by Berlin's Senate and document the political negotiations about mandatory ethics instruction. They included 142 parliamentary documents dating from February 3rd, 1993, through January 4th, 2018. All recorded parliamentary procedures in Berlin after 1995 are available online. The archive of Berlin's government organized them by case file (Vorgang) with abbreviated titles that included all consequences of a parliamentary motion or question. Documents produced before the 13th election period (before 11/30/1995) were not available as download but mentioned and organized within their case file and document number online. I obtained these documents through email contact with the archive.

The archive's database was searched for all documents and case files including the words "Ethik*" (ethic*) and "Werteunterricht*" (value education) from the January 1991 through April 2018, hits were then filtered for relevancy, that is all documents connected for example to the medical ethics committee were excluded. 102 procedures were identified that included 299 documents. After removing duplicates (as multiple procedures may have been discussed during the same parliamentary meetings) 142 documents remained including minutes of parliamentary hearings, sub-committee hearings, minor, oral and written interpellations, notifications, decision minutes, decision recommendations motions, notifications, draft bills, and bills. Documents had an average length of 27 pages, the parts of the documents where ethics was discussed specifically had an average length of five pages.

Curriculum Material: In addition to the policy material mentioned above, curriculum material was collected to gain in-depth knowledge about the state mandated content of instruction and the changes in it over time. These documents corroborated the topic foci of ethics instruction. The curriculum materials were published by Berlin's department of education but written by various ethics teachers who were compensated for this work. Curricula in Berlin are produced by working groups composed of multiple subject teachers. I collected the current as well as the two prior versions of the state curriculum (Rahmenlehrplan) for ethics (2006, 2011, 2015).

I further collected all newsletters (Fachbriefe). The newsletters were written by the subject representative at the Department of Education, a teacher who took on this leadership role in addition to their teaching responsibilities. They were published between 2006 and 2017. They discuss a variety of topics ranging from ideas for topics and content, student evaluations, subject implementation, additional training opportunities to changes in the curriculum and thus provide a more general idea of how ethics teachers are integrated into a larger network of teachers in Berlin. Although it is an official document published by the senate and distributed to schools, teachers are not required to read or follow these directives.

Instructional Material: My analysis is further informed by the instructional material I collected during my classroom observations and from a server hosted by Berlin's Department of Education that provides instruction materials to teachers and is freely accessible. Documents collected during observations were handouts, worksheets and tests distributed by the teachers I observed. They also include photographs of textbook pages that teachers used during my observations. This material also provided background information to my analysis and was used to triangulate larger tendencies within ethics teachers' interviews and classroom behavior.

3.4 Access and the Influence of the Socio-Political Context

Securing site access throughout my study was difficult as detailed in the introduction to this book. How teachers, principals and school administrators judged what categories of diversity were important to my study, was influential on my ability to secure access. When I initially started to procure possible participants for my study in January of 2015 the topic of how to accommodate religious and cultural diversity was ever present in media and public conception but not many schools felt it actually applied to them. Schools not wishing to participate in my study would justify their refusal by saying, they were too busy implementing the new curriculum or did not have any capacities to support the study (for example email communication 1/26/2015 and 9/8/2015). During early stages of communication with schools, even schools that were willing to participate would do so with caveats pointing to a lack of diversity within their student body – usually referring to students with migration background or Muslim students. The categories of diversity that teachers felt were important to my study thus became set and interpreted early on during recruitment, despite the fact that I did not mention the presence of students with migration backgrounds or Muslim students as a pre-requisite for participation or even the focus of my study.[22]

---

22 In the recruitment letter I describe my study as dealing religious diversity in everyday school life and particularly ethics classes. Example questions I gave were: How are

During the late summer, fall and winter of 2015 Europe and Germany experienced what would widely become known as the long summer of migration. As detailed in chapter 1, the profound uncertainty that arrived in Berlin's schools changed the ways in which categories of diversity were related to my study. To provide just a little anecdotal evidence that captures the chaos and uncertainty of this particular point in time: I witnessed conversations between a school secretary and German as a foreign language teachers about the arrival of new groups with uncertain numbers, and school vice principals questioned the age of deviant refugee students and whether or not that student should be at the school at all.

In addition, my field research was laced with international violence experienced in Western Europe and the US that received copious media attention in Germany starting in the pre-data collection phase with the attack on Charlie Hebdo in January 2015, the November 2015 Paris attacks, the attack in Orlando in June 2016, and the July 2016 attack in Nice to name just a few. At the same time Germany (and much of the rest of Europe) saw an increase in right wing violence and anti-diversity sentiments. In 2015 alone, refugee homes were violently attacked a total of 279 times (see Biermann et al., 5.24.2016 for a detailed analysis). And 6,330 criminal investigations due to xenophobic crimes (Landesjustizamt, 2016a, p. 1) were conducted compared to 5,317 in 2016 (Landesjustizamt, 2018, p. 1) and 2,666 (Landesjustizamt, 2016b, p. 1) in 2014. All of these events were directly and indirectly reflected in my interviewees' classrooms and interviews.

This context of uncertainty, upheaval, and violence is important to consider throughout the pages of this book even if they are not mentioned directly in the discussions that are to follow.

3.5 Data Analysis, Triangulation, and Validity

I analyzed data in Atlas.ti 8 in two separate project files: one for policy documents and one for ethnographic data. I approached my analysis as an inductive process build around reflection, memoing, and continuously consulting the literature. As Maxwell (2013) writes a qualitative researcher "begins data analy-

---

questions of inter-religious and inter-cultural coexistence dealt with in ethics instruction and how these questions are discussed with students? How is inter-religious conflict discussed in class? How are these topics discussed with students? Which teaching methodologies are used to do this? How do ethics teachers perceive their role? What kind of problems do ethics teachers see and in how far do they have suggestions for improvement? I never mention that I was interested in Muslim students in particular or in students with migration background more generally. However, these were the two categories that teachers inferred from my inquiry.

sis immediately after finishing the first interview or observation and continues to analyze the data as long as he or she is working on the research, stopping briefly to write reports and papers" (p. 104). As such my data analysis process was conducted in part at the same time as data collection. This way of analyzing data was also consistent with Rubin and Rubin's responsive interviewing strategy as it allowed for the preliminary analysis to inform interviews and observations. During data analysis I made use of three analytical options proposed by Maxwell (2013): "(a) memos, (b) categorizing strategies (such as coding and thematic analysis), and (c) connecting strategies (such as narrative analysis [profiles and vignettes]" (p. 105).

I developed codes according to three different categories: "organizational, substantive, theoretical" (Maxwell, 2013, p. 107) in multiple coding cycles (Saldaña, 2016). Organizational codes are "broad areas or issues" (Maxwell, 2013, p. 107) such as Approach, Diversity, Refugees, Legitimacy, Nation or Society in the analysis of interview and observation data or Content, Diversity, Goal, Islam in the document data analysis. These codes mainly served to organize the data into large topic groups. Substantive categories are "descriptive" (Maxwell, 2013, p. 108). This may include "descriptions of participants' concepts and beliefs" (ibid). Contrary to theoretical codes, substantive codes "don't inherently imply a more abstract theory" (ibid). Examples for these kinds of codes include demographics students and demographics teachers for the interview and observation data. The third category of theoretical codes organized the data "into a more general or abstract framework" (ibid). These codes were developed from "prior theory or from an inductively developed theory" (ibid). Examples in my interview and observation analysis include codes like "Ethics Definition - Citizenship Ed" or "Diversity - Contact Theory." This systematic approach to data coding allowed for a holistic analysis of my data. Data sources in Atlas.ti were also grouped into multiple categories (called document groups in the program) this allowed me to systematically analyze data by individual and school level of variation (see above) and thus discover commonalities and differences across these levels.

The myriads of different data sources I collected provided a way to check information and conclusions drawn from one source against other sources. This way of triangulation was essential to compensate for the weaknesses of individual methods (Maxwell, 2013, p. 102). Following Creswell (2013), I employed the four following approaches to check the validity of my findings. 1) "[P]rolonged engagement and persistent observation" (p. 250). 2) "[P]eer review and debriefing" (p. 251) was used to check findings and methods with other members of the research community. 3) "[N]egative case analysis" (p. 251): cases that did not fit into initial theories were evaluated closely throughout the analysis process and 4) "[C]larifying research bias" (p. 251). All of these approaches were used throughout to produce a sound and reliable analysis of the data I collected.

3.6 Role of the Researcher

I brought a unique position to my research subject. As a native German, I grew up in Germany and in fact spent most of my school summer vacations in Berlin with my father's family. I was educated through the German school system. During my time in high school, I took religious education classes engaging with the subject of religion and society from 7th through 13th grade and actually chose to do my oral high school exam (requirement in addition to three written examinations) in religion. For these reasons, I am deeply familiar with the questions presented by ethics instruction in Berlin. However, I have lived in the US for almost 10 years, removing me from German culture and attitudes. Throughout the interviews and conversations with teachers I sometimes struggled to find German words for concepts or switched between English and German for individual words or phrases – reflecting the disjunctions between vocabulary groupings in both languages. In fact, many of the people I talk to in Berlin frequently told me that I had an American accent when I spoke German (especially when they heard I was from New York University). Teachers also frequently engaged with me in conversations about how teaching diversity was handled in the US context.

I thus took a position in between insider and outsider for this research. This had certain advantages: My position as a native German provided me with a thorough understanding of German culture, attitudes and language. My position as a US-based graduate student provided an interesting starting point for conversation with teachers and principals in addition to affording the possibility of asking for further explanations of concepts and context. I was thus able to build rapport quickly with my research participants and have open and in-depth conversations with them about their understandings of diversity in ethics instruction.

3.7 Conclusion

The research underlying this study was carefully planned, conceptualized and conducted. I based my research design on an ethnographic vertical case study which helped me combine macro and micro level analysis to answer my overall research question. I collected multiple data sources (document, interview, and observation data) over a 1.5 years of field work which helped me to triangulate my findings and thus build a solid analysis and discussion. I sampled for maximum variation across Berlin's schools based on schools' track level and location in Berlin. Due to self-selection tendencies built into the recruitment design as well as the tumultuous times during which I conducted this research, there is a bias towards high track schools in the sample. In addition, the teachers that participated are better qualified than the overall population of ethics teachers in Berlin. However, these teachers were also generally interested in the topic of diversity integration and were actively shaping the future of their subject in various ways. They thus represent an ideal sample of informants to answer my research question and strengthen the validity of my findings.

Throughout my research, I engaged in analysis and reflection to check conclusions against personal biases and perceptions. I conducted data analysis in multiple cycles and included inductive and deductive coding. Data was also analyzed through various levels of variation by filtering across characteristics in Atlas.ti 8. I triangulated data in various ways to provide a well-founded analysis and discussion of results. Overall, my study design, data collection and analysis thus provided the data necessary to confidently answer my overall research questions.

4 Ethics and the Question of Diversity: Berlin's Quest for Value Education

"If children are to shape their lives on a clear and stable foundation of values, education must do more than simply provide facts – it must also impart values. These values cannot be conveyed neutrally; they must stem from a creed, a belief. That is why we advocate for a clear commitment to religious education, as it provides a framework for imparting values and convictions. Those who relegate religious education to the sidelines and claim it can be replaced by a neutral form of value education distort the issue – just as we see happening in Berlin today."
(Former Christian Democratic German Chancellor Angela Merkel, 2005, p. 6)

4.1 Value education in Berlin: A Contested Field

In Germany value education is by constitution a matter of religious education. It is stated in article 7.3 of the German constitution, which decrees mandatory confessional religious instruction for German public schools. Historically, both Christian denominations (Protestant and Catholic) have been the only providers of religious education in Germany and Berlin. This would not change until 1982 when the Humanistic Alliance entered Berlin's schools, closely followed by the Jewish community in 1986.[23] A remnant of the Weimar Republic,[24] the teaching of values has thus historically been situated within the confines of

---

23 The Humanistic alliance entered on a two-year probation but was established as a regular provider by 1984 (cf. Gräb & Thieme, 2011, p. 34; Häusler, 2007, p. 39). The Jewish community started to provide religious education in Berlin in 1986 and has since stayed predominantly within its own private schools – it only teaches in one public primary and one public secondary school in Berlin (cf. Häusler, 2007, pp. 42-43). Muslims would not gain the right to provide Islamic religious education in Berlin's schools until 2000. In 2015, a total of eight different organizations of various religious denominations and world views provided religious instruction in Berlin's schools: the Allevite Community of Berlin, the Buddhist Society of Berlin, the archdiocese of Berlin, the protestant church of Berlin and Brandenburg, the Humanistic Alliance, the Islamic Federation of Berlin, the Jewish community of Berlin, and the Syrian Orthodox Church Mor Afrem (cf. Abgeordnetenhaus von Berlin, 2018).

24 Religious education was also provided by the Catholic and Protestant churches during the NS regime in Germany. For the official agreement between the Catholic Church and the German Reich see the *Concordat between the Holy See and the German Reich* from July 20th, 1933, article 21 and 22 (in addition articles 23, 24, and 25 regulate private religious schools - *Concordat Between the Holy See and the German Reich [with Supplementary Protocol and Secret Supplement]*, 1933).

"Christian religious education" (cf. Ziemann, 2011, p. 704). As the quote from former Chancellor Merkel above, which was part of a speech given at the Christian Democrats protestant annual working group meeting, shows this connection remains unquestioned at the national level.[25]

In Berlin, city state and the only federal state today that combines both a former West German and East German part, the connection between value education and (Christian) religious education was not taken for granted. Instead, the Berlin model of value education relies on a legal exception to the national constitutional mandate of mandatory religious education.[26] Within the first decade of the 21st century Berlin's quest for a new regulation of value education turned into an all-out culture war (cf. Joffe, 2008; Posener, 2010). Against local and national pressures, Berlin's leftist government carved out a secular solution for value education unique among German federal states - ethics.

Overall, there is very little scholarly literature on ethics instruction, its history in Berlin, and its classroom practice. However, the few scholars who have written about the introduction of ethics in Berlin argue that the core issue was a differential understanding of the role of Christianity in society (cf. Gräb and Thieme, 2011; Häusler, 2007). They cite declining participation in religious education and decreasing church membership in the city as key factors. In contrast, this chapter challenges the notion that the changing status of Christian churches in society was the decisive factor in this political development. While secularization certainly played a role in putting value education on the political agenda, the formal secularization of society[27] alone did not generate enough

---

25 In fact, Berlin's approach to organizing value education was so controversial and deviated so sharply from established German principles on how to educate students in this area that even the German Parliament (Bundestag)—a governing body that typically does not intervene in federal state education policy—dedicated an entire session to the issue on April 13, 2005.

26 In contrast to most other federal states in Germany - with the exception of Bremen - Berlin does not follow the mandate for mandatory Religious Education of article 7.3 of the German Constitution. Instead, Berlin and Bremen claim article 141 or the "Bremer Klausel" due to a school law that regulated religious education prior to the German constitution becoming effective. The Bremer Klausel states that "paragraph 7.3 of the German Constitution does not apply to federal states that had a different state regulation predating January 1st, 1949". This exception has created a legal environment that made it possible for Berlin to find its own path in term of the value education of the city's students.

27 Formal church membership at least for the Christian denominations is measured in Germany through a tax that deducts between eight and nine percent (depending on the federal state of residence) of your income. Other factors that lead scholars to the conclusion that church memberships are declining are the attendance in mass and the participation in religious education. It should also be noted that secularization does not necessarily mean the decline of religiosity (see for examples arguments that consider soccer a form of religion, e.g. Xifra, 2008) and that secularization arguments in Europe – as this trend is not confined to Germany alone – are usually focused on Christian religions.

political momentum to drive a reorganization of value education in Berlin. Instead, I argue that the issue of diversity – particularly in debates linking youth, Islam, and violence – was the key driver of policy change.

This chapter demonstrates that the introduction of ethics instruction in Berlin's public schools in 2006/2007 was propelled by two main catalysts:

1. *Secularization*, understood as the declining social significance of religion (Wilson, 2016, p. 4), reflected in dwindling participation in religious education and the Christian churches' inability to garner sufficient support for the *ProReli* referendum.
2. *International fears and security concerns,* particularly regarding minority populations, which were translated into the local political context.

I argue that the debates were shaped by two competing logics of diversity, which I term *productive* and *destructive diversity*. Political conceptions of ethics as value education were driven by broader national and global discussions about diversity and what it means to be German. At stake in these debates was the fundamental question of how to manage diversity in order to foster a peaceful, pluralistic society – and how to structure education accordingly. Ethics instruction thus serves as a prime example of how debates over school curricula can evolve into broader political struggles over diversity integration and national identity. As such, this case study sheds light on the process by which global and national political discourses are translated into local educational policy, ultimately leading to organizational changes at the school level.

The history presented in this chapter is based on the analysis of 142 parliamentary documents ranging from minutes of parliamentary hearings, subcommittee hearings, minor, oral and written interpellations, notifications, decision minutes, decision recommendations, motions, notifications, draft bills, and bills dating from February 3rd, 1993, through January 4th, 2018. In addition, this chapter includes the analysis of two expert interviews (134 minutes and 112 minutes in length respectively), email communications with these experts, speeches given by Berlin's and national politicians outside of parliament and the scholarly literature.

This chapter focuses on the historical developments that led to the implementation of ethics. This history is marked by three distinct periods: The first period, which I call "losing faith," provides evidence of how the declining numbers of participation in Christian religious education slowly changed political and church perspectives on the organization of value education in Berlin. The second period, "diversity matters," shows how the introduction of diversity as a political argument, its connection to youth, local and global violence, and religion, drove policy change and essentially produced a new organizational solution. "The last rebellion" discusses the final attempt to bring religion back into the debates and the failure of the Christian Churches to mobilize enough political and public support to produce policy action. It also exemplifies a period that established a strong challenge to the legitimacy of ethics instruction in Berlin. In the discussion section of this chapter, I argue that the political debate relied on two logics – *productive and destructive diversity* – that were able to produce two distinct organizational models and political imaginations for value education although only one of these models was implemented.

4.2 Losing Faith: Putting Value Education on the Political Agenda

After the Second World War, Berlin's education laws were significantly shaped by the Allied forces occupying the city. They exerted their influence by downgrading mandatory religious education (*Ordentliches Lehrfach*) – which had been the standard form of value education in the Weimar Republic and later in West Germany – to an elective course. As a result, parents could choose whether their children would participate, and the course was taught and fully administered by representatives of the respective faith communities. Religious education was thus not under the control or jurisdiction of the state. Berlin only provided, room, electricity and a compensation for teacher salary. This regulation found entry into Berlin's school law of 1948 and remained the status quo until 2006 (cf. Beschorner, 2006; Giese, 1955). Berlin's model of value education was thus defined by a strict separation of state and church which took the state out of content decisions on religious education.

After Berlin's separation into East and West, West Berlin would continue to follow the model laid out in the school law of 1948.[28] From the 1950s until the late 1980s, the Protestant church in West Berlin advocated for keeping religious education as an elective in the sole responsibility of faith communities. However, as participant numbers declined, the Protestant church began to promote following the mandatory opt-out model of the West German constitution that would make religious instruction a regular subject under state control (cf. Gräb and Thieme, 2011, p. 34; Häusler, 2007).

During this same period, the Christian Democratic Union (CDU) tried multiple times to change the status of West Berlin's religious education to a

---

28 Since Berlin East would take over all regulations and school laws from Berlin West in the academic year 1991/92, I will not provide a detailed history of East Berlin. It should be mentioned, however, that the East German government from January 19th 1951 forward slowly pushed religious education out of its schools as "curriculum in schools and higher education are based on the theoretical foundation of Marxism-Leninism" (decision of the Central Committee of the SED, quote after Gräb & Thieme, 2011, p. 35) until religious education was no longer mentioned in the GDR's constitution from 4/6/1968 (Gräb & Thieme, 2011, p. 36).

mandatory subject under state control in accordance with the constitution. This failed again and again due to lack of political and until the late 1980s the Christian churches' support.[29] Therefore, no significant changes to the status of religious education as an elective were made in Berlin.

Figure 1: Participation in Christian Religious Education in Percent

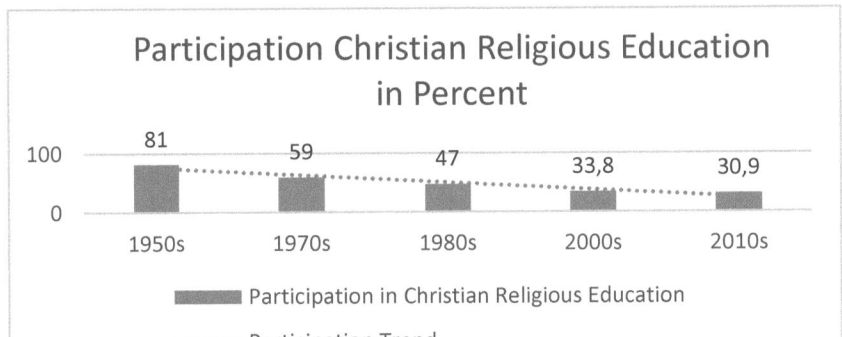

Source: Chart compiled from multiple sources: Abgeordnetenhaus von Berlin, 2008a; Gräb and Thieme, 2011, p. 33; Senatsverwaltung für Bildung, Jugend und Familie, n.d.–b; Statistisches Bundesamt, 2017[30]. Note: Data prior to 1990 shows West Berlin only, after 1990 data shown includes East and West Berlin

The early attempts by the Christian Democrats generally emphasized the low rate of participation in religious education and lack of reflection on questions of God and religion, as this comment by the Christian Democratic Senator for Education, Hanna-Renate Laurien, herself a converted Catholic, in 1988 shows:

---

29 After World War II Berlin's Christian Churches but especially representatives of the Protestant Church lobbied for the strict separation of church and state. They claimed that the church was its own governing body separate from the state and should take a position in accordance. Demands from the Protestant Church in Berlin went as far as claiming all of education for itself and requiring the establishment of Christian Schools, a request that the allied forces did not agree with. What both sides could agree on, however, was the independence of religious education from state influence, thus establishing the Berlin model of moral and value education (cf. Beschorner, 2006, pp. 43–47).

30 Numbers for the participation in catholic and protestant religious education provided in this figure refer to the middle of the decade, Gräb and Thieme (2011) unfortunately do not provide a specific school year for their numbers from the 1950s, 70s and 80s. The percentage for the 2000s are based on the school year 2005/06 (marking the school year before the introduction of ethics). The percentage for the 2010s are based on the numbers for the school year 2015/16 (marking the primary years of data collection for this study). For decades not included in this chart no data was available.

> Cutoff date: October 1st, 1987: In grades one through ten, 52.7% of students participated in religious instruction, up from 52.1% the previous year. When calculating these numbers for German students only – since it seems appropriate not to include the small number of Muslim students – the participation rate was 68.7% in 1987, compared to 67.4% the year before. In grades eleven and twelve, the participation rate for German students increased from 7.8% to 8.4%, though the subject does not contribute to the GPA.
>
> More than 90% of students, therefore, do not study religion or church in public schools during what is considered the age of reflection [*im Alter der Nachdenklichkeit*]. The example of Berlin clearly illustrates what it means to relinquish the status of mandatory subject [*Ordentliches Unterrichtsfach*]. (Laurien, 1989, p. 5)

Remarkable in this quote is the fact that Muslim youth, although admitted part of Berlin's student population, are not consequential for this debate. They are "counted out" by the senator. The question of value education in Berlin, thus, is not yet an issue of (unwanted) diversity.

After Germany's reunification in 1990 and confronted with the realities of uniting Berlin's western and eastern education regimes,[31] the government in Berlin again started to discuss the status of religious education as a subject to teach values and possible secular alternatives such as philosophy and ethics (cf. Beschorner, 2006; Zawatka-Gerlach, 2009). The city was suddenly confronted with a large influx of districts and citizens with no recent history of religious education and severe skepticism towards religion in general. Berlin's Christian Democrats felt obligated to provide a different form of value education to those students not interested in participating in voluntary religious education. The CDU, in power at the time, managed to set in motion a voluntary school trial of ethics/philosophy[32] in preparation for a change in Berlin's

---

31 Berlin is the only federal state that consisted of a former Western and Eastern part and thus struggled more than the newly formed federal states in the East to integrate East and West. New regulations for value education were, however, discussed all over Germany's federal states. The 1990s saw the introduction of Philosophy, Ethics, Practical Philosophy or other variations in multiple federal states as a compliment for those opting out of religious education (Ersatzfach). While Baden Wuerttemberg, Hamburg, Hesse, Lower Saxony, and Saarland introduced ethics as substitute for religious education in the late 1970s, Brandenburg, Schleswig-Holstein, Mecklenburg-Hither Pomerania, and North Rhine-Westphalia introduced either Ethics, Philosophy or a similar subject as electives or mandatory subjects in the 1990s (cf. Beschorner, 2006, pp. 22-25). Especially the introduction of Humanistic Life-skills, Ethics, and Religion (Lebenskunde Ethik Religion - LER) in 1992 as a mandatory subject in Brandenburg, the federal state surrounding Berlin, was monitored by Berlin's politicians with great interest.

32 In its first year, eleven schools participated in the trial. This number was steadily increased until a total of 37 schools participated - four low-track schools (Haupt- and Realschule), 21 high-track schools (Gymnasium), and eight comprehensive schools (Gesamtschule- combination of high and low track) with a total of nine schools in eastern Berlin (Abgeordnetenhaus von Berlin, 2000b). The number of students who partic-

school law towards the standard constitutional regulation with an opt out provision in 1994 despite little political support for making religious education a mandatory school subject. The introduction was legitimized politically by the CDU with a high interest of parents and school leaders (cf. Beschorner, 2006, p. 71). The content of the subject was based deeply in secular rational Kantian philosophy and thus distinct from religious education (cf. Beschorner, 2006).

The justification for this new test subject started to frame Berlin's youth as a problem within society, suffering "xenophobia, juvenile delinquency, and ethical disorientation" due to the "arbitrariness of the anti-church and anti-establishment norms in the thoughts and actions of the generation of 1968 in the West and the state dictated atheism in the east" (Richter-Kotowski, CDU, Abgeordnetenhaus von Berlin, 1998, p. 3707). Thus, the argument for mandatory religious instruction by Christian Democrats became contingent on a potentially violent youth population lacking moral values.

Opposition parties accused the Christian Democrats of trying to re-Christianize society in times, when Christian religions were simply no longer important for Berlin and former East Germany. They also employed the argument of a vital ethnically and religiously diverse city against Christian Democratic ambitions to implement mandatory religious instruction, claiming that with over 120 religions and faith groups in the city, mandatory religious education would not be feasible – or even wanted by Christian Democrats, as the government would have to extend the right to implement religious education to all faith groups due to the principle of equality established in the German Constitution (cf. Hoff, PDS, Abgeordnetenhaus von Berlin, 1999, p. 4848).

The period between 1950 and the late 1990s thus upheld Berlin's status quo of opt-in religious education as a voluntary subject with no secular alternative of value education. The declining numbers in participation in religious education especially after German reunification and the perceived increase in youth delinquency and xenophobia put value education on the political agenda as an area for possible intervention. Politicians were starting to consider models that would reach a broader student body than the current policy did. The issue of integrating diversity did not yet fully enter arguments but instead was used sporadically to counter Christian Democratic ambitions. Political support for a change to the status quo – in the form of mandatory religious education under state control with the option to opt-out – was slim. The policymaking process needed a second catalyst to move matters forward.

---

ipated in the trial almost doubled from 1995/96 with 2278 students to 1999/2000 with 4095 students in classes seven through ten (cf. Abgeordnetenhaus von Berlin, 2000b). In 2000 the subject was taught by about 170 teachers (cf. Abgeordnetenhaus von Berlin, 2000b). The school trial remained in effect until 2006 and the introduction of mandatory Ethics.

4.3 Diversity Matters: The Speedy Introduction of Ethics Instruction

Up until the late 1990s the concept of diversity had only played a minor role in political debates. With the discovery of diversity integration as a salient political topic in Germany overall in the late 1990s and early 2000s, however, the issue soon also took center stage in Berlin. The newly elected Social Democratic Senator (SPD) for Education in Berlin, Klaus Boeger, publicly advocated for a new regulation of Berlin's value education not – as the CDU had done previously – because of a lack of values due to a lack of religious education but because of the increasing uncertainties of a postmodern world and the diversity of the city:

> The cultural, religious, and ideological diversity of Berlin is also reflected in its schools. Despite these differences, there is a broad consensus that questions of identity and morality, the teaching of values, and making sense of the world are integral parts of public education. […] changes in society, the economy, and politics indicate that the challenges of the future – particularly the globalization of everyday life – are creating new complexities and increasing detachment within families and social communities. This makes it necessary to dedicate more time to questions of morality and values orientation in public schools, and a mandatory offer for all students seems essential. (Boeger, SPD, Abgeordnetenhaus von Berlin, 2000a, p. 1).

This inclusive vision of creating a common way to counter disorientation caused by global forces in all youth in Berlin, would soon be overshadowed by anxieties triggered by terror attacks in other countries, creating an argument that framed ethnic and religious diversity (especially Muslim minorities) in a destructive light – as a security threat and disruptive agent within society locally, nationally, and internationally (cf. Busher et al., 2017; Joppke, 2007a, 2007c; Mijs et al., 2016; Ríos-Rojas, 2014; Shain, 2013; Shirazi, 2017).

In Berlin, this perception of a possibly dangerous Muslim minority found its first expression in the legal fight around Islamic religious education. The Islamic Federation Berlin (an organization formed by 26 immigrant organizations in Berlin with the specific purpose to implement Islamic religious education in the 1980s (cf. Häusler, 2007, p. 40)) was suing Berlin for the right of implementation. The claimed reason for Berlin to deny this right to the Islamic Federation was the organization's supposed connection to a national Islamic political organization (Milli Görüş) that was suspected to be involved in criminal activities and not seen as representative of Islam in general (cf. Giese, 2000). After several rounds in local and federal court, Germany's highest administrative court (Bundesverwaltungsgericht) decided in February 2000 that Berlin's government had no acceptable reasons to deny the Islamic Federation its right to teach Islamic religious education (Urt. V. 23.02.2000, Az.: BVerwG

6 C 5/99, 2000). Berlin's unique solution for religious education that placed all curriculum and staff decisions in the responsibility of the faith communities allowed the Islamic Federation Berlin to implement Islamic religious education in public schools without the oversight of Berlin's politicians. This produced significant anxieties and fears in policy makers.

The anxieties of Berlin's politicians over not being able to control what happened in Islamic religious education classrooms only grew after the attacks on the World Trade Center in New York on September 11th, 2001. Especially the "blatant pleasure about and approval of the terror attacks by Muslim students" in Berlin's secondary schools (Dr. Gerhard Weil, Teachers' Union (GEW) Berlin and Aktionsbündnis ProEthik, personal email communication 10/19/2018), although not specifically mentioned in the Senate and committee debates, played a role in rethinking Berlin's model of value education according to stakeholders. The combination of the advent of the Islamic Federation of Berlin into public school classrooms and 9/11 served to anchor international anxieties in the local context:

> Today, we must note that, under the leadership of a social democratic government, an organization [Islamic Federation of Berlin] accused of extremism has gained access to Berlin's schools – where neither teachers nor the curriculum can be monitored. By opening the floodgates to all, including extremist proselytizing, within Berlin's schools, this is the most irresponsible action I can imagine for the city's public education system. (Schlede, CDU, Abgeordnetenhaus von Berlin, 2001, p. 1894)

As the example above shows, Berlin's schools were imagined by Christian Democrats to be a potential breeding ground for radicalization and violent religious extremism. There was a distinctive shift in conservative party conceptualization: those that constituted a danger to society and were in need of intervention were no longer youth in general but Muslim youth in particular. The violence invoked in these arguments was generalized into a non-specific constant threat that could endanger lives and the security of citizens wherever and whenever. Mandatory religious education under state control was now claimed to control and remove the Islamic Federation and the threat of extremism from Berlin's public schools.

These kinds of arguments, displaying a view of diversity as a destructive force aimed at majority society, were quickly countered by those opposed to mandatory religious education. They tried to expose the fear mongering and instrumentalization in the opposing sides arguments. In addition, proponents of mandatory ethics invoked a more productive view of diversity, highlighting an inherent potential to overcome conflict:

> In the days following the assassination of van Gogh,[33] I regret to say, much was conflated in public debates in Germany: Islam, Islamism, terrorism, forced marriage, failed multiculturalism, hate preachers [Hassprediger], religious education, juvenile offenders – these are terms that don't move us forward, they don't help. Immigrant societies are rarely conflict-free – everyone in this room should know this, as you've hopefully engaged with this issue for many years. In this regard, we need to think about how we can facilitate living together and ensure that those who live here finally feel at home. (Mutlu, Green Party, Abgeordnetenhaus von Berlin, 2004, p. 5030)

According to this argument, countering violent extremism and radicalization were thus not an issue of exercising more control but rather needed a more inclusive vision of national belonging. Wholesale stigmatization of entire minority populations was not seen as a viable solution by those opposed to mandatory religious education. Despite these heated discussions of the issue, however, neither the implementation of Islamic religious education in Berlin nor the 9/11 attacks produced enough political momentum to re-organize value education.

Instead the murder of Hatun Sürücü – a young woman of Kurdish descent – on February 7th 2005 in Berlin put extreme public and political pressure on the governing parties to change the status quo of value education.[34] The Sürücü murder was the latest in a series of so-called "honor murders" in Berlin[35] and elicited public outcry because Muslim students at a secondary school in Berlin were quoted by local media to endorse the murder (cf. Miller et al., 2005). The laissez-faire approach – where students could either choose voluntary religious education or have free time, often referred to in political discussions as "Religion or ice cream shop" (*Religion oder Eisdiele*) – was deemed no longer appropriate. This approach failed to provide value education to all of Berlin's students, particularly those from religious minority groups. From now on political discussions typically followed the trope of the illiberal Muslim, portrayed as lacking the democratic and moral values of host societies, a

---

33   Theo van Gogh was assassinated for producing and directing a film criticizing Islam. For German politicians this marked the end of a successful Dutch model of multiculturalism and the accommodation of diversity (cf. Sen, 2009).
34   In Germany more generally, the Sürücü murder sparked an intense debate about marriage laws lumping forced marriage and honor murders together. As Korteweg and Yurdakul (2010) show, national media and political debates employed extreme stigmatization of entire immigrant communities linking honor violence and Islam (pp. 14-15): "This has led to policies that generally restrict immigration rather than those that directly target gendered violence in immigrant communities" (Korteweg and Yurdakul, 2010, p. iii). Considering this more negative national tone of the debate it is even more exceptional that Berlin's government chose a policy path inclusive of local diversity in the education context as I show below.
35   Respectively since October 2004, six young women of migrant backgrounds had been murdered by family members. The motives are suspected to be damage to the family's honor (cf. Banse and Laninger, 2005).

narrative widely circulated in German and European media and reflected in academic inquiries (Abu-Lughod, 2015; Bendixsen, 2013; Cesari, 2004; Kepel, 2006; Klausen, 2005; Korteweg and Yurdakul, 2010; Özcan, 2013; Roy, 2004).

Both governing parties had since 2000 started to develop models that proposed a unified subject. Berlin's Social Democratic Senator for Education, Klaus Boeger, who had been working behind the scenes on proposals for the re-organization of value education, responded quickly to the Sürücü murder and introduced a bill to change the school law dated the very day of the murder (cf. Abgeordnetenhaus von Berlin, 2006a). This bill introduced ethics as a new mandatory subject for all of Berlin's secondary students while religious education remained a voluntary additional offering. The senator's proposal of the new subject was supposed to be grounded in the teachings of Western liberal philosophy – "no religion or intercultural aspects, that is no "Life Science, Ethics, and Religion" [Lebenskunde Ethik Religion as in Brandenburg], hence the name ethics, understood as sub-discipline of philosophy" (Dr. Gerhard Weil, GEW and ProEthik, personal Email communication 10/17/2018).[36] This new subject would keep Berlin's claim on the exception to the constitutional mandate intact. But the state would now take control of value education in Berlin's secondary schools with its new mandatory subject: ethics. The proposal was based on a deep concern over conflicts among different kinds of religions, cultures, and ideologies but saw potential in bringing together students of all different creeds, rather than separating them as mandatory religious education within one's creed with the option to opt-out and take ethics/philosophy would have done. Ethics was supposed to be taught in cooperation with the faith communities, offering them a place at the table in discussing the content as well as providing instruction in schools when needed.

By the time a hearing in the education sub-committee of the Senate was held to which all stakeholders in the matter – faith communities, union representatives, parent representatives, and notably Berlin's integration officer – were invited, teaching about world religions and intercultural aspects had been placed into the subjects' curriculum; the name, however, remained. The pro-

---

36 Both governing parties had decided that the new subject should explicitly teach content like religion and intercultural aspects during the party conventions in early 2005. And both parties had proposed titles similar to Brandenburg's Life-skills, Ethics, and Religion. The teachers' Union (GEW) was also thoroughly upset by the title and content of the subject proposed by the senator. Ethics and its content in this early proposal can thus be seen as a solo run of the Senator for Education in Berlin. Dr. Weil (GEW) goes on to suggest ("with high probability") in the email quoted above that this emphasis on content distinctly separate from what the Christian churches saw as their domain was a Compromise struck between the Senator and the Christian Church stakeholders. As chapter 6 of this book will show, however, the senator's wish for a uni-disciplinary subject based in only philosophy would ultimately be the model that teachers chose to advocate for.

posal was met with great skepticism by representatives of the Christian Church and the Jewish community who accused the government of wanting to control matters that were the sole responsibility of faith communities:[37]

> Let it be mentioned that the state seems to be clearly exceeding its competencies, if it claims sovereignty of interpretation of the different faith communities represented at this table in this subject. With this it claims the question of God for itself. (Seelemann, representative of the Protestant Church of Berlin and Brandenburg, Abgeordnetenhaus von Berlin, 2006c, p. 7).

Both Christian churches questioned the separation of church and state in this matter and accused the state of meddling in church affairs. In order to alleviate these concerns proponents of mandatory ethics re-emphasized the subjects' character as religiously neutral and secular and thus separate from confessional religious education (cf. Zillich, PDS, Abgeordnetenhaus von Berlin, 2006c, p. 21).[38] Basis for values taught in ethics would be the German Constitution and the Declaration of Human Rights.

The new law passed Berlin's Senate in late March 2006 and ethics started in grade seven of all secondary schools in Berlin the very next fall term. The implementation of mandatory ethics instruction was thus primarily the result of a political change in the perception of diversity. Specifically, the framing of the technical question of implementing value education moved away from an emphasis on Christian religious education and its importance for value education for youth in general towards an emphasis on intercultural conflict resolution and a solution that would reach all students (including Berlin's largest religious minority) without separating them into their different creeds and beliefs. Fears of an undemocratic Islamic religious education and international Islamic religious terror acts prompted political parties to re-position their agendas on value education.[39] While both sides of the argument (those in favor of mandatory religious education and those against it) recognized diversity as a

---

[37] While both representatives from the Christian Churches were present during the hearing, the Jewish community representative was absent. However, the Jewish community had previously voiced its concerns over the proposal and aligned its position with that of the Christian Churches. The representatives of the Islamic Federation of Berlin present at the hearing spoke in favor of the subject. However, other organizations representing Berlin's Muslim communities (DITIB) later aligned themselves with the Christian Churches and Jewish community (cf. Jung, 2011, p. 77).

[38] In this emphasis, proponents of ethics also espouse what is widely known as secularization theory: that is the seemingly tight connection between modernization and secularization. As a philosophical concept, neutrality is deeply connected to liberal secular traditions and is seen by some to be the ideal way to accommodate religious diversity in democratic nations (cf. Joppke, 2007b). For critiques of this connection see Asad (1993, 2003); Bruce (2017); Casanova (1994, 2006); Taylor (2007).

[39] The combination of legislation targeting diverse populations with fears over national security is also not unique to Berlin. In fact, Skrentny (2004) argues that this combination made the minority rights revolution in the USA possible.

potential threat to peace and security, their views on how to counter this threat differed substantially. In the end, those who saw diversity as productive and having the potential to bring society together despite religious differences won. Moreover, religious and cultural differences in these proposals were to build the basis for learning intercultural communication skills. However, also underlying this positive view was the fear of a violent local (Muslim) minority community that made ethics as a subject possible.

This debate showed how the localization of a national (one could even argue international) discourse about diversity, integration, national identity, and security was brought to bear on a very specific local political issue. It propelled the question of how value education in Berlin should be organized onto a national (and international) level of debate challenging those who were to implement the subject in schools to grapple with issues much larger than local concerns.

4.4 The Last Rebellion in a Lost Culture War? The Referendum for Mandatory Religious Education

After Berlin's government decided to implement ethics a private initiative, led by a Christian Democrat, formed with the goal to change Berlin's school law again. Specifically, the initiative ProReli wanted to make religious education a mandatory school subject under state control with the option to opt out and attend ethics instead. This would align Berlin's organization of value education with the German constitutional mandate. The campaign ran under the slogan "Values need God" referring to the stated aim of creating a sound foundation of values based in one's own faith tradition and advocated for "Free Choice [Freie Wahl]" emphasizing democratic principles. They thus aimed to recruit a broad base of voters for their cause.

However, underlying these efforts were still conceptualizations of diversity as a possible threat. In a subcommittee hearing ProReli founder Dr. Christoph Lehmann said the following about the intentions behind the referendum:

> We live [...] in a city with many religions and diverse ideological convictions. If we acknowledge that we don't all start with a common worldview, then we also have to accept that we must pick children and young people up where they are and where they came from at home. [...] Imagine a boy from a Muslim family who was taught in ethics that men and women are equal. Maybe after coming home in the evening, he will hear from his father, "That's fair enough, but the Quran says his sister has to be veiled, and that is why she will be doing that now." The boy will not be enabled by school to discuss this with his father on the same level; instead, he will be left in between two contradictory moral values – at least from his [the boy's] point of view. The goal of a proper religious education [...] – as

> well as any other ideological instruction – has to be to make clear to children how they can live in our society with their beliefs. (Lehmann, CDU, Abgeordnetenhaus von Berlin, 2008b, pp. 4–5)

While this statement tries to actively engage the criticism that mandatory religious education would foster separation rather than bring citizens together, the example used to illustrate this is problematic. Lehmann essentialized Islamic believes and ultimately casts Muslims as outside of "our society" in need of an education that would facilitate an ideological change within youth and by extension their parents.

While Lehmann here affirms that Islamic religious instruction would be part of the religious education portfolio in Berlin, its practical implementation would have been more than questionable. In Berlin religious education teachers are required by law to demonstrate knowledge of German (through expensive language certification) as well as a German (or comparable) university education in the religion in question. However, as such degree programs were just being founded throughout Germany at the time this requirement would have meant that no adequate staff for Islamic religious education would be available. As it had after the Islamic Federation won the right to implement Islamic religious education in Berlin, these specifications in the law would also have curtail the implementation of Islamic religious education after the referendum (cf. Häusler, 2007, pp. 40–43).

Proponents of mandatory ethics meanwhile would highlight again and again the unifying and integrative aspects imagined as part of mandatory ethics:

> We react with ethics to the special circumstances in Berlin. We are an international city. Christians, Moslems, Jews, Buddhists, and different cultures meet in the city and in its schools. We want students to discover differences and common values within their learning group [Klassenverband], we want them to talk to each other rather than about each other. (Mueller, SPD, Abgeordnetenhaus von Berlin, 2009b, p. 3741)

To those in favor of mandatory religious education – as had been the case from the beginning – the values to be taught in school were based in religious faith traditions especially an imagined Judeo-Christian heritage. Those opposing this plan located the values to be taught in the German Constitution and Declaration of Human Rights manifested in a claim that ethics content should be secular and neutral and thus inclusive of all.

The question of integration overall was a very contentious point in the campaigns and both sides tried to claim it for their arguments. While those in favor of mandatory ethics claimed that teaching everyone together would foster intercultural communication and integration the opposing side claimed that having sound foundations in one's own creed were the only way to promote integration (cf. Schneider, 2009 – an Op Ed by Berlin professor for practical theology). Some researchers have also argued that immigrant integration would have to foster religious education in immigrants' creeds (Collet, 2018). My point here is not to support either of these arguments but to show how different conceptions of diversity promoted one or the other.

The supporters of mandatory religious instruction successfully mobilized to force a referendum. This would be the last effort by conservative politicians for the time being to reclaim the right to value education and thus advance their view of destructive diversity in Berlin's education policy. After the initiative gathered enough signatures to force the referendum the Catholic and Protestant Churches openly supported the effort (cf. Jung, 2011). The referendum was lost in April 2009 with 51.4 percent of the votes against and 48.4 percent for the change in school law and a voter turnout of 29.2 percent (cf. Landesabstimmungsleiter Berlin, 2009, p. 3). Despite their support, Christian churches failed to mobilize their members to vote (cf. Schluß, 2010, p. 101). Although most districts in the former West of Berlin supported the effort, Eastern districts voted strictly against the change in law. This highlighted again the historical fault lines of religious affiliation in Berlin and the churches failure to establish a connection in the eastern part of the city (cf. Jung, 2011; Landesabstimmungsleiter Berlin, 2009; Schluß, 2010).

Figure 2: Results of Referendum Election in Percentage by District Group

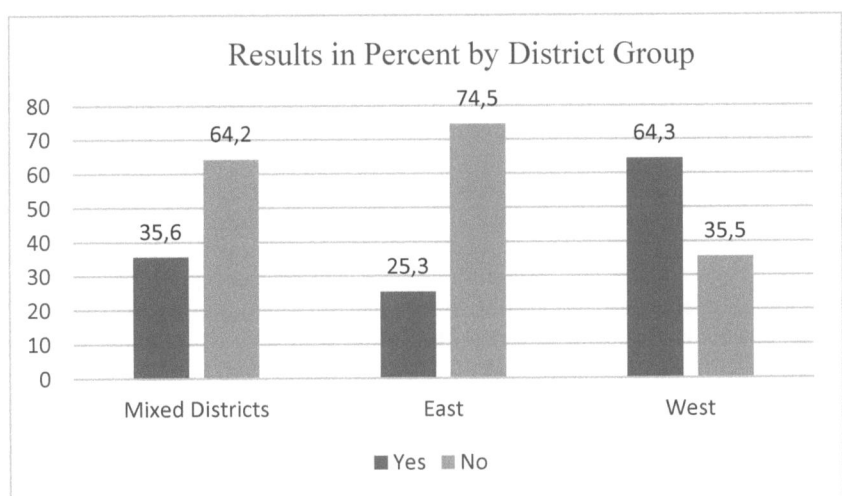

Source: Authors depiction following data from Landesabstimmungsleiter Berlin, 2009, p. 3

While the dwindling numbers of religious education participants certainly played a role in putting ethics on the political agenda, the reduced power of the Christian churches and their inability to mobilize voters in favor of mandatory religious education in East Berlin, kept ethics in place after the referendum (cf. Schluß, 2010, p. 101). The driving political force behind the introduction and implementation of ethics was the fear of a violent local minority youth population that did not abide by German (Christian) values, and the rule of law. In the political imagination, mandatory ethics instruction became the panacea to solve this problem and produce students with enough social competencies to be able to engage in intercultural dialog and ethical judgment based on the German constitution (cf. Schulgesetz für das Land Berlin/vom 26. Januar 2004, article 12.6). While the proponents of mandatory religious education lost the battle for Berlin's school law, their reasoning and challenge to ethics would echo on for years to come in public, education, and media challenges to ethics' legitimacy (cf. chapter 6). For both campaigns diversity was a key driver but the conceptions of diversity underlying them were very different.

4.5 Productive and Destructive Diversity

As the previous discussion has demonstrated the heart and soul of the debate about how best to organize mandatory value education in Berlin's secondary schools lay in different conceptions of diversity and its place within society. Both logics employed by politicans take for granted the potential danger of diversity for peace and security. That is, they start with the assumption of conflict but deal with this threat in very different ways. It should be made clear here that productive and destructive refers to the relationship of diverse groups to the mainstream (ethnic German-national) society. That is diversity may for example be seen as a productive resource for ethnic Germans, or as a destructive force acting on ethnic German culture. There may be a hidden third category of diversity that is situated predominantly in a minority perspective and calls for a view of diversity integration – that is greater acceptance and incorporation of diverse populations into the mainstream disrupting power relations in the discourse that generally tend to co-opt diversity for mainstream advantage.[40] Foroutan's (2019) post-migrant framework may provide the basis for one such perspective, although by 2015/2016 when the data for this study was collected, it had not yet emerged in political debates.

Those in favor of mandatory religious education with the option to opt-out espoused what I call a *destructive* view of diversity. Diverse minority populations, usually manifested in ethnic or religious difference, were seen as an imminent threat to society. Although more recently, this view has also been extended to gender-based diversity (cf. Stenzel, 2019). They were perceived as the breeding ground for individual or group acts of terrorism and distinctly

---

40 I thank Cynthia Miller-Idriss for this point.

marked as separate from the imagined national community (cf. Anderson, 2016). Group identities and cultures were thus seen as static and diametrically opposed on some levels following a "Huntington"-esk clash of civilizations theory (Huntington, 1996). Diversity thus marked a reason for intervention as it was perceived to destroy the imagined heritage and bond of the nation and society.

In Berlin, this view was expressed clearest in the arguments of the CDU. Their claim, as has been shown above, is that Muslim youth, and especially those taking part in Islamic religious education, are in danger of radicalizing and turning violent. Adherents of the destructive diversity position argued that the Muslim community as a whole lacked knowledge and the value system of the Judeo-Christian heritage and base of German nationhood and identity. Mandatory religious education under state jurisdiction was thus the only way to control the Islamic Federation and the threat it created to Berlin's security. In this way responsibility for curriculum and staff decisions would no longer be held by the Islamic Federation itself but rather fall under the authority of Berlin's Department of Education. However, since the school laws mandate for proof of German language skills and German teacher education (or its equivalent) had already successfully prevented Islamic religious education to take place in secondary schools (cf. Häusler, 2007, pp. 40–43) there was no reason to believe this would change under the new law.[41] In this argument the different faith groups would be educated separately to create a sound foundation of knowledge of one's own heritage (cf. Collet, 2018 for a similar argument). Without this sound foundation, it was argued no real dialog across difference would be possible as this critique of the ethics approach by a Christian Democrat shows:

> If one is to learn about all religions and tries to understand what guilt, sin, and sacrament mean within these religions, and if one is, in addition, to learn about humanistic life science [lebenskundliche Inhalte], it is relatively improbable that a certain standard can be reached. This results in arbitrariness, because everything is put next to each other indifferently. This, in turn, results in the juxtaposition of different things, but not a sound position [Standpunkt] from which new things

---

41 Berlin and Germany more generally did not have the organizational structure to produce university educated Islamic religious instruction teachers at the time. In fact, this area of study was first introduced in the fall term of 2012/2013 in Osnabrück (cf. Dreusicke, 2017). In addition, four other universities opened similar departments in Münster, Tübingen, Frankfurt Main/Gießen, and Nürnberg-Erlangen (cf. Wittmann, 2016). However, these departments cannot fill the demand for German educated imams and Islamic religion teachers (cf. Dreusicke, 2017; Wittmann, 2016). There were also no arguments produced within the ProReli campaign or before that hinted at plans to create the organizational structure needed for Islamic Religious Instruction to become a part of Berlin's curriculum.

could be extrapolated. (Schultze-Berndt, CDU, Abgeordnetenhaus von Berlin, 2006b, p. 6)

Cultures and religions were thus seen as static value systems that need to be taught in order to add to at a later point in time. Groups would remain separate even if they may talk to each other.

The logic of *productive diversity,* on the other hand, was taken up by proponents of mandatory ethics instruction. This view saw diverse minority and majority populations as having a potential common ground. That is within them lay the ability to create a new integrated form of society. Violence and terrorism were not attributed to minority populations wholesale but rather were seen as individual or small group acts that co-opt the identity of a specific minority population. Diverse minority groups were seen as part of the process of continued re-creation and re-negotiation of imagined nation or community (Anderson, 2016). Group identities and cultures were viewed as in flux and needed active negotiation and re-conceptualization with other groups in order to overcome conflict. Facilitating this act of active engagement was thus the reason for intervention not the fact that diverse groups exist within society per se.

As I show above, the main critique of mandatory religious education by those espousing a productive view of diversity was the separation of groups according to their creed. Proponents of mandatory ethics instead wanted value education to happen on the basis of a common ground they saw in the national framework of the German Constitution and in the international Declaration of Human Rights. This approach thus transcended the imagined nation in its contents source espousing a view of Berlin as a global city:

> Living peacefully with each other. Accepting core values. Learning together. The rules of our constitution are, just like human rights, the common basis of our society. Only knowledge about and observance of them make peaceful co-existence possible. The goal of joint ethics instruction is the deliberate acceptance [bewusste Akzeptanz] of these core values and fosters the non-violent resolution of conflicts and mutual understanding. (Joint Petition of SPD, Left, and Green Party, Abgeordnetenhaus von Berlin, 2009a, p. 2)

It was thus proposed that especially the coming together of different world views and religious faiths afforded the opportunities to learn, accept and use these core values to bridge difference and resolve conflicts. The transcendence of the nation in referencing international Human Rights while at the same time anchoring the subject's core values in the national fabric through the constitution invoked aspects of global citizenship education (cf. Gaudelli, 2016). The influx of international ideas like Human Rights is not an exclusive addition to Berlin's curriculum. It is a trend apparent throughout Western European textbooks and curricula – especially in history and social studies (e.g. Ramírez et al., 2007; Soysal, 2011; Soysal and Szakács, 2010; Soysal and Wong, 2007).

The opposing views of diversity held by both sides of the political debate were attached to different views of a pluralistic society. Mandatory religious education was connected to a destructive view of diversity, one where differences could only be managed by emphasizing one's own tradition and placing all faith communities (but especially Islam) under state control. This approach stayed distinctly within a bounded national imaginative of identity and heritage. Those favoring a more productive view of diversity sought to base their content in the German Constitution and Declaration of Human Rights thus attaching itself to secularism and neutrality. It transcended the national imagination to incorporate proposedly global values and saw only in coming together the potential for negotiating peace.

4.6 Arriving at Diversity

The organizational solution for value education in Berlin (opt in voluntary religious education in the full responsibility of the faith community) had been left untouched for more than 60 years. The introduction of secular mandatory ethics without an option to opt out represented a radical break from organizational solutions found elsewhere in Germany. Even in Bremen – the only other federal state where religious education is not a mandatory elective – students attend a distinctly Christian inflected subject called Biblical World Science. I argue that the change that occurred in Berlin and led to the introduction of mandatory ethics instruction, on the one hand was influenced by the 1) increasing *secularization* and on the other hand with the influx of 2) *international fears and security concerns* specifically related to minority groups. These two catalysts slowly eroded the conviction of church and government that the Berlin Model in the form it was introduced after the Second World War, that is voluntary religious education in the sole responsibility of the faith community, was the best way. Due to its exception to the constitutional mandate for mandatory religious instruction, Berlin's government was free to forge its own path on value education unique among German federal states. As noted throughout this chapter, at stake during the heated political struggle to arrive at a new model were two different views of diversity and its place within society, that I call *destructive* and *productive diversity*. The ideas, values, imaginations and taken for granted assumptions connected to each of these two logics had the potential to produce a unique organizational structure. The debates and solutions constructed by these two different logics build the institutional framework for teaching ethics in Berlin public schools. Both of these logics produced distinct political imaginations of the subject – one imagination providing the basis for the school law in effect today, the other became the basis for severe challenges to ethics' legitimacy as a subject. The logic that won political support in Berlin was significant in that it represented a new and highly contested form of organizational structure that carried the political conflicts into classrooms.

Ethics in Berlin, however, not only represents a case of institutional change that produced a new organizational solution, this case of organizational re-structuring also demonstrates how global debates were transitioned and rendered meaningful in the local context. Specifically, the political debates around value education in Berlin managed to transform international and global debates about diversity, nation, and integration into a local context. Ethics instruction thus became a site where these larger debates were translated and negotiated in everyday classroom interactions between teachers and students. As I will argue in the next chapter, inclusive and exclusive logics of diversity also significantly influence the ways in which teachers taught about diversity in various school contexts. And while I do not propose that there is a direct causal relationship between the logics operational in the political debates and those present in teaching practice, the similarity between them suggests that these opposing logics are operational in Germany more generally (cf. chapter 7).

5 Logics of Diversity in Ethics Teaching: Between Inclusion and Exclusion

> "The state alone cannot guarantee integration. Its laws and the actions of its organs build a framework, which needs to be given content by its citizens in their everyday behaviour. Integration is more than reciprocal toleration between non-Muslims and Muslims; it is, on the contrary, mutual acceptance. The prerequisite for this is the capacity for a dialogue of cultures [Dialog der Kulturen]."
> Standing Conference of the Ministers of Education and Cultural Affairs of the Länder [KMK], Weimar Appeal (Kultusministerkonferenz, 2003)

5.1 Striving for Integration

Over the past two decades, negotiating a place for minority populations in society has become a major policy issue. Especially Islam has drawn mainly negative attention by the general public, media, and politicians (Pew Research Center, 2011). This, as was discussed in previous chapters was also true for policymaking in Berlin. In fact, part of the reason for the CDU to so adamantly demand the reorganization of value education in Berlin was the advent of the Islamic Federation into Berlin's secondary schools (cf. chapter 4). Amid security concerns after 9/11 and anxiety over economic stability and social cohesion, Germany has increasingly focused on integration as a way to incorporate its growing and diversifying minority population. Although integration is a national priority, research finds that diversity policies, defined as "policies that acknowledge and accommodate the heterogeneity of the population," are especially common in Germany's urban areas (Martínez-Ariño et al., 2019, p. 667). The concept of integration itself is vague. However, the sociological literature defines it broadly as "the process of settlement, interaction with the host society, and social change that follows immigration" (Favell, 2014, p. 63). Yet, literature that examines how these policies are enacted and negotiated in everyday practice is still rare (cf. Martínez-Ariño et al., 2019, p. 668).

In education policy, Berlin's politicians were at the forefront of this drive for pro-diversity policy. As the previous chapter has shown, the issue of diversity and debates over what place it should occupy in society, were highly productive, albeit contested, drivers of the policymaking process. This chapter engages directly with the question of how teachers promote or discount prevalent logics about diversity in their classroom interactions with students. It thus considers a macro to micro negotiation of logics about diversity. That is not to say that teachers are causally affected by the logics in existence in the political debates as laid out in chapter 4. I rather show that within the sense-making about how to teach about diversity in ethics, teachers negotiate similar ideas and categories as the logics discussed in the previous chapter. Considering the important role teachers play as agents of the state who socialize students into their local and national communities, it is essential to understand how the dominant logics about diversity are negotiated by teachers in everyday classroom settings.

In this chapter, I argue that teachers negotiate two different logics of diversity in their sense-making about student populations and teaching. Both of these logics produce distinct teaching approaches in diverse and non-diverse context. Specifically, an exclusive logic of diversity is negotiated by teachers into what I call the *assimilationist* and *philosophical* teaching approach. An inclusive logic of diversity produces an *intercultural* and *critical* approach. I specifically chose to give these two logics a name different from the logics discussed in the previous chapter to highlight that there is no directly causal relationship between the political discourse and teachers' ideas about diversity. While the political discourse related to mandatory ethics in Berlin may certainly have provided these logics to some teachers there are also other ways that logics may find their way into social actors' cognition like textbooks, media discourses, professional training, or interpersonal communications.

I further show that these approaches are not strictly separate from each other and may co-exist in the same school context or an individual teacher's attempts to make sense. The existence of these two logics thus creates a multitude of responses to policy, which in some cases depart considerably from the political imagination of ethics as a way to create a peaceful pluralistic society. I further argue that the heterogeneity of approaches and the existence of two competing logics at work in ethics instruction in Berlin indicate an unstable institutional environment ripe for contest and change to the very imagination of what ethics instruction in Berlin is (cf. chapter 6).

In this chapter, I will focus on how teachers interact with (ethnic and religious) diversity in their classrooms on two levels: 1) by teaching diverse student bodies and 2) by teaching about different forms of diversity. Rather than focus my discussion on student body diversity as many other research projects interested in societal diversification and minority group integration processes do (cf. Abu El-Haj 2010; Bowen et al. 2013; Jaffe-Walter 2013, 2017; Rios-Rojas 2014; Schiffauer, 2015; Simel, 1995; Sunier, 2013), I consider student body diversity as an environmental stimulus that creates an organizational pressure on teachers. My discussion therefore focuses on how teachers teach about diversity. This content area was pivotal for the political imagination of mandatory ethics in Berlin. Furthermore, teaching about diversity plays a key role in educational interventions throughout Germany and the world in preventing (violent) inter-group conflict (UNESCO, 2017) and is often a crucial component in national education directives (Kultusministerkonferenz, 1996/

2013). Understanding how teachers negotiate diversity in different ways in all kinds of contexts, whether diverse or not, helps to overcome the limitations of studies that examine diversity only through the lens of diverse school populations (Abu El-Haj, 2010; Jaffe-Walter, 2013; Lelie et al., 2012; Mannitz and Schiffauer, 2005; Ríos-Rojas, 2014). In other words, I approach diversity integration as a two-way process that affects both minority and majority populations, rather than situating it only in contexts with high levels of diversity.

The main argument of this chapter is based on 39 semi-structured qualitative interviews with ethics teachers at 17 schools in Berlin. These schools differed according to academic track, socio-economic status and level of diversity in the student body (see chapter 3). At least one school in each of Berlin's twelve districts is represented in the study. Interviews were conducted between September 1st 2015 and July 18th 2016 and lasted between 25 and 98 minutes.

As detailed in chapter 3, my field work started in the middle of what would internationally be called the "European refugee crisis" in the summer and fall of 2015. In addition, the time of my field research was laced with international violence – with events impacting Western Europe and the US receiving copious media attention) and increased xenophobic and anti-refugee sentiments and violence in Germany. In 2015 alone, refugee homes were violently attacked a total of 279 times (see Biermann et al., 5/24/2016 for a detailed analysis). And 6,330 criminal investigations due to xenophobic crimes (Landesjustizamt, 2016a, p. 1) compared to 5,317 in 2016 (Landesjustizamt, 2018, p. 1) and 2,666 (Landesjustizamt, 2016b, p. 1) in 2014. These events were directly and indirectly reflected in my participants' classrooms and interviews.

Below, I first discuss the theoretical underpinnings used to analyze the empirical material. I then discuss the two approaches espousing an exclusive logic starting with the *assimilationist* approach found in diverse school contexts and continuing with the *philosophic* approach found in non-diverse school contexts. Next, I discuss the *intercultural* and *critical* approach of ethics teaching again starting with diverse school contexts and then discussing non-diverse school contexts. I then provide evidence of intersections between these four approaches and their two underlying logics before I analyze the commonalities and differences among these four ideal type approaches. Finally, my conclusion highlights the implications of the unstable institutional environment marked by the heterogeneity of practices found in ethics instruction throughout Berlin.

5.2 Heterogeneity of Practice and Teachers as State Agents

Teachers in many cases are the first government agents children and youth encounter and play a crucial role in socializing students into their "place in the political community" (Lipsky, 2010, p. 4). The ideas they project through their teaching approaches into ethics classrooms are hugely important to socialize minority and non-minority students into specific roles of national belonging and power structures (cf. Riggan, 2016). They determine how the state is imagined and re-imagined by citizens (cf. Anderson, 2016; Appadurai, 2010; Riggan, 2016). Teachers communicate ideas about citizenship, community, and belonging and may reproduce or challenge mainstream narratives in their classrooms. In the way ethics teachers specifically engage with diversity in their classrooms they negotiate the logics of community of the German nation.

I employ a conceptualization of logics as comprised of different elements decomposable by social actors. This allows me to systematically examine in what ways ethics teachers negotiate, mobilize, and complicate logics about diversity in their classrooms and what this might mean for the way diversity in German society is constructed for students. That is, the same logic may exist in different forms with an emphasis on different aspects depending on the organizational pressures actors are exposed to. In addition, there may be competing logics operating within ethics instruction, as suggested by the discussion of the previous chapter.

Actors do not make rational decisions about the logics they do or do not employ. Instead, actors are bounded within cultural constructs which may shape the problems and solutions they perceive in their everyday lives.

> Institutional logics represent frames of reference, that condition actors' choices for sense-making, the vocabulary they use to motivate action, and their sense of self and identity. The principles, practices, and symbols of each institutional order differentially shape how reasoning takes place and how rationality is perceived and experienced. (Thornton et al., 2012, p. 2).

Available logics thus provide the accessible building blocks for individual sense-making to each actor. Which elements or logics are activated is seen as mediated by the environment and situation teachers are in. In the sections below I discuss how school level diversity shapes the ways in which elements of particular logics are negotiated. However, I show that the two dominant logics are not mediated by school level environment but rather exist in both contexts.

Further, institutional logics theory predicts that the existence of competing logics within the same field – in this case ethics instruction in Berlin – creates a highly unstable institutional environment open to change. In other words, where multiple, possibly conflicting, logics are available, there is no stable social structure; social actors are not equally embedded in these logics, and as a result, there is no stable organizational practice. This has the potential to produce complexity or transformation within the organization, the field, and society (cf. Thornton et al., 2012, p. 99). A messy heterogeneity of practice thus hints at an unstable institutional environment, comprised of multiple competing logics, that is highly volatile and open to change.

Throughout this chapter I argue that two diversity logics (inclusive and exclusive) are negotiated by ethics teachers in various school environments. Depending on the school context they mobilize different elements within these logics producing four ideal type approaches: assimilationist, philosophical, intercultural, and critical. In addition, individual teachers may also cross logic boundaries in their sense-making. Thus, I show that ethics is situated in a highly unstable institutional environment with competing logics enacted simultaneously and not strictly separated from each other.

5.3 Teaching about Diversity: Exclusive and Inclusive Logics in Diverse and Non-Diverse Classrooms

Ethics is the only subject that has a description of its content inscribed into the school law in Berlin. By law ethics teachers were to engage students with diverse cultures, ideologies, and religions. As Berlin's school law states: "The goal of ethics instruction is to further the willingness and ability of students to engage with the fundamental cultural and ethical problems of individual life and societal cohabitation as well as different moral and spiritual explanations" (Schulgesetz für das Land Berlin/vom 26. Januar 2004, Section 12, Paragraph 6). Yet how ethics teachers teach about diversity in their classrooms varied significantly.

Most teachers viewed diversity in their student body and in society as a challenge requiring attention rather than an advantage. In my overall sample, only one teacher spoke exclusively positively about diversity, and just six teachers expressed more positive than negative views. Perceived student differences from the majority society (read: ethnic German) were thus framed as requiring intervention (cf. Sincer et al., 2019; van Middelkoop et al., 2017, for similar findings). Teachers especially saw encounters between different groups – usually between ethnic-German students and ethnic or religious minorities – as difficult. Likewise, interactions between ethnic-German teachers and minority students were perceived as equally, if not more, problematic than those between student groups.

Across the sample, in both diverse and non-diverse school environments, teachers' sense-making followed two distinct logics of diversity: one inclusive and one exclusive. However, teachers in each setting activated different elements of these logics, leading to distinct practices. I categorize these into four ideal-type approaches to teaching diversity in ethics: (1) *assimilationist*, (2) *philosophical*, (3) *intercultural*, and (4) *critical*. While the assimilationist and philosophical approaches are rooted in an exclusive logic, the intercultural and critical approaches follow an inclusive logic. At the same time, individual teachers sometimes drew on overlapping elements from both logics in their sense-making and practice.

5.3.1 Assimilationist Teaching: Exclusion in Diverse School Contexts

Teachers who espoused an assimilationist approach primarily focused on the perceived threat that ethnically and religiously diverse student groups posed to German cultural heritage as well as to societal – and, in some cases, personal – safety and well-being. Minority students were constructed as fundamentally different from their teachers, who positioned themselves as representatives of the majority culture and society. One way this perceived difference was expressed during the interviews was through descriptions of students with an exaggerated sense of "foreignness," sometimes contrasted with their formal citizenship status. As this example from Frau Smith shows:

> If it is the Turkish background, [the] Arabic migration background, we did not have any of this [at her old place of work]. So here at first, [I] experienced a little culture shock – in quotation marks... where you had to get acclimated at first. [...] With the students, you had to get used to it at first and that really took about a year, where I said to myself '[...] here you will get depressed, you can't really bear this.' [...] There is a specific kind of clique formation, especially [when it is] connected to [a] migration background. [...] Even though they were all born here, overall, they are all German, but they still get together in groups [according to country of heritage]. You notice, in terms of the constellation, they segregate themselves a little and try to remove themselves from others. (Frau Smith, Interview on 6/22/2016)

Frau Smith is a mid-career ethics teacher who used to teach at a high academic track school in a well-off neighborhood with low student diversity. At the time of the interview, she taught at a lower track school with a diverse student body in Berlin's Northwest. In contrast to Frau Smith's old place of work, she described her new school and its student body as producing a culture shock that she at first did not know how to deal with and that she feared would make her depressed and leave. Despite students at her new school all being "born here" and being "German", she still perceived them according to their ethnic-backgrounds (being Turkish or Arabic) and saw them grouping together, separating themselves from others, according to their heritage thus exaggerating their perceived foreignness.

While Frau Smith above describes her ethnic and religious minority students as a risk for her personal wellbeing, other teachers attributed a more general threat to their students' perceived identity:

> I think it [religion] is dangerous to be honest. [...] It is so close-minded [engstirnig], they are like this from home or wherever, [it] has to be from home... so drilled

on this. At 13 I did not know any of this. [...] I did not have a clue yet. And no one told me, even though my mother was very catholic. And that it is so hardened in them, so irrevocable, they don't debate it, this I think is horrid [grauenvoll]. [...] Because they don't even think anymore '[...] is this really what I want or believe? Or what does it mean to believe?' For them it is [simply] believe, it is completely clear, this is the way it is. And you cannot soften it. Very few take into account the different streams [within Islam], some are a little more open, but most of them are fixed. (Frau Singer, Interview on 3/1/2016)

Frau Singer, a late career teacher at the most diverse and socio-economically deprived schools in the sample who had been teaching ethics since its introduction in 2006, contrasted her own religious beliefs and conservative upbringing with that of her students. She went as far as claiming that Islam as lived and understood by her students was dangerous and that ethics instruction could not do anything to intervene in students' religious beliefs. After asking her whether softening these hardened religious beliefs was a goal of ethics in her opinion she replied: "Well, I try yes, but there I always feel like ... with the religion it doesn't make sense." (Frau Singer, Interview on 3/1/2016).

Throughout the interview and in her classroom teaching Frau Singer created rigid boundaries between presumably Christian ethnic-Germans and Muslim students – who were the majority in her classroom and school – repeatedly calling attention to her own and students' religious backgrounds. This went as far as calling on an ethnic-German student to explain the Ten Commandments to his 'Muslim classmates' [muslimischen Mitschülern] during a lesson on Hinduism (field notes, classroom observation on 10/1/2015). Religious identities and narratives were ever present in her classroom and a tool to divide students into (Christian) in- and (Muslim) outgroups.

The underlying goal of softening religious beliefs or at least getting students to think critically about religion and its role in their lives was prominent across the sample. The difference on what steps teachers would take to counter these beliefs, however, lay in the way they perceived the place of religious diversity in society. If conservative or hardened religious views were connected to teachers' fears (especially fears about majority culture survival) teachers asserted the "right values" more strongly as I discuss below.

Herr Stade, a late career German, physical education, philosophy, and ethics teacher with more than 40 years of experience, reflected on what it meant to be German in contrast to the religious orientation of his students. To him, Islam specifically threatened German cultural and religious identity. He emphasized that Germans needed to remember their Christian roots in order to be able to stand up to Islam and the possible threat of giving up one's identity:

[...] it would be really important, if we ehm remember, where we are coming from and what our intellectual roots are and that we should not so easily give them up. I think this is really important also for your own identity, which is more and more put into question. (Herr Stade, Interview on 9/1/2015)

Ethics to him was a way of protecting what he believed to be "our own identity" – that is a Judeo-Christian tradition and a certain understanding of German nationhood and belonging – against a foreign threat represented by Islam and ultimately his students (cf. Bowen et al. 2013; Mannitz, 2005; Mannitz and Schiffauer, 2005; Sunier, 2013 for similar findings and arguments). His perception of Islam as a threat was also apparent in his description of the religious composition of the neighborhood he taught in:

> Well secular ethics yes... is important in this neighborhood, because you need the lowest common denominator to talk with each other about morals and values at all. And that you still know, well, that one is let's say Christian, which has become really rare, or a Muslim, which massively manifests itself these days, or this one is a very mild Buddhist, which does also manifest. (Herr Stade, Interview on 9/1/2015)

As he explained, Christians had become rare. It was rather Muslims that provided the largest number and "massively manifest[ed]" themselves. His description of an overwhelming Islam also stood in stark contrast to the image of the "mild" [sanft] Buddhist (far less in numbers and not threatening) that followed his description of Muslims.

This description invoked the image of uncontrollable masses so common in right-wing narratives of the foreign invasion that immigrants and refugees pose and the "islamicization" feared by PEGIDA followers. That is not to say, that Herr Stade displayed right-wing tendencies, but rather that the narrative of a foreign threat connected to "waves" and "masses" that was for the longest time reserved to that political fringe has become mainstream and is invoked by middle-class teachers in Berlin. The mainstreaming of formerly right-wing narratives can be seen as a larger development in German society (cf. Miller-Idriss, 2017; Zick et al., 2019; Zick et al., 2023).

The creation of in- and out-groups between ethnic-German teachers and their minority students produced an assimilationist teaching agenda with the goal of imparting cognitive knowledge about majority culture and values. While Herr Stade talked about "secular ethics" as creating the smallest common denominator above, the knowledge of nationhood and heritage he wanted to impart on students led to an emphasis on Christianity and its advantages:

> Well, I believe that contrasting these different religions should make clear the advantages of Christianity... or of being Christian. If presented in the right way, everyone should be able to recognize the connections between these beliefs and how they relate to our current way of life and what was previously formulated as a goal [in the school law]. Right? [...] For instance, I teach a comparison, such as the Ten Commandments, from both the Christian and Muslim perspectives... Here, you try to identify commonalities within the Abrahamic religions… This is pretty good, but I think it is right to also make the differences clear. (Herr Stade, Interview on 9/1/2015)

This was part of his response to me asking directly about the goals of ethics written into the school law. To him, teaching about religious diversity and contrasting the Abrahamic religions with each other served to anchor an assimilationist agenda in ethics instruction. Combined with his negative assessment of Islam and belief that the Judeo-Christian heritage of German society needed to be protected, as described above, he emphasized that teaching Christianity "the right way" should make everyone understand its advantages. Other teachers also highlighted the importance of Germany's Christian heritage, its history and nationhood for students' education. The approach these teachers describe focused on reflection and gaining knowledge of majority culture values and differences to minority cultures informed by teachers' evaluation of ethno-religious diversity's place in society.

Teachers associated with this approach created static in- and out-groups based on their evaluation of students' Germanness and willingness to assimilate to majority culture. Often the interaction with minority students was connected with teachers' personal fears (Bender-Szymanski, 2000; Gutentag et al., 2018) or more general fears over the survival of national identity. The content taught was geared towards the acquisition of knowledge about majority culture and heritage.

5.3.2 *Philosophical Teaching: Exclusion in Non-Diverse School Contexts*

At schools with diverse student bodies the teachers argued that teaching about diversity happened to highlight German cultural standards. In non-diverse school contexts, many teachers did not see the need to engage students in learning about (local) diversity and brushed this off to schools with highly diverse student bodies. As Frau Mayer, student teacher instructor, and mid-career ethics, philosophy, and math teacher at a low diversity high academic track school in Southwest Berlin explained following my question on Berlin's school law:

> And especially this... I mean, we really don't have this as much at this school, this multicultural, but of course in other districts – I also train student teachers [Referendare] and I see many different schools – it is really really important, especial where maybe different cultures really collide with each other. (Frau Mayer, Interview on 4/26/2016)

Frau Mayer premised teaching about cultural difference and establishing intercultural skills on the existence of student body diversity. This perceived link was used here to produce a justification for not engaging with the topic and thus excluding diversity from teaching content. This sentiment was also echoed by Frau Zimmermann, a late career teacher with more than 30 years of experience who had recently transferred to a low diversity high academic track school in Eastern Berlin after many years at a low track school in diverse central Berlin:

> Yes, I mean, for example, that the topic of migration still feels like it hasn't arrived here yet. That is, we have almost no students – well, at least that's my impression – few students with migration background. I would say there are very few Turkish students, maybe a few Vietnamese students, whose parents have lived here for decades. [...] Well, in this way, I would say that the topic of different cultures is not the number one issue here. I would say that it was different in Neukölln when I worked there. There, it was present every day, of course. Well, it was clear there that there would be no pork in the cafeteria, because I would 70... Well not 70 percent but 50 to 60 percent of the students had a Turkish or Arabic migration background. (Frau Zimmermann, Interview on 3/3/2016)

Whereas teachers following an exclusive logic at highly diverse schools over-emphasized the foreignness of their students, teachers in non-diverse contexts emphasized their students' homogeneity, reflecting clear in and out-group boundaries. Moreover, out-group status was connected only to certain migrant heritages. Above Frau Zimmermann contrasted students of Vietnamese with those of Turkish heritage. While the parents of the Vietnamese students "have been here for decades" and have thus gained honorary belonging, the same was not true for German Turks, despite the fact that both of these migrant groups mainly came as part of guest worker agreements at similar points in German history. Due to the lack of perceived diversity, learning about cultural difference, according to Frau Zimmermann, was thus not part of the curriculum at her school as it represented a world far away from that of her students.

Frau Wels was a young early career teacher who had recently finished her student teacher training (Referendariat) and taught at the same high track, low diversity school as Frau Zimmermann. Below she elaborated on the teaching content she imagined for her students:

> Ethics is much more than just... right... than just this idea of intercultural understanding. In classes that are truly mixed, I can totally see it, where you say ethics is especially great for this, because these are really mixed classes. And now we have a platform to create a dialogue together. But at our school, this doesn't fit, because they all have the same opinions; they all come from the same... well, really, most of them come from the same cultural background. [...] Ethics is not meant to create a dialogue between all different cultures, because we simply don't have them. And I've already said that my focus in ethics is more on argumentation and reasoning. (Frau Wels, Interview on 5/27/2016)

Again, the sentiment expressed here was that learning about cultural difference and creating dialogue was reserved for highly diverse contexts. Instead, Frau Wels' focus was on cognitive skills rooted deeply in philosophical reflections developing reasoning and critical thinking skills.

Cognitive philosophical reflection was often referenced in this approach to teaching ethics. As Frau Mayer stated: "What says ethics on the cover is really filled with philosophy for junior high [Mittelstufe; grades 7-10]. That is, it is a school subject that operates on a cognitive level." (Frau Mayer, Interview on 4/26/2016). The interactions of diverse groups in Berlin and elsewhere in German society thus were not perceived as a topic for ethics instruction.

If actual examples of socio-cultural diversity were part of the curriculum, this diversity was portrayed to be far away in another part of the world:

> Then it is important to me that the kids learn not to wear blinders [über den Tellerrand hinaus sehen]. Well, for example, one topic that I always teach is something like street children, children in the Third World, children, well, not just in the Third World, but in other countries everywhere. That is really important to me. [...] We also have a project in Guatemala. [...] We also had guests from Guatemala. They introduced themselves to the children, talked a little about their country, and brought pictures, movies, and so on. Well, this is really important, that we have such a partnership, where the children, let me think... don't let me lie... each year they give five or ten euros so that multiple children can get an education. So, a sponsorship, where they also write or Skype with them. (Frau Muller, Interview on 5/26/2016)

Frau Muller was a late career teacher, ethics department head at her school and taught at a high academic track low diversity school in central Berlin, a mere five-minute walk from the most diverse school in my sample. Despite the ever-present diversity just outside the school's gates, diversity in her classroom was portrayed to be located in faraway countries.

Teachers following a philosophical approach thus projected a view of the German nation as non-diverse and homogeneous, where everyone shared the same cultural background reinforcing the stereotypes and exclusion associated with ethnic and religious diversity. Implicitly this teaching approach protects a culturally homogeneous view of the German nation and symbolically removes ethnic and religious diversity from within its borders locating it in faraway countries. Just like the assimilationist approach, teachers who followed the philosophical approach also strongly enforced the construction of in- and out-groups. The out-group, however, was not perceived to be present in students' everyday life.

5.3.3 *Intercultural Teaching: Inclusion in Diverse School Contexts*

While the teaching approach discussed above mainly saw diverse student populations as an overall threat to German cultural heritage or constructed an image of a homogeneous German nation, other teachers at diverse schools saw opportunities for creating a better society and bringing different groups together within their diverse student bodies. Frau Nehls, a mid-career language and ethics teacher who had recently joined school eight, a low academic track school with a diverse student body, saw diversity overall as something that made the world richer and wanted to transmit this sentiment to her students:

> [...] in the end we all meet each other at the basics. We are all not that different and we can really endure [each other] well. That we are completely different and diverse in certain things, it doesn't matter, it is just exciting. It is just exciting and interesting, that it is different... because otherwise it would be so damn boring (Frau Nehls, Interview on 6/28/2016)

The differences that each student brought to class and society were enriching everyone's lives as Frau Nehls stated. To her ethics afforded the chance to bring students of different creeds together and in the process discover meaningful conversations that would not have happened otherwise:

> [...] it is just so great, that we even have such a subject, where children sit together and talk about such topics. It is not like before... well the protestant students sit here; the catholic students sit here and who is nothing has free time, and you never talk together about the things that are important to everyone. I have had situations in my ethics classroom, where the Muslim girls heard for the first time from the Muslim boys, ehm. "Yes, of course, he was in a brothel before we get married. Of course, we actually want an untouched woman, but our fathers drag us to the brothel anyway, because we are supposed to learn this." This... this... to even talk about this, to have a place for this...where you can exchange opinions... Ehm... that was super fascinating... well for everyone... even if... if you belong to a community and for the rest as well...eh to contribute your share, "how is it even for us? I have never thought about it... because of you I am now thinking about it" ... a super exciting thing, this would not happen otherwise... In... no... you wouldn't have it. (Frau Nehls, Interview on 6/28/2016)

The example of the topic of conversation, she gave here, fell into a stereotypical gender discourse cast onto Muslim minorities in liberal Western democracies: the inequality between genders and the oppressed Muslim woman (cf. Abu-Lughod, 2015; Cesari, 2004; Jaffe-Walter, 2017). However, Frau Nehls went beyond the usual assertion of Western liberal values in this matter and saw these conversations in her classroom as a chance for other students to also think about their cultures. Differences and commonalities were thus part of students' knowledge, experienced by students, and discovered in conversation with each other rather than through the reflection on teacher-determined knowledge. It was not so much the difference between teacher values and students but rather the differences between diverse student groups themselves that were used as teaching tools and determinants of content.

Frau Summers, an early career math and ethics teacher at a diverse high academic track school and colleague of Herr Stade, saw the cultural exchanges that the law ascribed as something that happened naturally at her school and was not limited to ethics instruction:

> [...] Well that they... if they don't like something, that they don't just accept it, but that they work on it, that one changes it. And that of course beyond the cultural aspects somehow. But this is just a given at this school because we have so many different cultures in our classrooms. It is not a problem you need to draw people's attention to here. Because they have it in their classrooms and lessons every day. [...] they are really a diverse troop, so it is more or less natural that you somehow have cultural differences that you want to solve peacefully. (Frau Summers, Interview on 9/1/2015)

In an environment as diverse as that of her school, youth were naturally engaged in intergroup dialogue and possessed the skills needed for peaceful conflict resolution. Teacher intervention or ethics were constructed as almost unnecessary in this process (cf. Müller (2012) for similar findings in a study on CBO work in Amsterdam).

Herr Burkhardt, an early career science and ethics teacher was a little more cautious about his enthusiasm for the intergroup dialogue skills of his students. However, he also saw great potential in ethics as a subject to create intergroup understanding and a peaceful pluralistic society:

> Communication among each other, to also realize, "Man, multiple cultures live next to each other here and it still works somehow." This has many advantages, I think, and there is a lot of potential especially if you have such a heterogeneous group, if it is cultural, or religious or in whatever direction... that is of course something really exciting, but it always has a certain potential for conflicts that could develop theoretically as well, let's say it that way. (Herr Burkhardt, Interview on 7/11/2016)

While he saw the subject and the goal of intergroup communication as an exciting opportunity for students, he was also cautious about the potential conflicts that could "theoretically" develop in such interactions. This threat of conflict, however, was not attributed to a characteristic of the entire minority group but rather the result of interpersonal interactions between students. Just like Frau Summers above, Herr Burkhardt saw communication skills developing through student-led conversations.

Overall, teachers following this approach saw diversity as an opportunity to learn intergroup understanding and dialogue. To them ethics offered a chance for different creeds and cultures to come together and exchange their views, an opportunity that would not exist without ethics. Students learned through the conversations they had. And while there was the potential for conflict, this conflict seemed to stay only a theoretical possibility and on an interpersonal level. However, prerequisite for this approach seemed to be a heterogeneous student body, one in which inter-group dialogue happened naturally without much intervention from teachers.

The difference between the intercultural and assimilationist approaches to teaching diversity in ethics was not based on school context but rather the attitude of teachers towards diversity, that is, their embeddedness in a specific logic of diversity. Other social identities of teachers such as age, career level or religiosity also did not play a role in determining which logic teachers activated in their discussion of teaching diversity. The intercultural and assimilationist approaches existed simultaneously at the same schools, for example, Herr Burkhardt and Frau Nehls were colleagues of Frau Smith. All three of them taught at School Eight. While Frau Summers was a colleague of Herr Stade and both of them taught at School One. Teachers thus acted according to different logics when it came to the acceptance and inclusion of ethno-religious diversity in Germany not based on school environment.

5.3.4 Critical Teaching: Inclusion in Non-Diverse School Contexts

Similar to the co-existence of assimilationist and intercultural teaching approaches in diverse schools, not all teachers at non-diverse schools re-enforced a view that excluded local ethnic and religious diversity from their students' lived experience, as the philosophical approach did. In fact, even Frau Wels – who otherwise followed the philosophical teaching approach described above – was cognizant of the potential problems that not engaging with diversity could create:

> Our students here in Marzahn-Hellersdorf [Northeastern district, at the time known for little ethno-religious diversity but difficult socio-economic circumstances] on the one hand have the problem that they have almost no contact to foreign cultures and that... so to say, racism is here, I think, still a really big topic. That is probably really different at schools that are more central. (Frau Wels, Interview on 5/27/2016)

The quote above was part of her reflection on the school law mandate for intergroup dialogue and understanding and her overall teaching goals for ethics. As she stated, racism was a big topic for the students in her classroom compared to students situated in the central and more diverse areas of Berlin.

However, only a minority of teachers in low diversity contexts also expressed the need for intervention in their non-diverse student bodies. Frau Janka was a middle-aged early career ethics teacher at a high track low diversity school in Berlin's Southwest, who had been teaching ethics for five years and also taught ethics didactics at a university in Berlin. Below, she commented on the racism she had observed in students and teaching staff:

> There is no open racism here from my colleagues or the students, but there is a clear screening and that just affects those that have always been affected. But this is not being reflected, except by very very few colleagues, instead it is apparently [accepted] as objective "Well, this is how it is. They just are this weak [academically]. You can't do anything about it." (Frau Janka, Interview on 12/4/2015)

As she described, this racism was not openly voiced but rather the projection of un-reflected stereotypes onto "those who have always been affected" (students from "precarious" and/or migrant backgrounds). In order to challenge the racism, she sometimes tried to disrupt the underlying stereotypes by making use of citizenship categories:

> Foreigners here are usually English, American, Russian, and the migrants, that you usually have an eye on when you talk about migrants, are usually German but here they are perceived as foreigners, even by colleagues and their fellow students. That is why I always specifically emphasize this that I say… "well our foreigners here" not those, where you at first don't think… or don't have these prejudices, those are now the foreigners, it is those where one parent is British or Italian. (Frau Janka, Interview on 12/4/2015)

Being aware of the stereotypes her students and her colleagues had about who was German and who was not, Frau Janka tried to disrupt perceptions by talking directly about citizenship and showing her students that migrants are not just those "with head scarves and black hair who have little money" (Frau Janka, Interview on 12/4/2015). At the same time, however, she also creates clear groups in this approach to disrupting stereotypes. The difference to the teaching following an exclusive logic described above, however, is that to Frau Janka, all groups have an equal right to belong and be part of German society. Overall, the un-reflected and underlying racism present at her school, however, often tested Frau Janka's ability as a teacher and her methodology as she felt her approach (cognitive philosophical reflection) to counter racism was not sufficient:

> Well, a thing, where I am so to say…regularly overwhelmed [überfordert] I have to say, is when I observe everyday racism [Alltagsrassismus] in class that I don't really know what I should do against it. I can, of course, chose this cognitive reflective approach, but I always have the feeling that you should be trained completely differently didactically and pedagogically. And I am not trained at all, and neither are other ethics teachers. (Frau Janka, Interview on 12/4/2015)

For her inability and uncertainty in how to effectively combat racism in ethics Frau Janka faulted the education that ethics teachers received, despite being actively involved in this education herself. She felt that countering racism should receive a different focus in teacher training. This skepticism of an appropriate teacher education when it comes to teaching diversity is also prominent it the scientific literature on the subject. Often researchers site a lack of or ineffective education as the main reason why in-service teachers fail to deal with or teach diversity (cf. Bender-Szymanski, 2013; Cardona et al., 2018; Jafralie and Zaver, 2019; Szelei and Alves, 2018; Yuan, 2017, 2018 for a discussion of a teacher education project that aimed to combat this).

This sentiment of resignation and frustration with the teaching methodology, expressed by Frau Janka, was shared by others as well, and not limited to countering xenophobia, and racism. Herr Stark, a mid-career German, English, and ethics teacher who had been teaching ethics since the school trial in the mid-1990s described his experience with students' ableism. He questioned how far a cognitive reflective approach to teaching may be able to counter this:

> Ehm... I am a little fatalistic in this respect, because I have been homeroom teacher in an integration class [integration of students with disabilities] with three hearing-impaired students and one physically disabled student. And there you were able to measure if it is possible through all of these activities and ethics classes and of course the dialogue about it were part of this... and... well students quickly start to pay lip service [to these ideas] in class, you are able to nicely check this and they give presentations about equality [Gleichberechtigung], about equity [Gerechtigkeit] and so on, but in my bitter experience, this has no consequences for their personal behavior, right? [...] students gladly take up the theoretical site and eh eh reproduce it and then reflect and everything but in my personal experience this has little impact on their personal behavior. (Herr Stark, Interview on 6/30/2016)

In this quote Herr Stark reflected on the ability of ethics classes to help integrate different student groups. Although he did not state this directly, his example implied that ableism within his class did not abate after several attempts to counter it. Like Frau Janka, Herr Stark saw no merit in a theoretical text-based cognitive approach to countering discrimination. Students, he stated, would quickly understand and reproduce the theoretical argument about equity and equality, however, applying this to their daily behavior did not occur. In some ways he even questioned the ability of inter-group dialogue to counter the stereotypes his students held as not even daily interactions would decrease the amount of ableism displayed. Especially in connection to the assumed "natural" positive effect that un-mediated inter-group interaction may have as espoused by teachers of the intercultural approach, Herr Stark's critical evaluation is interesting. It confirms notion held in the scientific literature that argues for the inconclusiveness of evidence to support contact theory (Laurence, 2014).

Teachers following a critical approach to engaging with diversity in their classrooms in low diversity environments often perceived their majority group students as displaying or acting on un-reflected stereotypes and discriminatory notions. Diversity was perceived to be a part of German society and engaging with the stereotypes students had about it was perceived as a way to counter racism, xenophobia, and discrimination. Teachers in this category engaged with teaching about diversity through text-based cognitive theoretical reflection. In other words, discussions and analysis of concepts such as equality, freedom, and equity. However, they felt this was inadequate to counter discrimination. Overall, teachers saw themselves as ill-equipped to work against the discrimination they encountered in ethics classes.

5.3.5 Muddying the Waters: Heterogeneity and Crossing Logics within Teachers' Sense-making

The approaches discussed above were general tendencies within teachers' ways of teaching diversity in different school environments and thus represent ideal type categories. The reality of teachers' sense-making was even more heterogeneous. Teachers would, for example, express ideas found in other approaches staying within the same logic or they would espouse elements from a different logic. There were thus several examples of crossing and mixing logics and elements in my data.

In particular, the example of cross-logic reasoning described below shows how both inclusive and exclusive logics compete with each other within ethics teachers' ideas about diversity and its place in society. While I described the approach of Herr Stark above as falling within the critical teaching approach, this was only true for certain dimensions of diversity. After we had finished the interview protocol, Herr Stark continued the conversation by expressing his surprise about my questions:

> [I] had a completely wrong idea about what you wanted to know. […] Well, I thought you would be interested in the relationship to the Muslim student body and […] It does play a role. You can't deny it. Well yesterday I had... well I have a class that has one Muslim student. And he immediately closes his blinders [die Scheuklappen zu machen] when a westernized topic is coming up or so... well with gender equality and such.... There he completely closes himself off [macht völlig zu], he does not want to hear that. (Herr Stark, Interview on 6/30/2016)

In his description of the Muslim minority students in his classes, Herr Stark produced clear distinctions between the different value systems underlying ethnic German and Muslim minority. Gender equality as a topic was used here to ascribe an outsider status to this Muslim student based on a difference in values – creating clear in- and out-groups much like the teachers espousing an exclusive logic. Gender equality, as well as attitudes towards homosexuality were used by many teachers in the assimilationist approach to argue for a clear distinction between value systems of their Muslim, Arab, and Turkish students and their own. This tendency to focus on sex and gender in order to attest a lack of integration of minority but especially Muslim communities within Europe has also been documented in political discourse (cf. Uitermark et al., 2013). However, in describing his approach to teaching in environments with ethnic and religious minority students, Herr Stark reverted to a more critical and self-reflexive approach to teaching:

> Well, you are sometimes more careful […] you just have to move cautiously [behutsam], because at some point it may turn into a problem. […] to balance it in such a way that you ... you are always afraid yourself eh to to fall for some kind of stereotype... To say something, that in[cludes] stereotypes […] I usually try to deal

with [austragen] it at some point in some place... that you come to an agreement "how would you like to be treated [wie man dir begenet] ... should I call on you?" and so on. That you address it [...] with the class... because for the class it is also an experience, they usually already know it better than we [teachers] do... (Herr Stark, Interview on 6/30/2016)

Herr Stark was clearly conscious of the possibility for expressing or possibly reinforcing stereotypes and chose an open conversation to solve this problem. He thus modeled an inter-group engagement for the class while at the same time assuming that the classmates had already negotiated these differences elsewhere. Overall, therefore, teachers expressed elements from different logics in their reasoning. The co-existence of multiple logics within the same teacher's sense-making showed that these logics competed for attention within ethics teachers' sense-making. As the example of Herr Stark showed, teachers may negotiate between elements of both logics based on the type of diversity they perceive.

5.4 Creating a Peaceful Pluralistic Society: Teaching Approaches and Their Underlying Logics

As the discussion above showed, teachers relied on different elements of two diversity logics to develop different approaches of teaching. Moderated by the environment they were in, by the perceived category of diversity, and by their own views on diversity's place in society they either negotiated elements of an exclusive or an inclusive logic in their sense-making about teaching practice. Overall, I argue that the teachers in my sample produced four different ideal types for teaching diversity in ethics: *assimilationist, philosophical, intercultural,* and *critical*. An exclusive logic of diversity was negotiated by teachers into the assimilationist approach in diverse contexts and the philosophical approach in non-diverse contexts whereas an inclusive logic of diversity produced the intercultural approach in diverse school contexts and the critical approach in non-diverse school contexts.

Teachers espousing an approach that followed an exclusive logic of diversity viewed especially ethnic and religious diversity as external to German nationhood and belonging. Within their teaching approach they created static in- and out-groups. While these groups were present in the classroom for teachers in the assimilationist approach (represented by students and teachers respectively) the out-group was constructed as far away and in some cases beyond national borders in the philosophical approach. Teaching about diversity was a tool to highlight German cultural values, history and heritage to minority students by assimilationist teachers. Philosophical teachers relied on text-based engagement with philosophical content rather than teaching about lived experiences.

The approaches based on an inclusive logic share a common sense of providing a place for ethnic and religious diversity within German national belonging. Teachers generally had a sense that diversity was a positive influence on society and could produce new and exciting opportunities. Teachers in diverse school environments leveraged this by engaging students in intergroup conversations and discussions where teachers provided topics but the content and knowledge to be learned was based on student experiences. A critical approach used teaching about diversity in ethics to critically engage with stereotypes and discriminatory tendencies within ethnic German student groups.

Both logics co-exist in the same school context. Teachers espousing an intercultural approach would work side by side with those following assimilationist patterns, and teachers using critical ideas shared the same space as those following the philosophical approach. What differentiated these approaches from each other was not necessarily the school context but rather teachers' embeddedness in the logic of diversity they espoused. This heterogeneity of logics and their resulting approaches meant that ethics teachers did not construct a unified sense of belonging and place of diversity in society across Berlin's ethics instruction. Depending on the teacher, students would either learn that diversity was part of German society and worth engaging with, or they would learn that ethnic and religious minorities were not part of German society and posed a possible threat. Especially the approaches based on exclusive diversity logics significantly depart and, in some ways, actively resist the pro-diversity political imagination of the subject. Overall, the teachers represent a best case in terms of their interest in in the issue of cultural difference and intercultural relations (cf. chapter 3). As such the existence of these exclusive approaches in my sample is quite significant. It shows how powerful of an influence exclusive logics can be on practice.

The co-existence and competition of these logics in the same school contexts and sometimes even the same teacher's sense-making also implied the incomplete institutionalization of one dominant logic of diversity in the context of ethics instruction. Overall, this heterogeneity of logics and approaches indicated that ethics operated within an unstable institutional environment ripe for contests about the very meaning of ethics in Berlin. And as I show in the next chapter an exclusive logic was driving the way that teachers were re-imagining ethics in Berlin.

5.5 Political Actors and Diversity: Teaching Diversity in Ethics

While chapter 4 showed how the image of a potentially violent Muslim minority youth was pivotal in the political negotiation and creation of mandatory ethics, essentially producing two logics about the place of ethno-religious diversity in society, this chapter showed how teachers negotiated different logics within their ethics classroom. I looked specifically at how the level of school diversity may be related to teachers' teaching about diversity, thus facilitating an in-depth and systematic look at diversification processes in education across diverse and non-diverse school environments. Comparing diverse and non-diverse contexts, my analysis departs significantly from a research approach limited to diverse school contexts. It thus offers new ideas about how education in Germany responds to societal diversification processes and moves the focus of discussing integration to both minority and majority populations.

By looking at variation in the level of school context diversity, and how teachers engage with teaching diversity across these different contexts, I found larger underlying logics of diversity operational in each context. Specifically, I argued above that teachers created four different approaches to engage with diversity: *assimilationist, philosophical, intercultural* and *critical*. Each of the two logics about diversity were negotiated in one approach in diverse and one in non-diverse school contexts. While the level of student body diversity informed teachers' choices about teaching diversity, the content, approach, and emphasis they activated was critically dependent on interpretations of belonging, and the place of diversity in society. Furthermore, some teachers also engaged in negotiating elements of both logics simultaneously in their sensemaking. I argue that this heterogeneity of existing approaches and their underlying logics produced an unstable institutional environment in ethics with a potential to transform the purpose that was originally ascribed to the subject.

The next chapter engages with the question of how teachers imagined ethics instruction in Berlin. I look specifically at how ethics teachers try to unify the logics connected to ethics and what possible effect this may have on teaching about diversity. Specifically, I show that teachers use logics that ultimately exclude and stigmatize diversity to re-position ethics in Berlin's educational landscape.

6 The Struggle for Legitimacy: Removing the Stigma of Diversity from Classroom Teaching

"Dominant racial ideologies and practices are not simply produced and regulated by the state, nor are they merely manifestations of individual choices and preferences. On the contrary, racial ideas and practices that reflect the interests of the dominant group permeate all social institutions, small group formations, and individual actions in society (Bonilla-Silva 2003; Feagin 2001). Analysts must thus examine contentious racial politics in institutional settings outside of the state. Yet, in both popular thinking and academic accounts, the routine practices of social organizations tend to be "ignored or minimized" as processes that perpetuate racial inequality (Brown et al. 2003:19). In this view, racism is seen as a problem of a few bad apples, or a couple bigots acting contrary to the rules of supposedly egalitarian institutions, such that access to institutions that once excluded people of color is seen as the primary goal when it comes to dealing with racial injustice (Brown et al. 2003; Feagin 2001). The problem with this is that the form, ideas, and practices of these organizations were developed out of racial exclusion." (Bell, 2014, p. 7)

6.1 Reforming Berlin's Schools to Include Diversity?

The so-called intercultural opening of German schools, a process that seeks the integration of (ethnic and religious) diversity into schools' organizational practice, curricula, faculty, and content positions teachers as one of the main facilitators of this change (Georgi et al., 2011). Furthermore, German national policy frameworks that seek minority group integration, like the Integration Program, viewed teachers as untapped resources that will expedite the integration and inclusion processes (BAMF, 2010).[42] These policy conceptions of teachers as positive pro-diversity agents of change, however, neglect to take into account the organizational pressures and established logics underlying the teaching profession. Ethnicity and race scholars caution us that the mere inclusion of minority groups in a professional field does not necessarily facilitate im-

---

42 These frameworks see this potential especially in minority group teachers. However, given the ingrained anti-diversity logic underlying teaching in Germany that I will discuss below, it is doubtful whether mere inclusion can truly lead to the change imagined. Cem Özdemir is one of the most prominent German minority group politicians, former leader of Germanys Green Party, and long-standing representative in the German government. He also cautions against simply relying on minority teachers to do all the work. He argues schools also need improved financial support, better social work, and improved intercultural competency in ethnic-German teachers (cf. Özdemir, 2011, p. 12).

provement to ethnic and racial inequality, as the quote at the beginning of this chapter shows (Bell, 2014). In fact, research into the underlying logics of the German school system attest a general "dis-functionality for an immigration society" (Auernheimer, 2005), a "monocultural and monolingual habitus" (Gogolin, 2008; Gogolin and Neumann, 1997), institutionalized discrimination (Gomolla and Radtke, 2009) as well as a historical continuity in its emphasis on student body homogeneity and minority group exclusion (Krüger-Potratz, 2006). There are thus strong institutional and organizational pressures working against pro-diversity policy in school practice.

In this chapter, I discuss how these pressures are negotiated by Berlin's ethics teachers. I show how Berlin's ethics teachers engage in bottom-up institutional change. I focus specifically on how they re-imagine the place of diversity in ethic's classroom practice and teaching content. I argue that driving the re-imagination process is the severe challenge to ethics' legitimacy from various actors (cf. chapter 4; Keller, 2010; Vieth-Entus, 2016). In addition, contest to the pro-diversity policy imagination is possible because of the highly unstable institutional environment that ethics is situated in (cf. chapter 5). Specifically, I argue below that teachers rely on professional logics about pre-service requirements and the subject's disciplinary grounding to ensure the survival of mandatory ethics in Berlin. These professional logics are essential to frame exclusion and stigmatization of diversity content in ethics. Specifically, teachers seek to exclude teaching about religious diversity and deemphasize intercultural dialogue in teaching ethics. They thus perform a direct reversal of state policy actors' conscious effort to use inclusive logics of diversity to garner political power and legitimacy for their contentious policy innovation (cf. chapter 4; also, Skrentny, 2004). In this way, teachers directly confront and work against pro-diversity state policy and ultimately perpetuate a diversity exclusive status quo in Berlin.

This chapter understands teachers as political actors who work against the political imagination of ethics promoted by state law. In this process they reframe the goals of mandatory ethics in Berlin. As such the role of teachers in this understanding expands the one discussed in the previous chapter as it focuses on the disjuncture between political imagination and teachers' conceptualizations. In this chapter, I don't consider teachers to be acting as state agents, transmitters of state sanctioned knowledge. Rather, I show how teachers work to produce a form of ethics instruction that they consider beneficial. They do so by relying on institutional logics that are prevalent within their profession. In this way they may be considered agents of change, although the change they champion is a maintenance of the national anti-diversity status quo.

Like the previous chapter, the argument in this chapter builds on the analysis of 39 semi-structured qualitative interviews with ethics teachers and two interviews with experts. This chapter pays particular attention to teachers who were engaged outside of their school context through activities such as continued education workshops, state curriculum writing, and the training of student teachers (Referendare). Their experiences and perspectives proved especially important as they were actively engaged in shaping the future of the subject. I also pay close attention the voices of student teachers and early career professionals as these teachers will be the face of ethics in Berlin's classrooms in the coming years.

The chapter first lays out the theoretical background for the discussion. I then provide evidence of the challenges to ethics' legitimacy as described by the teachers in my sample. Next, I show how ethics teachers strive to counter these challenges by mobilizing elements from a professional logic about 1) entrance into the profession, and 2) ethics disciplinary direction. I further show how these elements of a professional logic are used to stigmatize and ultimately remove teaching about religious diversity and intercultural dialogue. Lastly, I provide a summary of the argument and its implications for ethics and an intercultural opening of German schools more generally.

6.2 Legitimacy, Diversity, and Change

The main factor that drives ethics teachers to engage in the renegotiation of ethics' purpose and content is the continued challenge to ethics' legitimacy. The concept of legitimacy is crucially important to institutional organization theory and sociology in general (cf. Deephouse et al., 2017; Meyer and Rowan, 2006; Meyer and Rowan, 1977). Legitimacy has been viewed as a "survival-enhancing phenomenon" that results from efficiency and conformity to "institutionalized myths in the organizational environment" (Meyer and Rowan, 1977, p. 353). Schools in particular are conceptualized as "securing success through processes of institutional conformity as opposed to technical efficiency" (Meyer and Rowan, 2006, p. 3). A lack of legitimacy may lead to societal questions and challenges of the organization (Hirsch and Andrews, 1984; Meyer and Rowan, 1977; Meyer and Scott, 1983). As such legitimacy is ultimately the deciding factor in the success or failure of educational reform efforts and the institutionalization of a new subject such as ethics.

The literature generally assumes an increase in legitimacy when organization align their structures with pro-diversity institutional logics (Meyer and Rowan, 2006; Meyer and Rowan, 1977) – such as Affirmative Action in the USA and other anti-discrimination laws. In the domain of politics, relying on the right logic of diversity also provides (political) power as it aligns political views with social movement goals and voter interests (Martínez-Ariño et al., 2019; Skrentny, 2004; Tarrow, 2012). In other words, in the right environment there is power and legitimacy in aligning one's policy goals with minority rights claims and anti-discrimination agendas. While the reverse is also true, in the case of ethics as I showed in chapter 4, Berlin's politicians used international pro-diversity logics (like Human Rights) to gain enough political power to sign pro-diversity education policy into law. However, teachers are not subject to voter interests and as I show below rely on different logics to facilitate their goals.

Given that legitimacy is so important for the success of education policy and thus ultimately for the successful institutionalization of mandatory ethics instruction in Berlin, it should not be surprising that teachers rely heavily on discourses regarding the need to improve the status of their subject and its legitimacy. For many of them improving ethics' legitimacy was tied to institutional change around the very imagination of what ethics' goals are. Institutional logics theory posits that change happens by mobilizing logics from different orders that have not previously been part of the conceptualization and linking them with existing elements (Friedland and Alford, 1991; Thornton et al., 2012). The main institutional orders theorized in institutional logics theory are profession, market, state, family, religion, corporation, and community (cf. Thornton et al., 2012). Social agents' negotiations of different orders of institutional logics have the capacity to "produce new truths, new models by which to understand themselves and their societies, as well as new forms of behavior and material practices" and inherently open ways to conceptualize change (Friedland and Alford, 1991, p. 254). I show below that teachers leverage elements of the logic of professionalism to facilitate resistance to pro-diversity state law. In contrast to existing scholarship, and indeed the practices of Berlin's politicians, teachers do not use diversity (and community logics) as a source of power and legitimacy for their cause. On the contrary, I show how teachers actively remove teaching about diversity from their ethics classrooms.

6.3 The Challenge to Ethics' Legitimacy: Not just a Waste of Time ("Laberfach")

In many ways, ethic's legitimacy had been challenged by various powerbrokers from the beginning. The most public and notable challenge was the referendum in 2009 (cf. chapter 4). Public media also continuously challenges the subject's right to exist, and overall value of the content taught (cf. Keller, 2010; Vieth-Entus, 2016). However, as teachers lamented throughout my sample these challenges were also expressed by school administration, teachers from other subjects, parents, and students.

Teachers in my interviews often spoke about the fact that neither the public, students, parents, nor teachers of other subjects really understood what the subject was actually about. For example, when I asked Frau Schuhmacher, a student teacher (Referendariat) who was finishing her training at the time of the interview, what challenges ethics faced, she responded by explaining what needed to change:

> More support in general in terms of attitude that you simply don't [see] Ethics as "there we just do ethics and ethics is a subject that is most easily canceled if you need a home room hour [Klassenleiterstunde] or so". But here I mean not necessarily school administration [Schulleitung], but the attitude in general of all teachers and of the parents as well. Well, I have had parent-teacher conferences in my short time, where I noticed here or there in a sub-clause by a parent, parents don't think much of ethics either – "it is just ethics" (Frau Schuhmacher, Interview on 3/2/2016)

Frau Schuhmacher, who taught at a lower secondary school (ISS) in Berlin's Northeast, described the lack of support from administration and parents that she felt. Her response to my question about which problems ethics faced echoed throughout the sample. Teachers described that ethics was deemed unnecessary or expandable by the school's administration and parents – as Frau Schuhmacher explained, it was not important to these parties whether ethics teaching happened or not.

This perception that ethics was a waste of time and did not offer valuable content to students went as far as other teachers high-jacking ethics lessons and content to resolve interpersonal problems in their classes:

> I am often asked by the home room teachers, things that have come up in their groups, if we could not talk about them in ethics. That is on the one hand good and possible, but on the other hand of course not this easy. If you are in the middle of teaching something and then they show up and say, "we are having a problem in this group, there is something going on with mobbing, could you not do something about it in ethics?" […] Of course, these topics you can teach once in a while, but on such short notice to just say "okay, I will just change my plans and do it" That is of course sometimes possible, but that should not be the norm. (Herr Lauda, Interview on 12/21/2015)

As Herr Lauda explained here, ethics was understood by many teachers as a kind of therapy session to deal with group dynamics and problems at the school or group level.

One of the most commonly used complaints by ethics teachers when it came to the subjects' standing and legitimacy within the overall school curriculum was its public reputation as a "waste of time subject" – "Laberfach" (cf. Keller, 2010). Literally "Labern" translates to something like chit chat and has a negative connotation. "Labern" is the act of talking without a point and no actual end result. Metaphorically this means that conversations in ethics are seen as a waste of time with no real student learning outcomes. As Herr Dorn, a mid-career philosophy, ethics, and Latin teacher at a high track secondary school in Berlin's Southwest, described after I asked him how he approached teaching ethics:

> I have also seen a lot of ethics instruction and I think, the biggest danger and the reason why ethics does not have a good reputation – because that is a fact – just lies in the lack of a concept. That they are doing some kind of nonsense, that they are crafting collages of dolphins or doing some kind of associative wandering around [associatives Rumgeirre] about Love and Friendship […] and on the other hand, I have observed this as well, ethics is transformed into some kind of testable [abfragbar] knowledge, along the lines of "I present a text to you" – generally the text is way too difficult, you will have John Rawls for ninth graders or something like that, […] and then they are tested and whoever is able to reproduce the text as much as possible verbatim receives an A. (Herr Dorn, Interview on 3/11/2016)

Herr Dorn framed the problem of ethics' legitimacy within the lack of a clear and unified objective. He described a vast variation in teaching quality in Berlin's ethics instruction – lying somewhere between nonsense, chit chat, and wasting time, on the one hand, and the production of testable knowledge about age (in)appropriate texts and concepts, on the other hand. Ethics teachers thus struggled to deal with the de-legitimization of their job, teaching, and engagement with students. All of them would like to see change in this area and hope for a better standing of the subject and more acceptance in the future. In order to achieve this goal, ethics teachers relied on elements of a logic of professionalism as I discuss below.

6.4 Invoking Elements of Professional Logics for Improvement: Teaching Degrees and the Disciplinary Grounding

The availability of well-trained teachers and unified goals were constructed to be a necessity for legitimate ethics instruction. The struggle for legitimacy in many ways had structural roots as the hasty introduction and implementation despite a severe lack of trained teachers and the lack of proper material at the beginning made the establishment of the new subject difficult. As Dr. Weil, representative of the teacher's union summarized: "The worse a teacher is qualified the more vulnerable a subject becomes." (Dr. Weil, Interview on 10/19/2016). He thus echoes one of the main arguments of ethics teachers to improve the subject: having the right credentials.

Teachers, framed improvement in terms of a professional logic that made 1) a university degree in philosophy and 2) a strong tie to philosophy as disciplinary grounding the only way to gain enough legitimacy for the subject. Within this professional logic they tied teaching about diversity to undesirable professional options and thus stigmatized it in their sense-making.

6.4.1 Guarding the Entrance into the Profession: The Importance of the Right Degree

Due to the speedy comprehensive introduction of ethics in 2006/07 finding teachers for the subject was a big problem. There was no university education for ethics in place at the time. Both of Berlin's big universities (*Freie Universität* and *Humboldt Universität*) have since created teacher education programs and have graduated the first cohorts. However, during the time of data collection ethics was for the most part still taught by a variety of different faculty, depending on the schools' resources. The teachers educated during the Philosophy/Ethics school trial in the mid-1990 through 2006 could not cover the need for ethics teachers in all of Berlin's secondary schools. New ethics teachers needed to be recruited and often this process was rather random, as Herr Dorn explained during the pilot phase of my study: "It was a little like asking all faculty: how do you spell Cicero? And whoever answered with a C got the job." (Personal communication, 1/21/2015). The sudden increase in need for ethics teachers lead to teachers being trained while already engaged in classroom teaching as Herr Vogel, a late-career philosophy and ethics teacher explained:

> Well, the problem is of course now the comprehensive implementation. The school trial [of the mid 1990s] was not a problem, everyone that taught during the school trial had a rock-solid education of four semesters. And now this education concept had to be renewed [...] and it of course had a bit of a makeshift character because colleagues came, started the education, and had to begin teaching at the same time. (Herr Vogel, Interview on 6/9/2016)

Herr Vogel was highly involved in curriculum creation and ethics' introduction in its early phase. At the time of the interview, he was also instructing student teachers (Referendare). He related the level of instructional quality directly to the form of education – explaining a hierarchy of university education, over early additional training during the school trial, to later additional training after 2006 (Zusatzausbildung) and no training at all.

The lack of trained ethics teachers and the fact that about 65.3 percent of ethics at lower track secondary schools and 35 percent at higher track secondary schools in 2013 was taught by teachers without a certification in ethics was widely cited in the press (cf. Anders, 2013). Compared to the statistics from 2013, not much had changed in the 2015/16 school year. There was a total of 1.025 certified ethics teachers in Berlin's primary and secondary schools – 42.3 percent (434) of whom had a university education in ethics/philosophy, 52.8 percent (541) had completed an additional qualification (Zusatzqualifikation), and 7.8 percent (80) were certified by principals with a competency for ethics (Kompetenzfach) with no training at all. At lower secondary schools (ISS) about one third (32.1 percent) of ethics teachers had a university qualification, compared to 42.8 percent at higher secondary schools (Gymnasium; cf. Senatsverwaltung für Bildung, Jugend und Familie, n. d.–a). Given the overall number of secondary schools in Berlin a large percentage of ethics instruction was still administered by non-certified teachers. And university educated ethics teachers were more likely to be employed at higher track secondary schools.

Interesting in these statistics is also the fact that 26.7 percent of university educated ethics teachers work at primary schools, where ethics is not taught. This was also a concern voiced by some of my early-career and novice teacher interviewees after the interview. They reported that some of their colleagues did not find jobs at secondary schools because the ethics positions there were taken by teachers with additional training. Young university graduates thus often had to take jobs at primary schools where they would not teach ethics at all (cf. Field notes, 5/27/2016 and 3/2/2016).

Most of my respondents directly connected the level of education of teachers with the quality of ethics instruction – even teachers who were certified by additional training themselves. The overall argument was that only university educated philosophy teachers would be able to teach ethics in a meaningful way. As Herr Dorn explains:

> And that [the lack of legitimacy] is also due to the fact that many ethics teachers have this additional qualification [Zusatzausbildung] the quality of which, and I can speak openly, is questionable in my opinion. It is not a university education. (Herr Dorn, Interview on 3/11/2016)

The ability of teachers who got certified through additional training is thus questioned if not denied.

Schools where only teachers with university degrees taught reported a clear improvement in the status of the subject within the student body. As Frau Janka, who was acting as the department head at her school and also worked at one of the local universities explained:

> Well, first of all by now students perceive ethics as a completely normal subject here at our school. It is not a subject that is somehow marginal, that you don't have to take seriously. That is due to the fact that here at this school no teachers with additional certification teach, but only people who studied philosophy. (Frau Janka, Interview on 12/4/2015)

The existence of an ethics faculty that received their qualification exclusively through university studies was seen as the sole reason for why the subject was "normal" at Frau Janka's school. She dismisses ethics instruction by teachers with other forms of certification as mere chit chat – "we all feel good and talk a little about what we just read in the newspaper" – without substance or a plan for student learning outcomes.[43]

Teachers thus created an environment that closely guarded the entrance to the profession. This resulted in an atmosphere where often especially those teachers who got certified through additional training felt insecure about their abilities to teach ethics. To them, this seemingly confirmed the fact that a university degree was needed to teach the subject well:

> We have too little knowledge. I have to learn so much on my own [...] I studied German and history... there I feel at home. I have the technical [fachlich] knowledge there [...] well and in ethics I sometimes feel like... ehm... Hobbes for example, I really should know much more... I should read the book... somehow eh ... it is too little [knowledge] for me [...] (Frau Mutombo, Interview on 9/2/2015)

Frau Mutombo, a late-career German, history, religion, and ethics teacher at a higher track secondary school in Berlin's Northwest explained her insecurity due to a perceived lack of deep subject knowledge and compared this to her confidence in the subjects she studied at university.

The influx of university educated young philosophy teachers was often seen as an increase in teacher professionalism that would ultimately improve the subject overall. As Frau Winkel, a mid-career music, French, and ethics teacher working at the same school as Frau Mutombo explained after I asked here where she saw ethics in Berlin in five years:

> Simply that really well-trained ethics teachers come to the schools with a philosophical... with a... with Philosophy knowledge as the basis... so that this subject eh just receives or gains a status that is eh appropriate (Frau Winkel, Interview on 9/8/2015)

The legitimacy of the subject was thus directly connected to the amount of university educated philosophy teachers in ethics classrooms. This focus on the right entry to the profession went hand in hand with a call for a strong disciplinary grounding of ethics instruction in philosophy as the next section shows.

---

43 While there certainly is ethics instruction that works along these lines in Berlin, I did not observe anything like this during my time in classrooms and schools. Teachers regardless of their certification had well-structured lessons plans and discussed concepts over longer periods. In addition, this attitude of closely guarding the entrance into the profession is problematic in times when states due to a severe lack of university certified teachers increasingly rely on recruiting people from other professions into teaching through a lateral recruitment and entry scheme. For the school year 2019/20 for example only four percent of newly recruited teachers in Berlin were university certified teachers (cf. Leinemann, 2019).

6.4.2 Linking a Strong Disciplinary Grounding

One of the main areas teachers blamed for the lack of ethics' legitimacy was the lack of unified content goals. Teachers often perceived ethics as taking on too many different things at once. The resulting openness was criticized by many ethics teachers as hurting the subject's legitimacy and, if done wrong, furthering its reputation as mere waste of time:

> I believe, well looking at it realistically, as a subject that is completely over fraught with expectations... to take on the entire moral-democratic education of students in only two hours a week... to in a sense absorb what parents and society at large cannot do and to look at religions, consumption, the culture of debate [Streitkultur], and the perception of women and so on and so forth, critical questions, organ donation, whatever else is added, and the preparation for philosophy [in grades 11 and 12]. Well... we are expected to achieve all of this. This is completely hopeless and it means that it deteriorates into superficial chit chat. (Herr Dachsen, Interview on 6/29/2016)

As Herr Dachsen, an early career P.E., ethics, and history teacher explained above, deep meaningful coverage of the range of topics and themes that ethics was supposed to engage with was "hopeless" to achieve. This lack of clear content would also lead to the variance of teaching quality in ethics instruction criticized by Herr Dorn earlier (from crafting collages about dolphins to reading John Rawls in ninth grade).

Just as important as emphasizing the right degree, teachers were eager to ground ethics instruction in the academic discipline of philosophy:

> Well basically ethics to me is Philosophy instruction from the higher grades [grades 11 and 12] modified for younger students and thematically limited to practical Philosophy. (Herr Dorn, Interview on 3/11/2016)

Herr Dorn unmistakably stated here that the right direction for ethics instruction was a change in the disciplinary focus. When asked about why they choose to be ethics teachers at the beginning of the interviews, many pointed out that they actually choose to be philosophy teachers and ethics came along with it: "Well I decided to become a philosophy teacher. And ethics in middle school was then so to say part of it." (Herr Anderson, Interview on 4/19/2016). Ethics was thus an add-on but something that teachers often thought of as philosophy for lower grades. Herr Anderson continued:

> I personally was skeptical at first, in general when it came to the introduction of the subject in Berlin. It [the skepticism] went as far as writing a seminar paper against it [the introduction of ethics] during my internship. [...] back then, if I remember correctly, ethics was introduced because of an honor murder in Berlin [...] and that seemed like as if an education component that usually parents are responsible for was moved into schools, introducing a sort of [moral] etiquette instruction [Benimmunterricht]. (Herr Anderson, Interview on 4/19/2016)

Herr Anderson, a philosophy, ethics, history, social studies, and political science teacher at a high academic track school in Central Berlin who also acted as the department chair at his school, was skeptical of the political imagination of the subject. That ethics was to establish some sort of moral grounding for students and help them sort out their lives was at the center of teachers' critique of the political imagination of the subject more generally. Initially, politicians imagined ethics to be modeled along a humanistic life-skills (Lebenskunde) approach and based their political imagination on the model of Brandenburg's Humanistic Life Sciences, Ethics and Religion class (LER - Lebenskunde-Ethik-Religion). Brandenburg introduced this subject shortly after German Reunification in 1992. Back then it was not entirely clear yet if Berlin would remain a separate federal state or if it would fuse with Brandenburg. Thus, many discussions in education policy evolved around an alignment of policies between these two federal states in order to make a possible fusion easier. This was one of the main areas the governing political parties and the teacher's union could agree on for their new subject. Politicians wanted the new subject to be close to students lived experiences based on culture studies, religious studies, and anthropology. This imagination of an interdisciplinary subject was justified with an imagined lack of morals and democratic values in ethnic-minority communities and emphasized the aspect of intercultural dialogue and teaching diversity.[44]

Herr Jagdmann, a 36-year-old student teacher at a high academic track school in Berlin's Northwest was at the time of the interview in his first year of training (Referendariat) and had studied philosophy at the university. He compared these different disciplinary foundations of ethics teaching as follows:

> Ethics as a subject always eh has a little bit this problem, exactly this conflict. Do I only want to be a "coping with life" [Lebensbewältigung], a place for encounter [Begegnungsstätte], then it is difficult to somehow sell it to students as a real subject. Well as one that they have to or should take seriously. And then it is difficult to make clear to them that it is not just chit chat, right? [...] If you do it in a qualified manner and that is again my background in philosophy [...] Yes and then I am worried that ethics is not able to achieve what was in a way the underlying idea, right? This mutual understanding (Herr Jagdmann, Interview on 11/25/2015)

---

44 In fact the Social Democrats adopted this resolution about the new subject on April 9th 2005: "A contemporary, norms-based education needs integrative forms of teaching - especially in the plural metropolis Berlin – in which students of different political, religious and ideological conceptions engage TOGETHER with questions of value orientation, different world religions, ideologies and conceptions of life and learn in dialogue with each other to develop their own perceptions and respect and understand foreign [fremde] views and forms of life. Berlin's SPD therefore supports the introduction of LER as mandatory subject without the option to opt-out". (Landesvorstand SPD Berlin, 2005, p. 3, emphasis in the original).

Herr Jagdmann argued, that if ethics was conceived of as subject that taught "coping with life," "mutual understanding" and created a "place for encounters," based on the multi-disciplinary life-skills imagination, it struggled to legitimize itself as a real school subject to its students and would become irrelevant "chit chat". However, if ethics was taught at a theoretical level, based on philosophy, ethics lost the connection to students. This dual identity of ethics was also evident in the existence of two professional teacher associations - one for ethics, in its conception as interdisciplinary, and one for philosophy. At the time of data collection, both claimed dominion over ethics teachers in Berlin and the subject's potential future.

Overall, many teachers were adamant in their connection of a strong disciplinary grounding in philosophy to an increase in subject legitimacy. The interdisciplinary approach politicians imagined was linked to less legitimacy and the subject running the risk of becoming a mere waste of time. The next section will show how both aspects of increasing legitimacy emphasized by ethics teachers – the university education and strong disciplinary grounding in philosophy – were connected to stigmatizing aspects of teaching about diversity in ethics instruction.

6.4.3 Linking Professional and Community Logics: The Stigma of Teaching about Diversity

In the accounts of how to improve ethics' legitimacy overall, especially by teachers who held positions influential to the future of ethics teaching and by early career teachers, elements from a professional teaching logic were often conceptualized as directly opposed to teaching about diversity. This perceived connection was used to discredit or remove teaching about diversity from a conception of "legitimate" ethics instruction.

The first aspect of classroom engagement with diversity in ethics that was targeted in the conception of teachers was content teaching about different religions. As Frau Janka explained:

> Well, a real challenge that my university students are always concerned with, and that was an issue here [at the school] as well, is that we are also asked to integrate this "studies of religions" part somehow. And I don't do it at all; it does not play a role in my classroom—I don't teach it. [...] There are many schools, for example, if you look at the internal curriculum of the xxx-Gymnasium [high track school nearby], they don't have it in there at all. We left it out of ours as well. We thought, if they can do it, we can too. (Frau Janka, Interview on 12/4/2015)

To Frau Janka, teaching about different religions was not part of her ethics instruction nor her school's internal curriculum. As a teacher educator at one of Berlin's universities this attitude directly influenced the way she taught future teachers and thus how the content of ethics would be viewed by them.

Often university educated teachers did not feel prepared to teach about religions as this was not part of university curricula:

> This is for once, something like the study of religions [Religionskunde] what we just did with Buddhism. It is the furthest removed from my university education. We never learned this in that sense, the study of religions. (Herr Lock, Interview on 4/8/2016)

While some teachers such as Herr Lock, a student teacher (Referendariat) at a lower secondary school in Berlin's Southwest, taught world religions in their classes despite his lack of knowledge others were not allowed to do so by their student teachers educators (personal email communication, 9/15/2015). The emphasis of a subject solely based in philosophy thus directly led to discrediting aspects from other disciplines like religious studies. Herr Lock thus concluded:

> I myself would not be too unhappy if I did not have to ... well if the study of religions was somehow transferred out a little or removed from the subject completely. (Herr Lock, Interview on 4/8/2016)

This did not necessarily mean that teachers thought teaching about religious diversity was not important. Herr Lock explained following this statement engaging with religious diversity was still important for students. But, in many teachers' understandings, the topic was not relevant for ethics instruction and should find a different home in school curricula.

The removal of teaching about religious diversity in ethics was the product of combining two elements from the professional logics ethics teachers employed. On the one hand, the vision of a undiscipline subject based in philosophy made it logical to teachers to remove aspects from other academic disciplines. This was reinforced by the preference towards university educated teachers who in their philosophy training did not learn about teaching about religious diversity and thus felt unable or unprepared to teach it.

At the same time, teachers who emphasized philosophy as the only disciplinary base for ethics instruction also ridiculed approaches closer to a life-skills understanding, discrediting them in the process. The aspect of developing intercultural skills was often a target of these arguments and directly linked to an undesirable form of ethics instruction:

> "We are all happy, you do it this way, he does it this way, and he does it like this, some believe in Allah, others in Jesus, and we are all human beings, and we are all nice after all." That is not thinking, that is chit chat. (Herr Dorn, Interview on 3/11/2016)

This sentiment that education about cultural differences in ethics is a pure waste of time and that learning the skills for intercultural dialogue was inferior to cognitive thinking and argumentation based in philosophical knowledge was expressed by many ethics' teachers. Frau Schuhmacher, an early career teacher, still engaged in her student teaching explains it like this focusing on conflict resolution:

> Well for me the biggest concern is that it does not become life science instruction. This fine line between I do a little life-skills... the typical blabla "and we talk, and we all think violence is bad" and so on, and to teach critical thinking in the sense of [...] well the difference between life science and ethics is that one is part of philosophy, where you always have to create a kind of problematization (Frau Schuhmacher, Interview on 3/2/2016)

Frau Schuhmacher also connects the life-skills approach to a lack of student learning outcomes calling it "the typical blabla" instruction without problem, point, or structure. She thus creates a stark contrast to a legitimate philosophy-based teaching agenda.

Many teachers voiced their agreement with the goal description for ethics in Berlin's school law. However, for teachers advocating a strong philosophical grounding furthering "the willingness and ability of students to *engage with the fundamental cultural and ethical problems of individual life and societal cohabitation* as well as different moral and spiritual explanations" (Schulgesetz für das Land Berlin/vom 26. Januar 2004, emphasis added) was imagined as this:

> We are in a secular state that provides us with very few guidelines on what is right and what is wrong, apart from the constitution. And even the constitution... well, what does it mean, "Human dignity shall be inviolable"? It has to be interpreted first; it has to be deconstructed—what is human dignity, and so on? And in this sense, I think it is really important that you practice together in ethics. (Frau Mayer, Interview on 4/26/2016)

After I read the school law description, Frau Mayer, a mid-career teacher at a high track school in Berlin's Southwest, and ethics department head, instructor for student teachers, and continued education workshops for in-service teachers, explained her students' engagement with diversity and discrimination remain at a theoretical, philosophical level. Students were not in contact with difference directly but reflect on what it means to be human instead.[45]

Thus, the emphasis of philosophy as a disciplinary grounding for ethics worked to discredit and in some schools remove aspects of teaching about diversity from the curriculum. This was reinforced by teachers closely guarded

---

45 The life-skills approach in contrast is more closely connected to ideas about caring and emotional closeness as this statement by Frau Mutombo shows: "Ethics is to me always a little closeness to humans and there ehm... empathy and emotion and closeness to human beings [Nähe zum Menschen] ... You cannot just let anyone lose on the students. Well, whoever thinks they have the disciplinary grounding [Wissenschaft]... eh Philosophy and now they are perfect [...] without trust no one will tell you what they think... Then the just read to you letter for letter what is in the book... But that does not work... that is not ethics." (Frau Mutombo, Interview on 9/2/2015)

expectations on entry into the profession, with a university study of philosophy as only acceptable option.

6.5 Changing the Idea of Ethics Instruction: From Multidisciplinary to Philosophy Instruction

While ethics teachers throughout the sample declared that ethics is an important subject for their students, they also described how this view was challenged from a variety of sources. Overall, ethics struggled with a reputation as waste of time (Laberfach) and was subject to a lack of recognition from administration, teaching staff, parents, students, and the wider public. Ethics was often challenged in its right to exist and in the appropriateness of its content for students' education.

To remedy this situation teachers relied on two distinctive elements from a professional logic, arguing that 1) university credentials and 2) a strong disciplinary anchor for the subject's content would ultimately bestow more legitimacy on ethics. In particular, teachers who were actively shaping ethics' future linked these elements of professional teaching logics to discredit certain elements of teaching about diversity. In their view 1) teaching about religious diversity, and 2) focusing on intercultural skills was to be removed from ethics instruction. They saw these elements as acting to de-legitimize and weaken the position of ethics by reducing teaching quality and student learning outcomes.

Teachers did not primarily base these assumptions on their understandings of diversity (as was the case in the previous chapter). They rather made assumptions about certain aspects of teaching about diversity and its relationship to instructional quality and student learning outcomes. Frau Janka is a good example of this. The previous chapter showed that she was eager to promote an inclusive world view to her students and tried to disrupt their racist stereotypes. In this chapter, I showed how she advocated for a strong disciplinary grounding in philosophy cutting out teaching about different religions entirely. So even for teachers that were in favor of pro-diversity teaching, the elements from professional teaching logics were detrimental to implementing pro-diversity policy in practice.

In their linking of the elements from professional logics with teaching about diversity, teachers were not primarily concerned with how to create a peaceful pluralistic society or mobilize community logics (as was the case with politicians) but with how to secure their subjects' survival despite pervasive challenges to its legitimacy. By introducing professional logics and linking them with a removal of pro-diversity content, teachers actively re-imagined what politicians had conceived of as a multi-disciplinary subject that focused on "*the fundamental cultural and ethical problems of individual life and soci-*

etal cohabitation as well as different moral and spiritual explanations" (Schulgesetz für das Land Berlin/vom 26. Januar 2004, emphasis added). They were engaged in creating an imagination of ethics instruction that did not contain certain aspects of teaching about diversity at all.

This change in imaginations about what ethics is and what it should teach was a slow-moving process facilitated by the recruitment of university educated philosophy teachers to fill ethics faculty positions and continued education workshops that emphasize the philosophical grounding of the subject. In this context it is also worth noting that while the philosophy teachers' association regularly hosts and promotes continued education workshops for in-service teachers, the ethics teacher association does not. The political actions of teachers to promote a specific version of ethics instruction is equivalent to a slow erosion of the political imagination of ethics to replace it with something teachers as professionals deem appropriate and legitimate for the subject. Contrary to what happened during the political debates around ethics introduction the idea of diversity was not perceived by teachers to add to the subjects' legitimacy. It was rather seen as a factor that detracted from ethics right to exist.

Within the context of Berlin, teachers thus acted as agents of change – re-imagining the very idea behind what ethics was supposed to be. However, in a national context in which education scholars attested an underlying education logic geared at excluding ethnic and religious heterogeneity (Auernheimer, 2005; Gogolin, 2008; Gogolin and Neumann, 1997; Krüger-Potratz, 2006) ethics teachers in Berlin promoted the status quo. This equated to leaving preconceived notions of ethnic and religious minority relations to the dominant group untouched. By introducing elements from the institutional order of professions into the negotiation process around ethics, teachers actively resisted and subverted pro-diversity policy turning it into exclusive practice.

6.6 Finding Legitimacy and Losing Diversity?

The success of education policy crucially depends on the decisions of classroom teachers. The previous chapter showed how conflicting logics of diversity found their way into teachers' approach to teaching diversity and created a heterogeneity of approaches and an unstable institutional environment. This chapter showed how teachers negotiated elements of professional logics and connected them to ethics and logics of diversity. Teachers were engaged in negotiating the relationship between teaching about diversity and the legitimacy of the subject – changing the very idea behind ethics instruction in Berlin. By reacting to institutional pressures, teachers engaged in re-configuring ethics content. Through their positions of influence outside of individual schools, they transmitted this new imagination of ethics to a wider audience actively shaping ethics' future.

Chapter 4 showed how certain assumptions about diversity may grant legitimacy and create enough political momentum to produce organizational change. In contrast, this chapter has shown how assumptions about diversity and their perceived linkages to other institutional orders led to stigmatization and the assumed reduction of legitimacy. The lack of a unified understanding about what ethics' content should actually include, visible in the heterogeneity of approaches to teaching diversity in ethics, provided a fertile ground for teachers to re-imagine what the subject should be.

In their efforts to re-imagine the subject by linking it to profession logics they did not actively engage in negotiating new logics about the position of diversity in society and in education. Instead espousing an imagination exclusive of diversity was a by-product of seeking more legitimacy and thus securing ethics' future. Teachers were concerned with ensuring the long-term survival of the subject. In fact, many teachers thought that teaching about diversity was important: just not in the context of ethics instruction. Instead, they argued that this topic should find a different home in schools. They thus created a subject imagination that reinforced a status quo marked by the exclusion of certain aspects of teaching about diversity. The relative ease at which teachers were able to stigmatize teaching about diversity by leveraging professional logics showed that within these logics there may be an inherent exclusion of diversity. Or to re-iterate the quote from Bell (2014) at the beginning of this chapter, professional teaching logics may have been developed out of minority exclusion and pro-diversity policy like ethics was not able to actively re-shape this.

7 Beyond Ethics Instruction: School Reform and Diversity Inclusion in Education

"Immigrant societies are rarely free of conflict [...] In this sense we have to think about how we can facilitate life together and how we can ensure that those who live here finally feel at home." Mutlu, Green Party, Abgeordnetenhaus von Berlin, 2004, p. 5030

7.1 Oscillating between Inclusion and Exclusion

In early 2018, Berlin's Senate decided that the amount of weekly instruction time for ethics would be reduced in favor of introducing political education as a separate, independent subject (cf. Vieth-Entus, 2018).[46] This move to curtail ethic's importance in Berlin's curriculum was the culmination of a decade long failure of the subject to gain enough legitimacy to secure its survival with school administrations, teaching staff, parents, and students. Despite teachers' efforts to link ethics to acceptable professional logics, the political imagination had moved on to privilege other social issues. Rather than highlight intercultural dialog, religious and cultural diversity, and peaceful co-habitation as the political imagination of ethics did in the early 2000s, political education in Berlin was to focus on democratic values (Grundwerte) and citizenship education. So, had ethics as representative of pro-diversity education policy failed in practice?

As a vertical case study (Vavrus and Bartlett, 2006, 2009) my research examined three distinct levels of a pro-diversity policymaking and institutionalization process in Berlin: the political level, the school organizational level, and the classroom level. I started at the macro level with a discussion of the logics underlying the political imagination of the subject and its challengers in a detailed policy analysis. I covered the post- World War II era, German reunification, the intense debates leading up to ethics' introduction in 2006 and the challenge to ethics in a referendum in 2009. What my analysis showed was that there were two different logics of diversity underlying the political dis-

---

46 This change in policy effective in the 2019/2020 school year places ethics, geography, history and political education into social sciences - with each receiving a separate grade on report cards. Due to the addition of political education in this area but no increase in weekly instruction time for the social sciences, ethics as well as history and geography will have to decrease their instruction time in order to accommodate political education. Since both history and geography currently only have one hour of weekly instruction time the task of reducing instruction time will fall on ethics. (cf. Anders, 2018).

courses about ethics: one inclusive that saw diversity as a productive force in society and the other exclusive that portrayed diversity as a threat to German national identity.

In addition, I looked at how ethics was institutionalized in schools a decade after its first introduction. Focusing on teachers, I showed how they made sense of diversity in relationship to their students and to the political imagination of the subject. I thus not only showed how the logics connected to ethics were expressed in different domains of public life, specifically in policymaking and in education practice, but also how teachers as political actors engaged with the demands put on them by their professional identities, political imaginations, and public expectations. Given teachers' special position as median actors, on the one hand, representative of the state to students and, on the other hand, as political actors exerting their potential for stasis or change, this examination was divided into two chapters examining each of these roles respectively.

At the classroom level, I compared diverse and non-diverse school contexts and showed that teachers in both settings espoused inclusive and exclusive logics of diversity. The school environment moderated the specific elements of the logics that teachers mobilized producing four different ideal type approaches: assimilationist, philosophical, intercultural, and critical. I argued that this heterogeneity of approaches indicated that ethics was situated in an unstable institutional environment. This instability made it more pressing for teachers to respond to challenges of ethics' legitimacy by positioning their subject in a way that would secure professionalism and a stable future. Teachers who were actively involved in shaping the subject's future by training student teachers, providing and coordinating continued education workshops for in-service teachers, and working on the state curriculum tried to link ethics to strongly national professional logics. Specifically, they sought to closely guard the entry into the profession by emphasizing the need for a university degree in philosophy and by linking ethics' content overall to a strong philosophical focus. This on the one hand, reduced or eliminated the engagement with different religions in ethics, as this content was thought to be outside of philosophical knowledge and part of the discipline of religious studies. Teachers argued that this was external to ethics undiscipline core. Teachers, even those with university degrees, also did not feel prepared to teach this component. In addition, ethics teachers linked developing intercultural skills with an inferior teaching approach and less desirable job qualifications. They thus also declared this teaching component to be undesirably and a factor of de-legitimization. Contrary to the level of political discourse, diversity thus did not function as a way to secure and increase legitimacy but in teachers' arguments was framed as producing fewer desirable outcomes.

Theoretically, I situated my findings within the larger discussions of teachers as political actors (e.g. Riggan, 2016) and the field of diversity studies (Vertovec, 2015). I used institutional logics as an overarching theoretical perspective to examine the underlying understandings and negotiations of diversity by policy makers and teachers. Specifically, my study discusses the components of power in neo-institutional organization theory and linked it directly to discourses about diversity. I thus provided insights into two under-theorized areas within neo-institutional organization theory. Berlin's mandatory ethics instruction served as a case study to understand better the larger phenomenon of societal diversification processes and their impact on education policy and practice. More specifically, I was interested in examining why discriminatory and exclusive education practices may exist in a context that is dominated by overwhelmingly inclusive and diversity friendly policy frameworks.

This chapter aims to summarize my findings overall and draw out larger themes, commonalities, and differences across levels and actors. It directs attention to the implications of my findings and the questions that my analysis opens up and points to areas for future research. Throughout this study, I argued that there was a remarkable continuity between constructions of diversity at the policy and practice levels. This does not, I contend, highlight any causal relationship between policy and practice but rather shows the more general existence of two logics of diversity within Germany. I further argue that there was also discontinuity between the policy and practice level in the way that national or international logics serve as a way to claim legitimacy for each specific imagination of the subject. This has important implications for practice as it shows the need to anchor diversity inclusive logics also into national and local professional imaginations. I content that the continuities and discontinuities within and between levels highlight the need to conceptualize the social situation as complex and fragmented, driven not by one logic, but by the negotiation and interaction of multiple logics.

In the next section I compare the way that categories of diversity were constructed by policy makers and teachers highlighting the continuities between policy and classroom. I then discuss the discontinuities between both levels in the way that each set of actors tried to add legitimacy to their cause. I conclude by adopting a broader perspective on the question of diversity integration in education in Germany.

7.2   A German Identity Crisis: Continuity in Diversity Constructions between Inclusive and Exclusive Logics

Throughout this book, I showed that the understandings and negotiations of policymakers and teachers relied on two logics of diversity: one inclusive and the other exclusive. Both logics interact with each other at the policymaking level and at the level of public education. The interaction is most clear at the level of policymaking. An inclusive logic of diversity won the negotiation process about how value education in Berlin should be organized, producing a subject that engaged with the topic of diversity in public education: mandatory ethics. The competing exclusive logic, predominantly favored by conservative politicians, created a severe challenge to ethics' legitimacy in public discourse by forcing a public referendum. These logics acted as antagonists to each other. However, an inclusive argument would not have been formulated without conservative politicians pushing the issue of value education into the political agenda. It was specifically conservatives' framing of value education in a way that would exclude and disadvantage religious minorities that made inclusive political support for mandatory ethics possible.

In teachers' interactions in relationship to their students and their sense-making about teaching diversity both logics were also present and institutionalized in practice in diverse and non-diverse school environment. My analysis relied on ideal type categories. I showed that an inclusive logic produced intercultural and critical teaching approaches while an exclusive logic facilitated assimilationist and philosophical teaching. I found both, inclusive and exclusive logics, to be present within the same school and even within the same teacher's sense-making. In their interaction vis-à-vis the political imagination of the subject teachers relied on elements of national professional logics excluding certain aspects of teaching diversity.

I contend that it is especially the construction of diversity used at both levels that showed the continuities in these two logics from one level to the other. That is not to suggest that there is a direct dissemination between policies and practice in this case but rather that these two logics are established beyond the local policy and school level. They are symptomatic of a more general identity crisis within Germany about what place in society immigrant and minority groups should have. This conflict revolves on the one hand around the exclusive conception of what Mecheril (2002) described as nation-ethno-cultural. On the other hand, there are elements of a more inclusive conception moving towards a post-migrant (Foroutan, 2019) understanding and negotiation of belonging. To make this point clearer, I return to examples from my empirical data. While both chapters 4 and 5 showed in detail how diversity was constructed for each level respectively, the juxtaposition of quotes from both, policy makers and teachers, below emphasize the continuities to highlight that these logics operate in a more general way. I first discuss how diversity was constructed under an exclusive or destructive logic of diversity in policy and practice. I then draw out the similarities in an inclusive or productive logic between both levels.

7.2.1 The Construction of Diversity within an Exclusive Logic

Constructions of diversity that relied on an exclusive logic utilized religion and Islam as the most prominent facets of identity categories evoked. Especially after the Islamic Federation won the right to provide religious instruction in Berlin, conservative politicians like the Christian Democrat below essentialized the organization and Muslims more generally into a threat for liberal democratic society:

> But the Islamic Federation holds a significant position in this city, and its religious instruction continues to expand. At many schools where the Islamic Federation provides religious instruction, we observe varying degrees of segregation tendencies, depending on the school's location. This is why it is crucial that Islamic religious instruction is also offered as a state-regulated, denominationally affiliated subject, taught by state-employed teachers who have been trained at universities in Berlin or elsewhere in Germany. It must be subject to state oversight because it is an untenable situation that Berlin's schools are required to admit so-called teachers who are not required to demonstrate any formal teaching qualifications to provide religious instruction. Furthermore, even the responsible school principal is not permitted to oversee the content of religious education. The Islamic Federation is merely required to submit a curriculum and is now free to operate as it sees fit. (Steuer, CDU, Abgeordnetenhaus von Berlin, 2008b, p. 15)

As I argued in chapter 4, the Islamic Federation was portrayed as a "significant" force in Berlin's society and its religious instruction was conceived of as "expanding" in schools. Steuer provided evidence of the negative consequences this had – increasing segregation. The segregation argument is closely tied to the accusations of multiculturalism and diversity inclusive politics furthering parallel societies and immigrant ghettoization that were popular around this time in many European political discourses (cf. Kymlicka, 2010; Vertovec and Wessendorf, 2010). Steuer went on to suggest that Islamic religion teachers were lacking all credentials to perform their job and that the Islamic Federation was circumventing the curriculum that was submitted to the Department of Education – "operate as it sees fit." By connecting the Islamic Federation, portrayed as acting outside the law, regulation, and common education standards, with Muslim youth who were the ones segregating themselves, the Muslim minority in Berlin was positioned as outside of German democratic, law-abiding society. Other conservative politicians made even more clear what Muslims were lacking by calling for "a minimal consensus in our society about the basis of state and society as they are established in the constitution following our occidental-Christian culture" (Schultze-Berndt, CDU, Abgeordnetenhaus von Berlin, 2005a, p. 5400). According to this framing Islam was a danger to Berlin's society and peaceful conviviality.

Secondary school teachers employed a similar way to frame Islam within the context of their school experience as argued in chapter 5 and exemplified here by this quote from Frau Smith:

> For me, it always felt like... well, we can talk as much as we want here [at school], but in the end, they are socialized at home, in Qur'an school, or wherever they go – perhaps even in the mosque, where they actively practice their religion. And I always have the impression, whether it's our student body or people with a migration background in general, including their parents, that they do not necessarily want to integrate. This is because men still hold a certain position, and religion occupies a privileged role that is upheld and practiced accordingly. They say, "We live here, we work here, we go to school here, we earn our degrees here," but the kind of integration [diese richtige Integration] that I envision – truly becoming part of society—is not something they seek. Even the parents do not seem to want it. (Frau Smith, Interview on 6/22/2016)

In this quote Frau Smith lamented the inconsequentiality of her teaching and schooling more generally with regard to her Muslim students – established by her reference to the Qur'an and Mosques – as they were socialized elsewhere. Their socialization was portrayed as outside of Western cultural norms referencing gender equality and the importance of religion in an individuals' life. The issue of gender equality more generally is frequently used by conservative politicians throughout Europe to justify Muslim discrimination and exclusion (cf. Uitermark et al. (2013) for a discussion of this in the Netherlands). Frau Smith also attested Muslims and people with migration background more generally an unwillingness to integrate, "the real integration that I envision," thus also accusing them of segregation.

Between these two levels, the conceptualization of Muslim minorities was thus remarkably similar. Both conservative politicians and some secondary school teachers connected Islam to societal segregation and highlighted the dangers that this created for peaceful conviviality. Muslims were a constant threat within an exclusive logic of diversity. They were generalized into a group that as a whole rejected integration, and German laws and values. Often these arguments were linked with references to citizenship and immigration status (as can be seen in Frau Smith's quote above but also throughout the evidence provided in chapters 4 and 5). Muslims were seen as possessing a uniform identity in constant opposition to German society.

7.2.2 The Construction of Diversity within an Inclusive Logic

Diversity categories invoked within an inclusive logic relied on a much broader group of identities. Policymakers, as I argued in chapter 4, constructed diversity as multi-dimensional:

> Especially in Berlin, where children come from such diverse backgrounds – in terms of family, culture, economic status, and religion – there are significant differences in educational levels within a single class. That is why it is crucial to engage collectively with democracy, non-violence, tolerance, equality, and the other values enshrined in our constitution, which are so important to us. Even in this multicultural, vibrant, and diverse city, where immigration is an opportunity and an asset [Bereicherung], we can no longer afford to look away or assume that cultural differences will naturally sort themselves out. No, we must actively foster consensus – there needs to be a shared agreement on fundamental values. (Müller, SPD, Abgeordnetenhaus von Berlin, 2006b, pp. 6970–6971)

Dimensions of diversity utilized in this argument went beyond someone's religion, including academic ability, socio-economic background, family situation and culture. While the exclusive arguments positioned Muslim minorities squarely outside of Berlin's society, Müller included them, other kinds of minorities, and immigrants into "multicultural, vibrant, diverse" Berlin and framed them as an asset. However, diversity still had to be managed to be productive for society in this argument.

As I showed in chapter 5, teachers espousing an inclusive logic also focused on the multi-dimensionality of diversity, as Frau Boehm did in the following quote, portraying difference of opinion more generally as a form of diversity fostering fruitful learning opportunities:

> I believe that as soon as you articulate your thoughts and hear the opinions of others—even if, in that moment, you are appalled by a differing viewpoint—the experience itself is valuable. Simply being able to endure this, to have an ethics teacher who says, "Here we have one opinion, and there we have another," is, in itself, a form of peacemaking... the experience that diversity can be endured, that you... [that] I don't have to hit the other because he thinks differently. (Frau Boehm, Interview on 4/15/2016)

To her these differences were not a cause for alarm but rather represented a chance to experience how to cope with differences in a constructive way. She even saw this sort of engagement with difference of opinion as peacemaking and thus overall positioned it as productive and worth engaging with.

Arguments relying on an inclusive logic of diversity therefore focused not on a single identity category but rather on the multidimensionality of constructions of social difference. Policymakers and some secondary school teachers alike argued that these differences were a constructive part of German society. While diversity in this logic also needed to be shaped and managed it was seen as an asset rather than a danger.

7.3 Discontinuities Between Political and Classroom Level: The Question of Gaining Legitimacy

While some of the data analyzed in this study points toward continuities between policymakers and secondary school teachers, there were also areas of disjuncture between these two levels. Especially, when it came to finding sources of legitimacy for their imagination of ethics both groups of actors relied on different levels of claims making. Two of the chapters in this book, chapter 4 and 6, dealt with the drivers behind the ways that policy makers and teachers were arguing for change in the imagination of the subject. While policy makers relied on linking their argument about mandatory ethics to international Human Rights, teachers relied on more national and local conceptions of the teaching professions to gain legitimacy. At both levels, I argued, diversity played a crucial role in finding arguments to increase the legitimacy of ethics instruction. However, while diversity was framed as a way to gain legitimacy at the political level, it was seen as a factor that de-legitimized ethics instruction at the classroom level.

As I argued in chapter 4, policymakers especially from the liberal left, that is those in favor of mandatory ethics, often evoked human rights and the German constitution as a basis for ethics and the need for the subject in Berlin's schools. They positioned themselves specifically against an understanding of value education that sought its basis in the Christian religion (i.e. the Christian Democratic imagination of the subject):

> I cannot imagine education in the Federal Republic of Germany—regardless of the governing party, whether it is the Christian Social Union (CSU), the Free Democrats (FDP), or the Green Party—without a common foundation for teaching and curricula: namely, our constitution. It establishes morals and values based on fundamental and human rights. The notion that school education could be value-free is absurd. Even more absurd is the claim that only the [Christian] churches are capable of providing value education. Where would that lead us? [Wo kämen wir dahin?] (Wowereit, SPD, Abgeordnetenhaus von Berlin, 2005c, p. 5831)

In this quote, the acting mayor of Berlin at the time, summarized the main point of contention in the discussions about mandatory ethics in Berlin: where norms and values should come from. At stake was the question of whether or not the German constitution was based on a Christian cultural tradition and could thus be claimed for either side of the argument. The acting mayor's clear answer to this question was no. In fact, many political arguments from the left pitted Human Rights directly against a conception of national values based on religion – in the German context often summarized with the concept *leading culture* (Leitkultur). Human Rights was thus a powerful tool to establish the legitimacy and importance of mandatory ethics for a modern, liberal, and diversity inclusive Berlin; for a Berlin that imagined itself as a global city. It invoked a multilateral, international consensus on what values and rights human existence as a whole (beyond individual nation states) should be based on and thus created a powerful tool for political mobilization (cf. Skrentny, 2004 for an analysis of this mechanism in minority rights in the USA). Appealing to and invoking diversity in Berlin was thus at the very center of overcoming exclusive nationalistic policy imaginations. It also provided the political appeal for opposition parties, specifically the green party, to add their voices and vote. Pro-diversity education policy in Berlin was thus in part also based on appealing to pro-diversity international frameworks.

Conservative political voices rarely invoked Human Rights as a source of legitimacy for their argument or mentioned them at all in their arguments. One example is from a Christian Democrat, trying to critique the superficiality of content on religion in ethics:

> Real tolerance is based on strong points of view. It refers to matters of conscience, to deep personal convictions. It develops from the respect for the dignity of human beings. But what SPD and PDS want is to have no individual convictions. But without your own opinions are the real argument about the truth and the search for a sustainable consensus impossible. The ragbag of things that they prescribed to students – today, Christianity, tomorrow Buddhism and the day after tomorrow Islam – cannot create deep personal convictions. That is how you create arbitrariness and indifference. (Zimmer, CDU, Abgeordnetenhaus von Berlin, 2005b, p. 5547).

To the conservatives, only religion could provide the meaningful basis of values. While the quote above shows that this is somewhat linked with the constitution by Zimmer's reference to human dignity, this in their view is not enough.

At the school level, as I showed in chapter 6, teachers argued that the only way to find a common basis of values that could foster conviviality was to create a sound basis in philosophy and move teaching of diversity to other subject areas:

> I think that ethics talks about a lot of things that are important for students but that don't necessarily need to be consolidated in one subject. Well we teach of course in history, in social studies and even in biology [...] in biology you talk about pregnancy or something like that and I don't know in English you talk about Blacks in New York or something like that [...] especially for this age group I would rather see it if instead of ethics in grades 7 through 10 the other subjects would take place there and we would have a philosophy basic course in grades 11 and 12. I would think that makes more sense because then student can talk at a different more abstract level about ethics and philosophy and morals and that would really bring new insights. (Herr Alkim, Interview on 11/25/2015)

Ethics teachers were not advocating for removing teaching about diversity (in this case talking about race in the USA) from school entirely, but for moving these topics out of ethics and into other subjects. While Herr Alkim here advocates for removing ethics entirely, this is an outlier opinion within my sample.

For the most part ethics teachers were convinced that ethics is an important, if not one of the most important subjects students had.

As I argued in chapter 6, teachers relied on elements of national professional logics to claim legitimacy for their imagination of ethics. It was not Human Rights but rather the established academic discipline of philosophy they argued would grant legitimacy to their imagination of the subject. They thus advocated for university educated teachers and a sound basis of ethics in philosophy. Both of these areas would in their own right remove teaching about diversity from ethics classrooms.

While diversity inclusion came to be imagined as a marker of Berlin's international and global ambitions by politicians, teachers firmly grounded their imagination of the subject in national professional logics, removing teaching about diversity in the process. Given the dominant logic of monoculturalism, monolingualism, and exclusive approach towards immigrant and diverse populations in German schooling this is problematic (Auernheimer, 2005; Gogolin, 2008; Gogolin and Neumann, 1997; Krüger-Potratz, 2006). As I argued in chapter 5, basing teaching on a philosophical approach might project a false sense of national homogeneity and perpetuate discrimination and exclusion in majority population imaginations of the national community. In other words, the difference in claims making and gaining legitimacy for policy ambitions might be one important factor that turns inclusive policy into exclusive and discriminatory school practice.

7.4 The Implications of Logic Continuity and Discontinuity between Policy and Practice

Across this case study, I thus analyzed the continuity and discontinuity of logics of diversity between policymakers and teachers. Overall, both groups of political actors relied on very similar construction paradigms with regard to group identities and socio-cultural differences among citizens and students. To be clear, that is not to suggest that policy views and arguments caused ethics teachers to think this way. What the continuity between these two levels shows was rather the more general existence of these two logics of diversity within German society. They are evidence of a deep-seated identity crisis within German society about its integration of minorities.

Returning to my larger question from chapter one of how an environment that was dominated by diversity-inclusive policy may still produce discriminatory education practice, this research has shown that explanations cannot rely on the assumption of a homogeneous underlying cultural logic that actors either adhere to or not. The discontinuities between political and classroom level negotiations of an imagination of mandatory ethics proofs that we need to pay careful attention to how diversity is negotiated in different settings. That is to say, the divergence between diversity-friendly policy and discriminatory practice was not the result of individuals' adherence to, or rejection of, a homogeneous underlying logic (Ortloff, 2009; Sunier, 2013), neither was it the result of mere window dressing at the policy level (Edelman, 1990, 1992; John W. Meyer and Rowan, 1977; Nonet and Selznick, 1978), or the lack of expertise at the top (Dobbin and Kalev, 2017). What certainly contributed to teachers turning to exclusive logics were structural issues that politicians did not address in their reform effort. In the case of ethics instruction, there was no teacher education system or higher education structure in place to prepare teachers to fulfil the imagination of mandatory ethics as a multidisciplinary subject that could bring students together. While the introduction of the subject itself was quite progressive in terms of creating inclusive schools in Berlin, to paraphrase Bell (2014), it did so in a structural and institutional environment developed out of exclusion.

Overall, the fact that both logics are influential at the national, local and classroom level and that they are constantly negotiated by political and social actors may need to be addressed in the long run if Germany (and Europe) wants to create a truly inclusive environment for diverse populations. Diversity in society should also not have to be sold as productive to the majority. Instead, it should be able to exist in its own right in a truly post-migrant society. What my data demonstrates is that there were ideological and structural deficiencies that need to be addressed before education in Berlin, and Germany more generally, can be inclusive.

In fact, especially politicians from a minority background did try to point this out in the negotiation process around mandatory ethics as early as 2004:

> Earlier, someone asked: Why do you not feel German? – I will tell you. Whenever I have to answer this question—and I have to answer it often, especially in the presence of American journalists—it is difficult for me to say that I feel German. And do you know why, Mr. Wansner? Because mainstream society has still not accepted, even after 40 or 50 years of immigration, that this country has changed. That even an Özcan Mutlu, an Ülker Radziwill, or a Giyasettin Sayan are German, that they belong to this society. As long as German society, as a whole, refuses to acknowledge this reality and accept these people, it should not be surprised when certain demagogues [Rattenfänger] come along and preach about the importance and greatness of "the" Islamic religion or the supposed superiority of Turkish nationhood and culture. (Mutlu, Green Party, Abgeordnetenhaus von Berlin, 2004, p. 5030)

During the ethics debate these voices, however, were subsumed in measures that did not go far enough. Instead, they built on old structures that were not meant to be inclusive. In other words, the debates around ethics were driven by ethnic and religious majority voices. This of course has to do with larger structural inequities about the representation of minorities in policy and the teaching profession. Both sides of the debate as well as some of the teachers in my sample imagined diversity to be a potential danger to a peaceful society – only the degree to which this danger was located either in the entire minority group or within rogue individuals was different between the two logics I discussed (see chapter 4). Politicians and teachers were caught up in and reproduced argumentative structures produced for and by majority society. As Stevens et al. (2018) explain in their study of universities:

> Imagine a research university as a coral reef: a composite of organisms at varying stages of development and decay. New life does not fully replace what came before it. Instead, the older entities provide scaffold and succor for the younger ones as the entire ecosystem evolves. While hardly the result of any rational planning, the overall entity nevertheless has integrity, coherence, and even beauty as it sustains intellectual lives and livelihoods over time. (Stevens et al., 2018, p. 19)

This description of research universities and their organization of area studies is also accurate for the discursive structures around diversity analyzed in this study. In many ways the path dependencies in discursive practices around diversity that drove political debates, and teaching approaches exposed the differential power structures still operational in German society.

7.5 Teaching Diversity: Towards a new Pedagogy?

The fact that mandatory ethics got entangled in the German diversity and integration debate was detrimental to its survival. It is thus not surprising that policy recently turned against openly advocating for diversity-inclusive teaching as the primary focus of education reform in Berlin. As discussed at the beginning of this chapter, the new focus in Berlin's public education moved toward political education and away from teaching about diversity. That is not to say that both subjects could not be related. They certainly are (cf. Achour, 2023; Fereidooni, 2025; Koschmieder and Koschmieder, 2025). Conflicts around diversity are deeply implicated in the transformation of democracies around the world in 2025.

The shift in Berlin's policy focus came with a specific justification for the new subject of political education. The imagined threat to society no longer emanated from potentially violent minority groups and the possible conflicts inherent in a hyper-diverse classroom but rather from a new more general rise in intolerance, anti-Semitism, xenophobia, and right-wing attitudes in the population and amongst youth (Zick et al., 2019; Zick et al., 2023). Berlin thus in some ways pre-empted the current concern over a new strong far-right in Germany caused by its mainstreaming (cf. Sponholz et al. 2025) and far-right acts of violence. For example, the attack in Hanau, Germany in February 2020 in combination with the detection of a right-wing terror network earlier that same month and the attack on a synagogue in Halle in 2019 caused many politicians to emphasize the need for a vigilant fight against these right-wing sentiments.

As Berlin's Senator for Education stated in her introduction to a pamphlet introducing political education:

> For some time, we have witnessed that the core values that support our democracy are no longer shared by all people who live in Germany. Extreme-right, white supremacist and radical religious mindsets [Gedankengut] are spreading in a way that we did not think possible a couple of years ago. (Senatsverwaltung für Bildung, Jugend und Familie, 2019, p. 4)

A focus that includes right-wing tendencies and radical religiosity was not problematic and given the discourse about diversity driving policymakers in the past possibly an improvement, as it no longer singled out an ethnic minority group as threat. The relative ease at which right-wing and populist political forces have used democratic structures for their causes, however, should at least warrant a careful investigation into the merits of democracy education as a counter measure to right-wing radicalization (cf. Christodoulou and Szakács-Behling, 2018, Achour 2025, Koschmieder and Koschmieder, 2025). In its conception this new subject focused on "democracy as a way of life." With regard to diversity this new focus in curriculum and pedagogy highlights the following goal:

> Political education enables young people to perceive mechanisms of exclusion and strategies of discrimination in the political public and in everyday life. It also enables them to critically reflect their own role in this and to actively work towards change. We have to find answers to the complex interaction of multiple factors in the migration society that transcend populist solution strategies. (Senatsverwaltung für Bildung, Jugend und Familie, 2019, p. 19)

This focus was echoed in policy directives throughout Germany (Die Bundesregierung, 2016; Kultusministerkonferenz, 2009/2018). The fact, that in Berlin political education was curtailing and superseding a subject imagined teaching about diversity, however, could be potentially detrimental. Given the fact that teachers were already split on if and how to teach about diversity in ethics instruction, a new subject that does not focus on diversity at all may afford enough room to cast the topic out completely. Recent studies also found that political education varies greatly in Berlin (Achour and Wagner, 2019). The failure to establish a concrete place for teaching about diversity in Berlin's public schools could thus be seen as contributing to legitimizing a community logic that casts diversity outside of school curriculum and state mandated knowledge. By not giving learning about diversity a proper place in youth's education, schools may inadvertently re-enforce an exclusive logic denying minority groups in Germany a right to belong. Given the racist undertones of recent attacks by the far-right in Germany a focus on democracy and especially the anti-establishment political dimension of far-right movements, may not be enough.

That is not to say that ethics was the perfect solution to achieve diversity integration and a peaceful pluralistic society. Far from it, an assimilationist classroom might be just as harmful in its overall message to minority and majority students as a school that completely neglects the existence of diversity in German society. However, in times that are seeing significant election successes of populist and right-wing political parties, large anti-immigrant and anti-diversity civil society movements, and the success of racist populist leaders with autocratic tendencies worldwide to gain positions of power, choosing one over the other may not be the right move for education.

Researchers have shown that a rise in right-wing party success oftentimes comes with an increase in xenophobic and racist political discourse and tendencies in civil society (cf. Rydgren, 2015). Countering them, I argue can only work by integrating diversity in Germany overall. The demotion of the importance of ethics in Berlin's curriculum shows that preventing right-wing extremism through the promotion of democracy and teaching about diversity are still decoupled from each other. At least in the political imagination they are not seen as working together to prevent violence, radicalization, and extremism.

As I showed in chapter 5, the way that political actors like teachers include or exclude diversity in their teaching is important not just in diverse classroom settings. It also frames the way that majority youth may come to imagine the nation they live in, who belongs and who does not belong. At present, democratic values have come to be an unreliable protection against discrimination and mistreatment based on one's group identity. While I do not wish to suggest that teaching youth about democracy is the wrong path to create inclusive societies, it cannot be the only path to achieve this goal. Teaching about diversity in a positive and inclusive manner; showing that modern societies are by their very nature heterogeneous has to be part of educational efforts. This also needs a firm place in the curriculum as teachers otherwise may choose not to engage with this topic. Conceptualizing diversity in society more generally, not just in hyper-diverse settings, is also crucial for future research agendas and scholarly discussions. As I argued in this book, categories of diversity are not just created in hyper-diverse settings and only in comparative approaches considering both can we fully understand how and why diversity positive policy frameworks may fail in practice.

7.6 Beyond Ethics Instruction

The story of mandatory ethics in Berlin was a story of attempted but failed organizational and institutional change. Ethics was imagined at a time when Germany was desperate to find ways to make room for a new type of citizen, one that was connected to Germany by birth but not necessarily by blood or cultural heritage. Mandatory ethics represented one way to change school structure to accommodate a logic of creating a new and different type of communality. As I argued this change was quite revolutionary in Germany overall and broke with established logics about if and how values should be taught in school. Rather than privileging religious education as the standard option, Berlin's politicians chose a subject that moved the idea of diversity front and center in the curriculum. That is to say, my argument here is not that either one of these organizational structures (mandatory ethics or mandatory religion) were better suited for the task at hand but rather that the conceptualization of diversity was more inclusive in one case than in the other.

However, overall mandatory ethics in Berlin was only incompletely institutionalized. The efforts of Social Democrats, Left, and Green Party did not fail completely as the school reform did produce a new subject in Berlin's secondary schools. However, it did fail in establishing a legitimate area within schools to learn about diversity and intergroup interactions, to be a conduit for producing a peaceful pluralistic society – the goal that ultimately garnered enough buy-in to produce political action. Ethics was thus the story of a failed political imagination. While some teachers within Berlin's secondary schools chose to follow an agenda of inclusiveness those with a potentially high impact on the direction of the subject did not. The heterogeneity of teaching approaches to ethics produced an unstable institutional environment that allowed neither logic of diversity to fully take hold of the subject and thus contributed to its ultimate decline in importance.

In addition, the failure of ethics can be attributed more widely to a failure in reforming the structures that govern schooling more generally. Within the ethics teacher community and profession there were no strong logics that would support change towards diversity inclusive teaching or question the support of majority dominated structures and logics. That is not to say that teachers did not think teaching about diversity was not important but rather that it was not an important topic for ethics instruction. The ease at which ethics teachers were able to use professional logics to stigmatize teaching about diversity suggests that the logic behind teacher professionalism overall warrants work to become inclusive. The statistics of where minority teachers find work (that is in the lower academic tears of public education and in trade schools) also suggest that there is some form of institutionalized discrimination (Doğmuş, 2022; Fereidooni, 2016).

While the political imagination of mandatory ethics was inclusive of diverse populations, it still followed a logic that saw diversity as something to be managed overall and a possible problem for societal peace. Those voices that sought to expose unequal power were subsumed under a majority dominated imagination. Furthermore, policy makers responded to local and international pressures directly by using Human Rights and the German constitution as underlying moral models for mandatory ethics conception and content. As I argued above in an environment where schooling is still imagined as monoliguistic, monocultural, and unfit for diverse populations this is problematic. It did not provide a logic that teachers could mobilize for legitimizing their work.

There is a progression in this story although it is by no means linear. It rather shows continuity and discontinuities between political imaginations, challenges to this imagination, and actual practice. My findings highlight the heterogeneity of co-existing logics and the ways in which they are constantly negotiated with each other but also amended, re-interpreted, and re-inscribed in different settings. Ethics represents a prime example of how the question of organizing school content morphed at the political level into the much broader questions of diversity integration and national identity. This case illuminates how these questions were then removed from practice by teachers. As such this case study highlighted the process of translating global and national debates into the local level and organizational change at the school level. In many ways, the case of ethics is exemplary of negotiations around diversity driving policymaking in German society more generally. These are processes happening throughout policymaking imagining how diversity may be included into the national fabric.

Given the challenges around diversity for Germany and Europe that are still to come, my research underlines the deeply complex and contradictory nature of policymaking and practice with regard to diversity. Broader political and social oscillations and negotiations that are occurring between two different ideas of diversity management: 1) an inclusive view that acknowledges the productive potential of diverse populations for Germany overall, and 2) an exclusive view of diversity that seeks to protect the heritage of German belonging from a "foreign" threat. While these two ideas about diversity management have been present in politics about citizenship and national belonging for many years and in other contexts (cf. Kymlicka, 2010; Vertovec and Wessendorf, 2010), it is their simultaneous existence, their oscillating influence in different settings, and how they are negotiated by different social and political actors that brings new theoretical insights.

Germany and Europe more generally will have to come to terms with diversity. Diverse populations are not going to decrease. A new influx of refugee is already waiting at the southern borders of the EU. Political power plays, economic tensions, natural disasters and other factors are bound to increase migrant and refugee populations in some of the most affluent countries around the world. In addition, Germany and Europe more generally need immigration in order to secure their economic stability.

Diversity integration and the creation of peaceful conviviality are going to be some of the most important topics for years to come. As I have argued throughout, we need to pay particular attention to how categories of diversity are negotiated in different societal settings and by different political actors. This also needs to include careful attention to the underlying power structures and the question of who is negotiating diversity overall. Institutional logics theory and especially careful attention to the institutional order of community can be an invaluable analytical tool in this process. We need more studies that pay close attention to how community logics are negotiated across different societal levels to fully understand how pro-diversity policy may turn exclusive in practice. But we also need studies that compare the processes and negotiations taking place in diverse and non-diverse contexts within one level. That is, we cannot just focus our investigations of diversity integration on hyper-diverse settings, imaginations of the nation and who is included and excluded from national belonging are produced in every German classroom whether it is diverse or not. Understanding the differences and similarities between these settings may help inform policy initiatives and teacher education programs that can facilitate inclusive practice in the future.

References

Abgeordnetenhaus von Berlin. (1998). Plenarprotokoll 13/48: 48. Sitzung Berlin, Donnerstag, 3. September 1998.
Abgeordnetenhaus von Berlin. (1999). Plenarprotokoll 13/66: 66. Sitzung Berlin, Donnerstag, 1. Juli 1999.
Abgeordnetenhaus von Berlin. (2000a). Kleine Anfrage Nr. 14/548 des Abgeordneten Özcan Mutlu (Bündnis 90/ die Grünen) über: Modell zur Zukunft des Religions-, Weltanschauungs- und Ethikunterrichts in Berlin.
Abgeordnetenhaus von Berlin. (2000b). Kleine Anfrage Nr. 14/550 des Abgeordneten Özcan Mutlu (Bündnis 90/ die Grünen) über: Ergebnisse des Berliner Schulversuchs Ethik/Philosophie.
Abgeordnetenhaus von Berlin. (2001). Plenarprotokoll 14/35: 35. Sitzung vom 27. September 2001.
Abgeordnetenhaus von Berlin. (2004). Plenarprotokoll 15/60: 60. Sitzung Berlin, Donnerstag, 25. November 2004.
Abgeordnetenhaus von Berlin. (2005a). Plenarprotokoll 15/64: 64. Sitzung vom 24. Februar 2005.
Abgeordnetenhaus von Berlin. (2005b). Plenarprotokoll 15/66: 66. Sitzung vom 14. April 2005.
Abgeordnetenhaus von Berlin. (2005c). Plenarprotokoll 15/69: 69. Sitzung vom 2. Juni 2005.
Abgeordnetenhaus von Berlin. (2006a). Drucksache 15/4698: Vorlage – Zur Beschlussfassung – Erstes Gesetz zur Änderung des Schulgesetzes.
Abgeordnetenhaus von Berlin. (2006b). Plenarprotokoll 15/81: 81. Sitzung Berlin, Donnerstag, 16. Februar 2006.
Abgeordnetenhaus von Berlin. (2006c). Wortprotokoll JugFamSchulSport 15/72: Ausschuß für Jugend, Familie, Schule und Sport 72. Sitzung 2. März 2006.
Abgeordnetenhaus von Berlin. (2008a). Drucksache 16/12675: Kleine Anfrage des Abgeordneten Matthias Brauner (CDU) Teilnahmezahlen am Religionsunterricht.
Abgeordnetenhaus von Berlin. (2008b). Wortprotokoll BildJugFam 16/24: Ausschuss für Bildung, Jugend und Familie 24. Sitzung 22. Mai 2008.
Abgeordnetenhaus von Berlin. (2009a). Drucksache 16/2198: Antrag Gemeinsam statt getrennt. Für einen gemeinsamen Ethikunterricht!
Abgeordnetenhaus von Berlin. (2009b). Plenarprotokoll 16/41: 41. Sitzung Berlin, Donnerstag, 29. Januar 2009.
Abgeordnetenhaus von Berlin. (2018). Schriftliche Anfrage Nr. 18/13 029 der Abgeordneten Frank Kerker (AfD) zum Thema: Schule und Religion.
Abu El-Haj, T. R. (2010). "The Beauty of America": Nationalism, Education, and the War on Terror. Harvard Educational Review, 80(2), 242–275.
https://doi.org/10.17763/haer.80.2.hw3483147u83684h
Abu El-Haj, T. R., Ríos-Rojas, A., Jaffe-Walter, R. (2017). Whose race problem? Tracking patterns of racial denial in US and European educational discourses on Muslim youth. Curriculum Inquiry, 47(3), 310–335.
https://doi.org/10.1080/03626784.2017.1324736

Abu-Lughod, L. (2015). Do Muslim women need saving? (First Harvard University Press paperpack edition). Harvard University Press.

Achour, S. (2023). Politische Bildung für eine (nicht) distanzierte Mitte. In A. Zick, B. Küpper, N. Mokros (Eds.), Die Distanzierte Mitte: Rechtsextreme und demokratiegefährdende Einstellungen in Deutschland 2022/23 (pp. 355-376).

Achour, S. (2025). Gesellschaftspolitische, didaktische und pädagogische Perspektiven auf Demokratiebildung: Ein Überblick über Kontroversen, Synergien, Chancen und Desiderate. In S. Achour, M. Sieberkrob, D. Pech, J. Zelck, P. Eberhard (Eds.), Handbuch Demokratiebildung und Fachdidaktik: Bd. 1: Grundladen und Querschnittsaufgaben (pp. 19-43). Wochenschau.

Achour, S. & Wagner, S. (2019). Wer hat, dem wird gegeben: Politische Bildung an Schulen. Bestandsaufnahme, Rückschlüsse und Handlungsempfehlungen. Friedrich Ebert Stiftung. https://library.fes.de/pdf-files/studienfoerderung/15611.pdf

Alba, R. D., & Foner, N. (2015). Strangers no more: Immigration and the challenges of integration in North America and Western Europe. Princeton Univ. Press. https://www.loc.gov/catdir/enhancements/fy1614/2015932635-b.html

Allemann-Ghionda, C. (2009). From intercultural education to the inclusion of diversity: Theories and policies in Europe. In J. A. Banks (Ed.), Routledge international handbook series. The Routledge international companion to multicultural education (pp. 134–145). Routledge.

Anders, F. (2013, July 7). Der Ethik-Unterricht an Berliner Schulen ist gefährdet. Berliner Morgenpost. https://www.morgenpost.de/berlin-aktuell/article117796785/Der-Ethik-Unterricht-an-Berliner-Schulen-ist-gefaehrdet.html

Anders, F. (2018, January 24). Politik wird zum Pflichtfach an Berliner Schulen. Berliner Morgenpost. https://www.morgenpost.de/berlin/article213214377/Politik-wird-zum-Pflichtfach-an-Berliner-Schulen.html

Anderson, B. R. (2016). Imagined communities: Reflections on the origin and spread of nationalism (Revised edition). Verso.

Appadurai, A. (2010). Modernity at large: Cultural dimensions of globalization (9. print). Public worlds: Vol. 1. Univ. of Minnesota Press.

Asad, T. (1993). Genealogies of Religion. Johns Hopkins University Press. https://doi.org/10.1353/book.16014

Asad, T. (2003). Formations of the secular: Christianity, islam, modernity. Cultural memory in the present. Stanford University Press. https://doi.org/10.1515/9780804783095

Auernheimer, G. (2005). The German Education System: Dysfunctional for an Immigration Society. European Education, 37(4), 75–89. https://doi.org/10.2753/EUE1056-4934370406

Bade, K. J. (2011). Von der Arbeitswanderung zur Einwanderungsgesellschaft. In S. Stemmler (Ed.), Multikultur 2.0: Willkommen im Einwanderungsland Deutschland (pp. 154–185). Wallstein Verlag.

Baethge, M., Solga, H., & Wieck, M. (2007). Berufsbildung im Umbruch: Signale eines überfälligen Aufbruchs; [Studie (1. Aufl.). Netzwerk Bildung. Friedrich-Ebert-Stiftung. https://library.fes.de/pdf-files/stabsabteilung/04258/studie.pdf

Ball, S. J. (1993). What is Policy? Texts, Trajectories and Toolboxes. Discourse: Studies in the Cultural Politics of Education, 13(2), 10–17.

https://doi.org/10.1080/0159630930130203
Ball, S. J. (2015). What is policy? 21 years later: reflections on the possibilities of policy research. Discourse: Studies in the Cultural Politics of Education, 36(3), 306–313. https://doi.org/10.1080/01596306.2015.1015279
BAMF. (2010). Bundesweites Integrationsprogramm: Angebote der Integrationsförderung in Deutschland – Empfehlungen zu ihrer Weiterentwicklung. https://www.bamf.de/SharedDocs/Anlagen/DE/Integration/Integrationsprogramm/bundesweitesintegrationsprogramm.pdf?__blob=publicationFile&v=5
Banks, J. A. (2009). Multicultural education: Dimensions and paradigms. In J. A. Banks (Ed.), Routledge international handbook series. The Routledge international companion to multicultural education (pp. 9–32). Routledge.
Banse, D., & Laninger, T. (2005, February 16). Mordmotiv: Blut für die Ehre. Die Welt. https://www.welt.de/print-welt/article425556/Mordmotiv-Blut-fuer-die-Ehre.html
Barnes, L. P. (2018). Religious Education in Northern Ireland: Conflict, Curriculum and Criticism. In M. Sivasubramaniam & R. Hayhoe (Eds.), Oxford studies in comparative education: Volume 27, Number 2. Religion and education: Comparative and international perspectives (pp. 273–288). Symposium Books.
Bartlett, L., & Vavrus, F. K. (2016). Rethinking case study research: A comparative approach. Routledge.
Bassey, M. (1999). Case study research in educational settings. Doing qualitative research in educational settings. Open University Press. http://www.loc.gov/catdir/description/mh051/98030734.html
BBC (2011, February 5). State multiculturalism has failed, says David Cameron. BBC Politics. https://www.bbc.com/news/uk-politics-12371994
Beauchamp, C., & Thomas, L. (2009). Understanding teacher identity: an overview of issues in the literature and implications for teacher education. Cambridge Journal of Education, 39(2), 175–189. https://doi.org/10.1080/03057640902902252
Bechky, B. A. (2003). Sharing Meaning Across Occupational Communities: The Transformation of Understanding on a Production Floor. Organization Science, 14(3), 312–330. https://doi.org/10.1287/orsc.14.3.312.15162
Bell, J. M. (2014). The Black power movement and American social work. EBL-Schweitzer. Columbia University Press. http://www.jstor.org/stable/10.7312/bell16260
Bender-Szymanski, D. (2000). Learning through Cultural Conflict? A longitudinal analysis of German teachers' strategies for coping with cultural diversity at school. European Journal of Teacher Education, 23(3), 229–250. https://doi.org/10.1080/02619760120049120
Bender-Szymanski, D. (2013). Argumentation integrity in intercultural education: a teaching project about a religious-ideological dialogue as challenge for school. Intercultural Education, 24(6), 573–591. https://doi.org/10.1080/14675986.2013.845932
Bendix, R. (2017). Nation-Building and Citizenship: Studies of Our Changing Social Order (Third edition). Taylor and Francis. https://permalink.obvsg.at/
Bendixsen, S. (2013). The Religious Identity of Young Muslim Women in Berlin: An Ethnographic Study. Muslim Minorities. Brill. https://library.oapen.org/bitstream/id/c942e5d8-9293-4658-a02c-03319ab34726/1000351.pdf
Bentrovato, D. (2015). Narrating and teaching the nation: The politics of education in pre- and post-genocide Rwanda. Eckert. Die Schriftenreihe: Band 138. V&R unipress.

Berkovich, I. (2011). No, we won't! Teachers' resistance to educational reform. Journal of Educational Administration, 49(5), 563–578. https://doi.org/10.1108/09578231111159548

Berrey, E. (2014). Breaking Glass Ceilings, Ignoring Dirty Floors. American Behavioral Scientist, 58(2), 347–370.

Beschorner, J. (2006). Der Berliner Schulversuch Ethik/Philosophie in der Sekundarstufe I: Möglichkeiten und Grenzen ethischer Bildung in der Schule [Dissertation]. DataCite. https://refubium.fu-berlin.de/handle/fub188/5194

BiBB. (2021). Datenreport zum Berufsbildungsbericht 2012: Informationen und Analysen zur Entwicklung der beruflichen Bildung. http://datenreport.bibb.de/html/dr2012.html

Biermann, K., Faigle, P., Geisler, A., Polke-Majewski, K., Soltau, H., Stahnke, J., Steffen, T., & Venohr (5.24.2016). Plumbing the Depths of Racist Terror. Die Zeit. https://www.zeit.de/politik/deutschland/2016-05/racism-violence-emergency-accommodations-refugees-right-terror

BMI, & BAMF. (2016). Migrationsbericht des Bundesamtes für Migration und Flüchtlinge im Auftrag der Bundesregierung: Migrationsbericht 2015. https://www.bmi.bund.de/SharedDocs/downloads/DE/publikationen/themen/migration/migrationsbericht-2015.pdf?__blob=publicationFile&v=5

Boss-Nünning, U. (2006). Berufliche Bildung von Migrantinnen und Migranten: Ein vernachlässigtes Potential für die Wirtschaft und Gesellschaft. In Friedrich-Ebert-Stiftung (Ed.), Kompetenzen stärken, Qualifikationen verbessern, Potenziale nutzen: Berufliche Bildung von Jugendlichen und Erwachsenen mit Migrationshintergrund (pp. 6–29). bub Bonner Universitätsbuchdruckerei.

Bowen, J. R. (Ed.). (2013). Cambridge studies in law and society. European states and their Muslim citizens: The impact of institutions on perceptions and boundaries (1. pbk. ed.). Cambridge Univ. Press.

Bowen, J., Bertossi, C., Duyvendak, J., Krook, M. (Ed.). (2013). European States and their Muslim Citizens: The Impact of Institutions on Perceptions and Boundaries. Cambridge University Press.

Boxenbaum, E. (2006). Lost in Translation: The Making of Danish Diversity Management. American Behavioral Scientist, 49(7), 939–948.

Bracho, C. (2015). Mobilized Maestros: revolutionary Teacher Movements in Oaxaca, Mexico, Dissertation.

Brint, S. (2001). Gemeinschaft Revisited: A Critique and Reconstruction of the Community Concept. Sociological Theory, 19(1), 1–23. https://doi.org/10.1111/0735-2751.00125

Bruce, S. (2017). Secularization elsewhere: it is more complicated than that. Política & Sociedade, 16(36), 195–211. https://doi.org/10.5007/2175-7984.2017v16n36p195

Bundesministerium für Arbeit und Soziales. (Oktober 2022). Fachkräftestrategie der Bundesregierung.

Die Bundesregierung. (2007). Der Nationale Integrationsplan: Neue Wege. Neue Chancen. https://www.bundesregierung.de/resource/blob/2065474/441038/acdb01cb90b28205d452c83d2fde84a2/2007-08-30-nationaler-integrationsplan-data.pdf

Die Bundesregierung. (2016). Federal Government Strategy to Prevent Extremism and Promote Democracy.

https://www.bmfsfj.de/resource/blob/115448/cc142d640b37b7dd76e48b8fd9178cc5/strategie-der-bundesregierung-zur-extremismuspraevention-und-demokratiefoerderung-englisch-data.pdf

Burde, D. (2014). Schools for conflict or for peace in Afghanistan. Columbia University Press. https://doi.org/10.7312/burd16928

Bush, K. D., & Saltarelli, D. (2000). The two faces of education in ethnic conflict: Towards a peacebuilding education for children. Research Report. unicef. https://eprints.whiterose.ac.uk/80473/1

Busher, J., Thomas, P., Harris, G., & Choudhury, T. (2017). What the Prevent duty means for schools and colleges in England: An analysis of educationalists' experiences. Research Report. Aziz Foundation. https://eprints.hud.ac.uk/id/eprint/32349/

Bushnell, M. (2003). Teachers in the Schoolhouse Panopticon: Complicity and Resistance. Education and Urban Society, 35(3), 251–272. https://doi.org/10.1177/0013124503035003001

Cardona, M., Tichà, R., & Aber, B. (2018). Education for Diversity in Initial Teacher Preparation Programmes: a Comparative International Study. Journal of E-Learning and Knowledge Society, 14(2). https://www.learntechlib.org/p/184467/

Casanova, J. (1994). Public religions in the modern world (6 [reprint]. University of Chicago Press.

Casanova, J. (2006). Rethinking Secularization: A Global Comparative Perspective. The Hedgehog Review, 8(1/2), 7–22.

Castles, S. (2000). Ethnicity and Globalization: From Migrant Worker to Transnational Citizen. SAGE Publications. https://doi.org/10.4135/9781446217733

Cesari, J. (2004). When Islam and Democracy Meet: Muslims in Europe and in the United States (1st ed. 2004). Palgrave Macmillan US; Imprint Palgrave Macmillan. https://doi.org/10.1057/9781403978561

Cherng, H.-Y. S., & Davis, L. A. (2019). Multicultural Matters: An Investigation of Key Assumptions of Multicultural Education Reform in Teacher Education. Journal of Teacher Education, 70(3), 219–236. https://doi.org/10.1177/0022487117742884

Chisholm, L. (1999). The Democratization of Schools and the Politics of Teachers' Work in South Africa. Compare: A Journal of Comparative and International Education, 29(2), 111–126. https://doi.org/10.1080/0305792990290202

Christodoulou, E., & Szakács-Behling, S. (2018). Preventing violent extremism through education: International and German approaches. Georg-Eckert-Institut für Internationale Schulbuchforschung.

Çil, N. (2007). Topographie des Außenseiters: Türkische Generationen und der deutsch-deutsche Wiedervereinigungsprozess (1. Aufl., dt. Erstausg). Schriftenreihe Politik und Kultur am Otto-Suhr-Institut für Politikwissenschaft der Freien Universität Berlin: Vol. 9. Schiler.
http://www.socialnet.de/rezensionen/isbn.php?isbn=978-3-89930-192-2

Çil, N. (2011). Diversity und Multiculturalität: Macht und Ausgrenzung in modernen Gesellschaften. In S. Stemmler (Ed.), Multikultur 2.0: Willkommen im Einwanderungsland Deutschland. Wallstein Verlag.

Clycq, N. (2017). 'We value your food but not your language': Education systems and nation-building processes in Flanders. European Educational Research Journal, 16(4), 407–424. https://doi.org/10.1177/1474904116668885

Collet, B. A. (2018). Migration, religion, and schooling in liberal democratic states (First edition). Routledge Research in Religion and Education. Taylor and Francis.

https://doi.org/10.4324/9781315624945

Comaroff, J. L., & Comaroff, J. (2009). Ethnicity, Inc (2. print). Chicago studies in practices of meaning. Univ. of Chicago Press.

Concordat between the Holy See and the German Reich [with Supplementary Protocol and Secret Supplement]. (1933). https://www.concordatwatch.eu/kb-1211.834

Creswell, J. W. (2013). Qualitative Inquiry and Research Design: Choosing Among Five Approaches (3. Auflage). SAGE Publications.

Crossley, M., & Vulliamy, G. (1984). Case-study Research Methods and Comparative Education. Comparative Education, 20(2), 193–207. https://doi.org/10.1080/0305006840200202

Crul, M. (2016). Strangers no more. Debunking major theoretical assumptions. Ethnic and Racial Studies, 39(13), 2325–2331. https://doi.org/10.1080/01419870.2016.1203444

Crul, M., & Lelie, F. (2023). The new minority: People without a migration background in the superdiverse city. VU University Press.

Crul, M., Schneider, J., & Lelie, F. (2013). Super-diversity: A new perspective on integration. VU University Press. https://repub.eur.nl/pub/50358/

Deephouse, D. L., Bundy, J., Tost, L. P., & Suchman, M. C. (2017). Organizational Legitimacy: Six Key Questions. In R. Greenwood, C. Oliver, T. Lawrence, & R. Meyer (Eds.), The SAGE Handbook of Organizational Institutionalism (pp. 27–52). SAGE Publications Ltd. https://doi.org/10.4135/9781446280669.n2

Bundesministerium des Innern. (2014, September 12). Bundesminister de Maiziere zum Verbot der Betätigung der Terrororganisation „Islamischer Staat" in Deutschland [Press release]. http://www.bmi.bund.de/SharedDocs/Audio/DE/OToene/Minister/verbot-islamischer-staat.html;jsessionid=25C0EC4ABF99CDE60EC-BEF9DC689C100.2_cid295

DiMaggio, P. & Powell, W. (1991). Introduction. In W. Powell & P. DiMaggio (Ed.), The New Institutionalism in Organizational Analysis (pp. 1–38). The University of Chicago Press.

Dobbin, F., & Kalev, A. (2017). Are Diversity Programs Merely Ceremonial? Evidence-Free Institutionalization. In R. Greenwood, C. Oliver, T. B. Lawrence, & R. E. Meyer (Eds.), The SAGE Handbook of Organizational Institutionalism // The SAGE Handbook of organizational institutionalism [Second Edition], pp. 808–828). SAGE.

Doğmuş, A. (2022). Professionalisierung in Migrationsverhältnissen. Springer Fachmedien Wiesbaden. https://doi.org/10.1007/978-3-658-37721-2

Dreusicke, L. (2017, July 1). Uni Osnabrück spürt Trend: Studienfach Islamische Religion auf Lehramt immer beliebter. Neue Osnabrücker Zeitung. https://www.noz.de/deutschland-welt/panorama/artikel/uni-osnabrueck-spuert-trend-studienfach-islamische-religion-auf-lehramt-immer-beliebter-23240918

Dryden-Peterson, S. (2016). Refugee education in countries of first asylum: Breaking open the black box of pre-resettlement experiences. Theory and Research in Education, 14(2), 131–148. https://doi.org/10.1177/1477878515622703

Dryden-Peterson, S. (2017). Refugee education: Education for an unknowable future. Curriculum Inquiry, 47(1), 14–24. https://doi.org/10.1080/03626784.2016.1255935

Dryden-Peterson, S., Adelman, E., Alvarado, S., Anderson, K., Bellino, M. J., Brooks, R., Bukhari, S., Cao, E., Chopra, V., Faizi, Z., Culla, B., Maarouf, D., Reddick, C., Scherrer, B., Smoake, E., & Suzuki, E. (2018). Inclusion of Refugees in National Education Systems: Migration, displacement and education: Building bridges, not walls. Background paper prepared for the 2019 Global Education Monitoring Report. UNESCO.

Edelman, L. B. (1990). Legal Environments and Organizational Governance: The Expansion of Due Process in the American Workplace. American Journal of Sociology, 95(6), 1401–1440. https://doi.org/10.1086/229459

Edelman, L. B. (1992). Legal Ambiguity and Symbolic Structures: Organizational Mediation of Civil Rights Law. American Journal of Sociology, 97(6), 1531–1576. https://doi.org/10.1086/229939

Elrick, J., & Farah Schwartzman, L. (2015). From statistical category to social category: organized politics and official categorizations of 'persons with a migration background' in Germany. Ethnic and Racial Studies, 38(9), 1539–1556. https://doi.org/10.1080/01419870.2014.996240

Euler, S. S. (2017). Utilizing the Project Method for Teaching Culture and Intercultural Competence. Die Unterrichtspraxis/Teaching German, 50(1), 67–78. https://doi.org/10.1111/tger.12022

Favell, A. (2014). Immigration, integration and mobility: New agendas in migration studies: Essays 1998-2014. ECPR Press essays. ECPR Press.

Fereidooni, K. (2016). Diskriminierungs- und Rassismuserfahrungen von Referendar* innen und Lehrer* innen ‚mit Migrationshintergrund ‚im deutschen Schulwesen. Eine quantitative und qualitative Studie zu subjektiven bedeutsamen Ungleichheitspraxen im Berufskontext [Inauguraldissertation, Ruprecht-Karls-Universität Heidelberg, Heidelberg]. RIS. https://archiv.ub.uni-heidelberg.de/volltextserver/20203/1/dissertation%20karim%20fereidooni(1).pdf

Fereidooni, K. (2025). Rassismuskritik: Ein Baustein für die Demokratiebildung. In S. Achour, M. Sieberkrob, D. Pech, J. Zelck, P. Eberhard (Eds.), Handbuch Demokratiebildung und Fachdidaktik: Bd. 1: Grundladen und Querschnittsaufgaben (pp. 142-153). Wochenschau.

Flick, U. (2016). Qualitative Sozialforschung: Eine Einführung (8. Auflage). Rowohlt.

Foroutan, N. (2015). Die Einheit der Verschiedenen: Integration in der postmigrantischen Gesellschaft. Kurzdossier. http://www.bpb.de/gesellschaft/migration/kurzdossiers/205183/integration-in-der-postmigrantischen-gesellschaft

Foroutan, N. (2019). Die postmigrantische Gesellschaft: Ein Versprechen der pluralen Demokratie. X-Texte zu Kultur und Gesellschaft. transcript.

Foucault, M. (1982). 'The subject and power', an afterword. In H. L. Dreyfus & P. Rabinow (Eds.), Michel Foucault, beyond structuralism and hermeneutics. University of Chicago Press.

Foucault, M. (1995). Discipline and Punish: The Birth of the Prison (2. Auflage). Vintage Books. A Division of random House.

Foucault, M. (2013). Archaeology of Knowledge. Routledge. https://doi.org/10.4324/9780203604168

Frey, W. H. (2018). Diversity Explosion: How new racial demographics are remaking America. Brookings Institution Press. https://permalink.obvsg.at/

Friedland, R., & Alford, R. R. (1991). Bringing Society Back In: Symbols, Practices, and Institutional Contradictions. In W. Powell & P. DiMaggio (Ed.), The New Institutionalism in Organizational Analysis (pp. 232–263). The University of Chicago Press.

Friedland, R., & Arjaliès, D.-L. (2019). X-Institutional Logics: Out or In? SSRN Electronic Journal. Advance online publication. https://doi.org/10.2139/ssrn.3403131

Fuchs, J., Kubis, A., & Schneider, L. (2019). Zuwanderung und Digitalisierung: Wie viel Migration aus Drittstaaten benötigt der deutsche Arbeitsmarkt künftig? https://doi.org/10.11586/2019013

Gardinier, M. P. (2012). Agents of Change and Continuity: The Pivotal Role of Teachers in Albanian Educational Reform and Democratization. Comparative Education Review, 56(4), 659–683.

Gaudelli, W. (2016). Global citizenship education: Everyday transcendence. Routledge. https://www.taylorfrancis.com/books/9781315683492 https://doi.org/10.4324/9781315683492

Geddes, A. (2010). The politics of migration and immigration in Europe (Repr). Sage politics texts. SAGE. https://doi.org/10.4135/9781446280492

Geiger, K. F. (2003). Multicultural Society and Intercultural Education: Debates in the Federal Republic of Germany. In B. S. A. Yeoh (Ed.), Approaching transnationalisms: Studies on transnational societies, multicultural contacts, and imaginings of home (pp. 141–159). Kluwer Acad. Publ.

Georgi, V. B., Ackermann, L., & Karakaş, N. (2011). Vielfalt im Lehrerzimmer: Selbstverständnis und schulische Integration von Lehrenden mit Migrationshintergrund in Deutschland. Waxmann.

Gessler, T., & Hunger, S. (2023). The Politicization of Immigration and Radical Right Party Politics in Germany. In M. Weisskircher (Ed.), Contemporary Germany and the Fourth Wave of Far-Right Politics (pp. 115–139). Routledge.

Giese, G. (1955). Die Kirche in der Berliner Schule. Lettner.

Giese, K. (2000). Islamische Förderation versus Land Berlin. In R. Busch (Ed.), Integration und Religion: Islamischer Religionsunterricht an Berliner Schulen; [den Kern des vorliegenden Buches bilden die Beiträge einer Tagung zum Thema „Integration und Religion. Muslime in der Christlichen Gesellschaft. Islamischer Religionsunterricht an Berliner Schulen?", die am 5.12.1999 in der Freien Universität Berlin stattfand (pp. 75–82). Dahlem Univ. Press.

Gogolin, I. (2008). Der monolinguale Habitus der multilingualen Schule (2., unveränderte Auflage). Internationale Hochschulschriften: Bd. 101. Waxmann.

Gogolin, I., & Neumann, U. (Eds.). (1997). Interkulturelle Bildungsforschung: Vol. 1. Großstadt-Grundschule: Eine Fallstudie über sprachliche und kulturelle Pluralität als Bedingung der Grundschularbeit. Waxmann.

Gomolla, M. (2020). Direkte und indirekte, institutionelle und strukturelle Diskriminierung. In A. Scherr, A. El-Mafaalani, & A. C. Reinhardt (Eds.), Springer Reference Sozialwissenschaften. Handbuch Diskriminierung (pp. 1–24). Springer Fachmedien Wiesbaden. https://doi.org/10.1007/978-3-658-11119-9_9-2#DOI

Gomolla, M., & Radtke, F.-O. (2009). Institutionelle Diskriminierung: Die Herstellung ethnischer Differenz in der Schule (3. Auflage). VS Verlag für Sozialwissenschaften.

Gosh, R., & Chan, A. (2018). The Role of Religious Education in Countering Religious Extremism in Diverse and Interconnected Societies. In M. Sivasubramaniam & R. Hayhoe (Eds.), Oxford studies in comparative education. Religion and education: Comparative and international perspectives (pp. 335–350). Symposium Books.

Gräb, W., & Thieme, T. (2011). Religion oder Ethik? Die Auseinandersetzung um den Ethik- und Religionsunterricht in Berlin. Arbeiten zur Religionspädagogik: Vol. 45. V&R unipress. https://swbplus.bsz-bw.de/bsz335205011kla.htm

Gräfe-Geusch, A. (2020). Vignette 2: When the global comes crashing in – A chance for GCE? Reflections on teaching refugees in ethics instruction in Berlin. Tertium Comparationis Journal Für International Und Interkulturelle Vergleichende Erziehungswissenschaft, 26(2), 122–130.

Gräfe-Geusch, A., & Okroi, J. (2024). Education and Integration: The Importance of Incorporating Refugee Youths' Agency and Perceptions. In M. Otto & T. Saeed (Eds.), Peace and human rights education. Critical perspectives on refugee and migrant integration in education: Grassroots narratives from multiregional settings (pp. 151–166). Bloomsbury Academic; Bloomsbury Publishing (UK).

Gutentag, T., Horenczyk, G., & Tatar, M. (2018). Teachers' Approaches Toward Cultural Diversity Predict Diversity-Related Burnout and Self-Efficacy. Journal of Teacher Education, 69(4), 408–419. https://doi.org/10.1177/0022487117714244

Guven, O. (2018). Undoing Forty Years of Public Lies: Fear, Mistrust, and Resentment in Resistance and Silence Among Exiled Syrian Teachers in Turkey (New York University ProQuest Dissertations & Theses 10815345) [Dissertation, New York University, New York]. RIS.

Hansen, R. (2011). The Two Faces of Liberalism: Islam in Contemporary Europe. Journal of Ethnic and Migration Studies, 37(6), 881–897. https://doi.org/10.1080/1369183X.2011.576192

Häusler, U. (2007). Religion unterrichten in Berlin. Zeitschrift Für Religionspädagogik, 6(1), 25–49. https://www.theo-web.de/zeitschrift/ausgabe-2007-01/5.pdf

Helbig, M., & Nikolai, R. (2015). Die Unvergleichbaren: Der Wandel der Schulsysteme in den deutschen Bundesländern seit 1949. Verlag Julius Klinkhardt.

Herold, M., & Schäller, S. (2023). Germany's Anti-Islamic Pegida Movement. In M. Weisskircher (Ed.), Contemporary Germany and the Fourth Wave of Far-Right Politics (pp. 39–56). Routledge.

Hilferty, F. (2008). Theorising teacher professionalism as an enacted discourse of power. British Journal of Sociology of Education, 29(2), 161–173. https://doi.org/10.1080/01425690701837521

Hirsch, P. M., & Andrews, J. A. Y. (1984). Administrators' response to performance and value challenges: Stance, symbols, and behavior. In T. J. Sergiovanni (Ed.), Illini Books edition. Leadership and organizational culture: New perspectives on administrative theory and practice (pp. 170–185). Univ. of Illinois Pr.

Huntington, S. (1996). The Clash of Civilizations and the Remaking of World Order. Simon & Schuster.

Ingram, P., & Rao, H. (2004). Store Wars: The Enactment and Repeal of Anti-Chain-Store Legislation in America. American Journal of Sociology, 110(2), 446–487. https://doi.org/10.1086/422928

Ingram, P., Yue, L. Q., & Rao, H. (2010). Trouble in Store: Probes, Protests, and Store Openings by Wal-Mart, 1998–2007. American Journal of Sociology, 116(1), 53–92. https://doi.org/10.1086/653596

Jackson, R. (2008). Teaching about Religions in the Public Sphere: European Policy Initiatives and the Interpretive Approach. Numen: International Review for the History of Religions, 55(2-3), 151–182. https://doi.org/10.1163/156852708X283032

Jaffe-Walter, R. (2013). "Who would they talk about if we weren't here?": Muslim Youth, Liberal Schooling, and the Politics of Concern. Harvard Educational Review, 83(4), 613–635. https://doi.org/10.17763/haer.83.4.b41012p57h816154

Jaffe-Walter, R. (2017). "The More We Can Try to Open Them Up, the Better It Will Be for Their Integration": Integration and the Coercive Assimilation of Muslim Youth. Diaspora, Indigenous, and Minority Education, 11(2), 63–68. https://doi.org/10.1080/15595692.2017.1288616

Jafralie, S. N., & Zaver, A. (2019). Teaching Religious Education: The Ethics and Religious Culture Program as Case Study. FIRE: Forum for International Research in Education, 5(1), 89–106. https://doi.org/10.32865/fire201951136

Joffe, J. (2008, December 17). Kulturkampf lite: Der Staat muss Freiheit von Religion gewähren. Die Zeit (52). https://www.zeit.de/2008/52/Zeitgeist-52

Joppke, C. (2007a). Beyond national models: Civic integration policies for immigrants in Western Europe. West European Politics, 30(1), 1–22. https://doi.org/10.1080/01402380601019613

Joppke, C. (2007b). State neutrality and Islamic headscarf laws in France and Germany. Theory and Society, 36(4), 313–342. https://doi.org/10.1007/s11186-007-9036-y

Joppke, C. (2007c). Transformation of Immigrant Integration: Civic Integration and Antidiscrimination in the Netherlands, France, and Germany. World Politics, 59(2), 243–273. https://doi.org/10.1353/wp.2007.0022

Jung, O. (2011). Direkte Demokratie in Berlin: Der Fall "Pro Reli" 2007-2009. Berliner Wissenschaftsverlag. https://www.steiner-verlag.de/direkte-demokratie-in-berlin/9783830527145

Katz, Y. J. (2018). Religious Education in the Israeli State School System. In M. Sivasubramaniam & R. Hayhoe (Eds.), Oxford studies in comparative education. Religion and education: Comparative and international perspectives (pp. 251–270). Symposium Books.

Keating, J., Preston, R., Burke, P. J., Van Heertum, R., and Arnove, R. F. (2013). The political economy of educational reform in Australia, England and Wales, and the United States. In R. F. Arnove, C. A. Torres, & S. Franz (Eds.), Comparative education: The dialectic of the global and local (Fourth edition, pp. 229–270). Rowman & Littlefield Publishers Inc.

Keller, C. (2010, June 1). Qualitätskriterien für die „Laberstunde". Der Tagesspiegel. https://www.tagesspiegel.de/berlin/schule/ethikunterricht-qualitaetskriterien-fuer-die-laberstunde-/1848932.html

Kelly, E., & Dobbin, F. (1998). How Affirmative Action Became Diversity Management. American Behavioral Scientist, 41(7), 960–984. https://doi.org/10.1177/0002764298041007008

Kepel, G. (2006). The war for Muslim minds: Islam and the West (1. paperback ed.). The Belknap Press of Harvard Univ. Press.

Kiel, E., Syring, M., & Weiss, S. (2017). How can intercultural school development succeed? The perspective of teachers and teacher educators. Pedagogy, Culture & Society, 25(2), 243–261. https://doi.org/10.1080/14681366.2016.1252421

King, E. (2013). From Classrooms to Conflict in Rwanda. Cambridge University Press.

Klausen, J. (2005). The Islamic challenge: Politics and religion in Western Europe (Repr). Oxford Univ. Press https://doi.org/10.1093/acprof:oso/9780199231980.001.0001

Knorr-Cetina, K. (2022). Epistemic cultures: How the sciences make knowledge. Harvard University Press. https://doi.org/10.4159/9780674039681

Kober, U., & Süssmuth, R. (2012). Nachholbedarf: Vom Einwanderungsland wider Willen zu einem Land mit Willkommenskultur. In Bertelsmann Stiftung (Ed.), Deutschland, öffne dich! Willkommenskultur und Vielfalt in der Mitte der Gesellschaft verankern (pp. 13–24). Verlag Bertelsmann Stiftung.

Kögel, A. (2015, December 14). Flüchtlinge in Berlin: Sechs Gründe für das Chaos am Lageso: Jede Menge Formulare, ständig neue Termine, unklare Ansagen: Das Durcheinander am Lageso ist erklärbar. Tagesspiegel. https://www.tagesspiegel.de/berlin/sechs-grunde-fur-das-chaos-am-lageso-6316249.html

Korteweg, A. C., & Yurdakul, G. (2010). Religion, Culture and the Politicization of Honour-Related Violence: A Critical Analysis of Media and Policy Debates in Western Europe and North America (Gender and Development Programme Paper No. 12). United Nations Research Institute for Social Development. https://www.files.ethz.ch/isn/124186/2010_No12_KortewegYurdaku.pdf

Koschmieder C. & Koschmieder, J. (2025). Schule als Gründünger für die Demokratie. Rechtsextremismus und Demokratiebildung. In S. Achour, M. Sieberkrob, D. Pech, J. Zelck, P. Eberhard (Eds.), Handbuch Demokratiebildung und Fachdidaktik: Bd. 1: Grundladen und Querschnittsaufgaben (pp. 127-141). Wochenschau.

Kottmann, B. (2006). Selektion in die Sonderschule: Das Verfahren zur Feststellung von sonderpädagogischem Förderbedarf als Gegenstand empirischer Forschung. Vollst. zugl.: Bielefeld, Univ., Diss., 2004 u.d.T.: Selektion von Grundschulkindern durch die Feststellung von sonderpädagogischem Förderbedarf. Klinkhardt Forschung. Klinkhardt.

Krüger-Potratz, M. (2005). Migration als Herausforderung für Bildungspolitik. In R. Leiprecht & A. Kerber (Eds.), Reihe Politik und Bildung: Vol. 38. Schule in der Einwanderungsgesellschaft: Ein Handbuch (3. Aufl., pp. 56–82). Wochenschau-Verl.

Krüger-Potratz, M. (2006). Präsent, aber "vergessen": Zur Geschichte des Umgangs mit Heterogenität im Bildungswesen. In M. Göhlich, H.-W. Leonhard, E. Liebau, & J. Zirfas (Eds.), Beiträge zur pädagogischen Grundlagenforschung. Transkulturalität und Pädagogik: Interdisziplinäre Annäherungen an ein kulturwissenschaftliches Konzept und seine pädagogische Relevanz (pp. 121–139). Juventa-Verl.

Kühn, H. (September 1979). Stand und Weiterentwicklung der Integration der ausländischen Arbeitnehmer und ihrer Familien in der Bundesrepublik Deutschland: Memorandum des Beauftragten der Bundesregierung. https://germanhistory-intersections.org/de/migration/ghis:document-125

Kultusministerkonferenz. (1996/2013). Interkulturelle Bildung und Erziehung in der Schule: Beschluss der Kultusministerkonferenz vom 25.10.1996 i. d. F. vom 05.12.2013. https://www.kmk.org/fileadmin/veroeffentlichungen_beschluesse/1996/1996_10_25-Interkulturelle-Bildung.pdf

Kultusministerkonferenz. (2003, March 14). Das deutsche Bildungswesen und der Dialog mit den Muslimen: Weimarer Aufruf. https://www.kmk.org/fileadmin/Dateien/pdf/PresseUndAktuelles/Beschluesse_Veroeffentlichungen/Lerngemeinschaft_10.pdf

Kultusministerkonferenz. (2009/2018). Demokratie als Ziel, Gegenstand und Praxis historisch-politischer Bildung und Erziehung in der Schule: Beschluss der Kultusministerkonferenz vom 06.03.2009 i. d. F. vom 11.10.2018. https://www.kmk.org/fileadmin/veroeffentlichungen_beschluesse/2009/2009_03_06-Staerkung_Demokratieerziehung.pdf

Kultusministerkonferenz. (2015, October 8). Darstellung von kultureller Vielfalt, Integration und Migration in Bildungsmedien - Gemeinsame Erklärung der Kultusministerkonferenz, der Organisationen von Menschen mit Migrationshintergrund und der Bildungsmedienverlage: Beschluss der Kultusministerkonferenz vom 08.10.2015. https://www.kmk.org/fileadmin/veroeffentlichungen_beschluesse/2015/2015_10_08-Darstellung-kultureller-Vielfalt.pdf

Kymlicka, W. (2010). The rise and Fall of multiculturalism? New debates on inclusion and accommodation in diverse societies. In S. Vertovec & S. Wessendorf (Eds.), The multiculturalism backlash: European discourses, policies and practices (pp. 32–49). Routledge.

Labaree, D. (2009). What Schools can't do. Understanding the Chronic Failure of American School Reform. Zeitschrift Für Pädagogische Historiographie, 15, 12–18.

Landesabstimmungsleiter Berlin. (2009). Bericht des Landesabstimmungsleiters: Volksentscheid über die Einführung des Wahlpflichtbereichs Ethik/Religion am 26. April 2009. Endgültiges Ergebnis zugleich Statistischer Bericht B VII 4-1. Amt für Statistik Berlin-Brandenburg. https://www.wahlen-berlin.de/historie/abstimmungen/Landeswahlleiterbericht_VE09.pdf

Landesjustizamt. (2016a). Erhebung der Landesjustizverwaltung über Verfahren wegen rechtsextremistischer/fremdenfeindlicher Straftaten in der Bundesrepublik Deutschland (1. Januar bis 31. Dezember 2015). https://www.bundesjustizamt.de/SharedDocs/Downloads/DE/Justizstatistiken/Straftaten_2015.pdf?__blob=publicationFile&v=4

Landesjustizamt. (2016b). Erhebung der Landesjustizverwaltungen über Verfahren wegen rechtsextremistischer/fremdenfeindlicher Straftaten in der Bundesrepublik Deutschland: 1. Januar bis 31. Dezember 2014. https://www.bundesjustizamt.de/SharedDocs/Downloads/DE/Justizstatistiken/Straftaten_2014.pdf?__blob=publicationFile&v=4

Landesjustizamt. (2018). Erhebung der Landesjustizverwaltungen über Verfahren wegen rechtsextremistischer/fremdenfeindlicher Straftaten in der Bundesrepublik Deutschland: 1. Januar bis 31. Dezember 2016. https://www.bundesjustizamt.de/SharedDocs/Downloads/DE/Justizstatistiken/Straftaten_2016.pdf?__blob=publicationFile&v=4

Landesvorstand SPD Berlin. (2005). Beschlussprotokoll Landesparteitag der Berliner SPD am 9. April 2005. https://parteitag.spd.berlin/app/uploads/2005_apr09_beschlussprotokoll_gesamt.pdf

Laurence, J. (2014). Reconciling the contact and threat hypotheses: does ethnic diversity strengthen or weaken community inter-ethnic relations? Ethnic and Racial Studies, 37(8), 1328–1349. https://doi.org/10.1080/01419870.2013.788727

Laurien, H. R. (1989). Die Bedeutung des Religionsunterrichts für die Gesellschaft. Schönberger Hefte, 19(2), 3–9.

Lawrence, T. B., & Buchanan, S. (2008). Power, Institutions and Organizations. In R. Greenwood, C. Oliver, T. B. Lawrence, & R. E. Meyer (Eds.), The SAGE handbook of organizational institutionalism (Second edition, pp. 477–506). SAGE.

Leinemann, S. (2019, August 1). Lehrermangel: Berlin setzt weiterhin auf Quereinsteiger. Berliner Morgenpost. https://www.morgenpost.de/berlin/article226652987/Lehrermangel-Berlin-setzt-weiterhin-auf-Quereinsteiger.html

Lelie, F., Crul, M., & Schneider, J. (2012). The European Second Generation Compared: Does the Integration Context Matter? Does the Integration Context Matter? Amsterdam University Press. https://doi.org/10.26530/OAPEN_426534

LeTendre, G. (1994). Guiding Them on: Teaching, Hierarchy, and Social Organization in Japanese Middle Schools. Journal of Japanese Studies, 20(1), 37. https://doi.org/10.2307/132783

Levin, H. M. (2009). Foreword. In F. K. Vavrus & L. Bartlett (Eds.), International & development education. Critical approaches to comparative education: Vertical case studies from Africa, Europe, the Middle East, and the Americas (1st ed.). Palgrave Macmillan US.

Levinson, B. A. (1999). Resituating the Place of Educational Discourse in Anthropology. American Anthropologist, 101(3), 594–604. https://doi.org/10.1525/aa.1999.101.3.594

Lipsky, M. (2010). Street-level bureaucracy: Dilemmas of the individual in public services (Updated edition). Publications of Russell Sage Foundation. Russell Sage Foundation.

Loescher, G., Milner, J., Newman, E., & Troeller, G. (Eds.). (2008). Protracted Refugee Situations. Political, Human Rights and Security Implications. United Nations University Press.

Lofland, J., Snow, D. A., Anderson, L., & Lofland, L. (2006). Analyzing Social Settings: A Guide to Qualitative Observation and Analysis (4. Auflage). Wadsworth Cengage Learning.

Lounsbury, M. (2008). Institutional rationality and practice variation: New directions in the institutional analysis of practice. Accounting, Organizations and Society, 33(4-5), 349–361. https://doi.org/10.1016/j.aos.2007.04.001

Luchtenberg, S. (2009). Migrant minority groups in Germany: Success and failure in education. In J. A. Banks (Ed.), Routledge international handbook series. The Routledge international companion to multicultural education (1st ed., pp. 463–474). Routledge.

Luykx, A. (1999). The citizen factory: Schooling and cultural production in Bolivia. SUNY series, power, social identity, and education. State University of New York Press.

MacQuarrie, C. (2009). Othering. In A. J. Mills (Ed.), Encyclopedia of case study research (pp. 635–639). SAGE Publications.

Mannitz, S. (2005). The Place of Religion in Four Civil Cultures. In W. Schiffauer, G. Bauman, R. Kastoryano, & S. Vertovec (Eds.), Civil enculturation: Nation-state, schools and ethnic difference in the Netherlands, Britain, Germany and France. Berghahn Books.

Mannitz, S., & Schiffauer, W. (2005). Taxonomies of Cultural Difference: Construction of Otherness. In W. Schiffauer, G. Bauman, R. Kastoryano, & S. Vertovec (Eds.), Civil enculturation: Nation-state, schools and ethnic difference in the Netherlands, Britain, Germany and France (pp. 60–87). Berghahn Books.

March, J. G., & Olsen, J. P. (1976). Ambiguity and choice in organizations. Universitetsforlaget.

Marquis, C., & Battilana, J. (2007). Acting Globally but Thinking Locally? The Influence of Local Communities on Organizations (Working Paper 08-034). https://www.hbs.edu/faculty/Publication%20Files/08-034_189964be-e3ce-46f8-b58c-eadc0eba68da.pdf

Martínez-Ariño, J., Moutselos, M., Schönwälder, K., Jacobs, C., Schiller, M., & Tandé, A. (2019). Why do some cities adopt more diversity policies than others? A study in France and Germany. Comparative European Politics, 17(5), 651–672. https://doi.org/10.1057/s41295-018-0119-0

Massumi, M., Dewitz, N. von, Grießbach, J., Terhart, H., Wagner, K., Hippmann, K., & Altinay, L. (2015). Neu zugewanderte Kinder und Jugendliche im deutschen Schulsystem: Bestandsaufnahme und Empfehlungen. https://international.uni-koeln.de/sites/international/aaa/92/92pdf/92pdf_REFUGEES_PUBL_MI_ZfL_Studie_Zugewanderte_im_deutschen_Schulsystem_final_screen.pdf

Maxwell, J. A. (2013). Qualitative research design: An interactive approach (3rd edition). Applied social research methods series: Vol. 41. SAGE.

Mazawi, A. E. (1994). Teachers' Role Patterns and the Mediation of Sociopolitical Change: the case of Palestinian Arab school teachers. British Journal of Sociology of Education, 15(4), 497–514. https://doi.org/10.1080/0142569940150404

McGinty, P. J. W. (2009). Teachers and Teaching During Educational Restructuring and Reforms. In L. J. Saha (Ed.), Springer international handbooks of education. International handbook of research on teachers and teaching (pp. 1135–1152). Springer. https://doi.org/10.1007/978-0-387-73317-3_74

Mecheril, P. (2002). Natio-kulturelle Mitgliedschaft - ein Begriff und die Methode seiner Generierung. Tertium comparationis, 8. https://doi.org/10.25656/01:2924 (Tertium comparationis 8 (2002) 2, S. 104-115).

Zukunft für Deutschland in christdemokratischer Perspektive: Rede der Bundesvorsitzenden der CDU Deutschlands, Dr. Angela Merkel MdB, anlässlich der 42. Bundestagung des Evangelischen Arbeitskreises der CDU/CSU vom 10.–11. Juni 2005 in Heidelberg, redigierte Bandabschrift (2005).

Meyer, H.-D., & Rowan, B. (2006). Institutional Analysis and the Study of Education. In H.-D. Meyer & B. Rowan (Eds.), New Institutionalism in Education (pp. 1–13). State University of New York Press.

Meyer, J. W., Kamens, D., & Benavot, A. (1992). School knowledge for the masses: World models and national primary curricular categories in the twentieth century (1. publ). Studies in curriculum history series: Vol. 19. Falmer Press.

Meyer, J. W., & Rowan, B. (1977). Institutionalized Organizations: Formal Structure as Myth and Ceremony. American Journal of Sociology, 83(2), 340–363. https://doi.org/10.1086/226550

Meyer, J. W., & Scott, W. R. (Eds.). (1983). Organizational environments: Ritual and rationality. SAGE Publications.

Mijs, J. J. B., Bakhtiari, E., & Lamont, M. (2016). Neoliberalism and Symbolic Boundaries in Europe. Socius: Sociological Research for a Dynamic World, 2, Article 2378023116632538. https://doi.org/10.1177/2378023116632538

Miller, T., Vorbringer, A., & Raich, S. (2005, February 17). Neuköllner Schüler haben einen Mord aus verletzter Familienehre gutgeheißen. Die Schule toleriert das nicht: „Wir dulden keine Hetze". Berliner Zeitung. https://www.berliner-zeitung.de/neukoellner-schueler-haben-einen-mord-aus-verletzter-familienehre-gutgeheissen---die-schule-toleriert-das-nicht--wir-dulden-keine-hetze--15462494

Miller-Idriss, C. (2009). Blood and Culture: Youth, Right-Wing Extremism, and National Belonging in Contemporary Germany‹br›. Politics, History, and Culture. Duke University Press. https://doi.org/10.1515/9780822391142

Miller-Idriss, C. (2017). The extreme gone mainstream: Commercialization and far right youth culture in Germany. Princeton studies in cultural sociology. Princeton University Press.

MIPEX. (2015). Migration Integration Policy Index: Germany. https://www.mipex.eu/germany

MIPEX. (2020). Migration Integration Policy Index: Germany. https://www.mipex.eu/education

Moland, N. A. (2015). Can Multiculturalism Be Exported? Dilemmas of Diversity on Nigeria's Sesame Square. Comparative Education Review, 59(1), 1–23. https://doi.org/10.1086/679014

Morning, A. (2011). The nature of race: How scientists think and teach about human difference. Univ. of California Press.

Müchler, B. (2015, September 21). In Berlin versinken Flüchtlinge im Behörden-Chaos: Asylanträge. Welt. https://www.welt.de/politik/deutschland/article146663316/In-Berlin-versinken-Fluechtlinge-im-Behoerden-Chaos.html

Müller, F. (2012). Making contact. Generating interethnic contact for multicultural integration and tolerance in Amsterdam. Race Ethnicity and Education, 15(3), 425–440. https://doi.org/10.1080/13613324.2011.585341

Niehaus, I. (2017, April 27). Schulbuchstudie Migration und Integration – Ergebnisse und Empfehlungen für die Bildungspolitik und -praxis. DIW Berlin, & Leibniz-Forschungsverbund Bildungspotenziale (LERN). LERN-Jahrestagung. http://www.leibniz-bildungspotenziale.de/pdf/LERN%202017_Niehaus.pdf

Niehaus, I. (2018). How Diverse Are Our Textbooks? Research Findings in International Perspective. In E. Fuchs & A. Bock (Eds.), Palgrave handbooks. The Palgrave handbook of textbook studies (pp. 329–343). Palgrave Macmillan. https://doi.org/10.1057/978-1-137-53142-1_24

Nonet, P., & Selznick, P. (1978). Law and society in transition: Toward responsive law. Octagon Books.

Nowakowski, G., Vieth-Entus, S., & Zawatka-Gerlach, U. (2004, November 22). „Ja, wir alle haben versagt": Bildungssenator Klaus Böger (SPD) über Integration, Werteunterricht und die Lehren aus den Fehlern der Vergangenheit. Tagesspiegel. https://www.tagesspiegel.de/berlin/ja-wir-alle-haben-versagt-1172695.html

Ortloff, D. H. (2009). Social Studies Teachers' Reflections on Citizenship Education in Bavaria, Germany. Race/Ethnicity: Multidisciplinary Global Contexts, 2(2), 189–214.

Ortloff, D. H., & Frey, C. J. (2007). Blood Relatives: Language, Immigration, and Education of Ethnic Returnees in Germany and Japan. Comparative Education Review, 51(4), 447–470. https://doi.org/10.1086/520865

Özcan, E. (2013). Lingerie, Bikinis and the Headscarf. Feminist Media Studies, 13(3), 427–442. https://doi.org/10.1080/14680777.2012.712382

Özdemir, C. (2011). Vorwort. In V. B. Georgi, L. Ackermann, & N. Karakaş (Eds.), Vielfalt im Lehrerzimmer: Selbstverständnis und schulische Integration von Lehrenden mit Migrationshintergrund in Deutschland (pp. 11–12). Waxmann.

Panayi, P. (2004). The Evolution of Multiculturalism in Britain and Germany: An Historical Survey. Journal of Multilingual and Multicultural Development, 25(5-6), 466–480. https://doi.org/10.1080/01434630408668919

Pearson, J. (2015). Berlin's Appalling Conditions at Refugee Registration Center LaGeSo. http://needleberlin.com/2015/09/29/berlins-appalling-conditions-at-refugee-registration-center-lageso/

Pew Research Center. (2011, July 21). Muslim-Western Tensions Persist: Common Concerns About Islamic Extremism (Report). https://www.pewresearch.org/global/2011/07/21/muslim-western-tensions-persist/

Pew Research Center. (2015). The Future of World Religions: Population Growth Projections, 2010-2050. http://www.pewforum.org/files/2015/03/PF_15.04.02_ProjectionsFullReport.pdf

Pinson, H., Arnot, M., & & Candappa, M. (2010). Education, asylum and the non-citizen child: The politics of compassion and belonging. Palgrave Macmillan. https://link.springer.com/book/10.1057/9780230276505

Posener, A. (2010, December 26). Auf der Suche nach dem Kulturkampf um die Religion. Die Welt. https://www.welt.de/politik/deutschland/article11834674/Auf-der-Suche-nach-dem-Kulturkampf-um-die-Religion.html

Ramírez, F. O., Suárez, D., & Meyer, J. W [John W.]. (2007). The Worldwide Rise of Human Rights Education. In A. Benavot & C. Braslavsky (Eds.), CERC studies in comparative education: Vol. 18. School knowledge in comparative and historical perspective: Changing curricula in primary and secondary education (pp. 35–52). Comparative Education research Centre The University of Hong Kong; Springer. https://doi.org/10.1007/978-1-4020-5736-6_3

Riggan, J. (2016). The Struggling State: Nationalism, Mass Militarization, and the Education of Eritrea. Temple University Press. https://library.oapen.org/handle/20.500.12657/30057

Ríos-Rojas, A. (2014). Managing and Disciplining Diversity: The Politics of Conditional Belonging in a Catalonian Institut. Anthropology & Education Quarterly, 45(1), 2–21. https://doi.org/10.1111/aeq.12044

Rojas, F. (2017). Race and Institutionalism. In R. Greenwood, C. Oliver, T. B. Lawrence, & R. E. Meyer (Eds.), The SAGE Handbook of Organizational Institutionalism / The SAGE Handbook of organizational institutionalism [Second Edition], pp. 786–807). SAGE.

Rösch, A. (2018). Das Spannungsfeld von Wertbezogenheit und Neutralität im Ethikunterricht. In Z. Štimac & R. Spielhaus (Eds.), Eckert: Band 143. Schulbuch und religiöse Vielfalt: Interdisziplinäre Perspektiven (1st ed., pp. 79–92). V & R unipress. https://doi.org/10.14220/9783737007481.79

Roßmann, R. (2018, September 6). Seehofer zeigt Verständnis für Demonstranten: Cheminitz. Sueddeutsche Zeitung. https://www.sueddeutsche.de/politik/horst-seehofer-chemnitz-1.4118883

Roy, O. (2004). Globalized Islam: The search for a new ummah. The CERI series in comparative politics and international studies. Columbia Univ. Press.

Rubin, H. J., & Rubin, I. S. (2011). Qualitative Interviewing: The Art of Hearing Data. SAGE.

Rydgren, J. (2015). Xenophobia: The role of political articulation. In S. Vertovec (Ed.), Routledge international handbooks. Routledge international handbook of diversity studies (pp. 310–316). Routledge Taylor & Francis Group.

Sachverständigenrat für Integration und Migration. (2025, January 23). Ungleiche Bildungschancen: Fakten zur Benachteiligung von jungen Menschen mit Migrationshintergrund im deutschen Bildungssystem. https://www.svr-migration.de/wp-content/uploads/2025/01/SVR-Fakten-zu-ungleichen-Bildungschancen-2025.pdf

Saldaña, J. (2016). The coding manual for qualitative researchers (3. edition). SAGE.

Schiffauer, W. (2015). Schule, Moschee, Elternhaus: Eine ethnologische Intervention (Originalausgabe). Edition Suhrkamp: Vol. 2699. Suhrkamp Verlag.

Schluß, H. (2010). Die Kontroverse um ProReli: ein Rück- und Ausblick. Zeitschrift für Pädagogik und Theologie(2), 99–111. https://www.degruyter.com/document/doi/10.1515/zpt-2010-0202/html

Schmidtke, H.-P. (2005). Entwicklung der pädagogischen Betrachtungsweise – Ausländerpädagogik, interkulturelle Pädagogik, Pädagogik der Vielfalt. In R. Leiprecht & A. Kerber (Eds.), Reihe Politik und Bildung: Vol. 38. Schule in der Einwanderungsgesellschaft: Ein Handbuch (3. Aufl., pp. 142–161). Wochenschau-Verl.

Schneider, R. (2009, February 24). POSITIONEN: Der Unheilsprophet: Jürgen Zöllner war früher für ein Wahlpflichtfach Religion – und nun das! Tagesspiegel. https://www.tagesspiegel.de/meinung/der-unheilsprophet-7094182.html

Schönwälder, K. (2010). Germany: Integration policy and pluralism in a self-conscious country of immigration. In The Multiculturalism Backlash (pp. 162–179). Routledge. https://doi.org/10.4324/9780203867549-12

Seibert, H., Hupka-Brunner, S., & Imdorf, C. (2009). Wie Ausbildungssysteme Chancen verteilen: Berufsbildungschancen und ethnische Herkunft in Deutschland und der Schweiz unter Berücksichtigung des regionalen Verhältnisses von betrieblichen und schulischen Ausbildungen. Kölner Zeitschrift für Soziologie und Sozialpsychologie, 61(4), 595–620. https://doi.org/10.1007/s11577-009-0084-3

Sen, S. (2009, November 1). Der Tag, der Holland veränderte: Mord an Theo van Gogh. Der Spiegel. https://www.spiegel.de/geschichte/mord-an-theo-van-gogh-a-948574.html

Senatsverwaltung für Bildung, Jugend und Familie. (n. d.–a). Interne Statistik, Ethik Lehrer*innen 2015/2016. unveröffentlicht.

Schulgesetz für das Land Berlin. https://www.schulgesetz-berlin.de/berlin/schulgesetz/teil-ii-schulgestaltung/abschnitt-ii-gestaltung-von-unterricht-und-erziehung/sect-12-unterrichtsfaecher-lernbereiche-und-querschnittsaufgaben-lernfelder-ethik.php

Senatsverwaltung für Bildung, Jugend und Familie. (n.d.–b). Teilnehmerinnen und Teilnehmer am freiwilligen Religions- und Weltanschauungsunterricht im Land Berlin. unveröffentlicht.

Senatsverwaltung für Bildung, Jugend und Familie. (2015). Zahlen. Daten. Fakten: Ausgewählte Eckdaten Allgemein bildende Schulen 2015/2016. https://digital.zlb.de/viewer/api/v1/records/15331500_2015_2016/files/media/eckdaten_allgemeinbildende_schulen_2015_16.pdf

Senatsverwaltung für Bildung, Jugend und Familie. (2017, February 28). Anmeldezahlen für die weiterführenden Schulen 1.055 Plätze sind noch frei! [Press release].

https://www.berlin.de/sen/bjf/service/presse/pressearchiv-2018/pressemitteilung.680223.php

Senatsverwaltung für Bildung, Jugend und Familie. (2019). Politische Bildung an Berliner Schulen: Eine integrative Gesamtstrategie. https://www.berlin.de/sen/bildung/unterricht/politische-bildung/gesamtstrategie_politische_bildung_an_berliner_schulen.pdf

Shain, F. (2013). Race, nation and education. Education Inquiry, 4(1), 63–85. https://doi.org/10.3402/edui.v4i1.22062

Shamim, M. (2017). Muslims, schooling and security: Trojan Horse, Prevent and Racial Politics. Palgrave Macmillan. https://link.springer.com/content/pdf/10.1007/978-3-319-52335-4.pdf

Shen, J., D'Netto, B., & Tang, J. (2010). Effects of human resource diversity management on organizational citizen behaviour in the Chinese context. The International Journal of Human Resource Management, 21(12), 2156–2172. https://doi.org/10.1080/09585192.2010.509622

Shiao, J. L. (2005). Identifying talent, institutionalizing diversity: Race and philanthropy in post-civil rights America. Duke University Press.

Shirazi, R. (2017). When Schooling Becomes a Tactic of Security: Educating to Counter "Extremism". Diaspora, Indigenous, and Minority Education, 11(1), 2–5. https://doi.org/10.1080/15595692.2016.1253555

Shooman, Y. (2014). „… weil ihre Kultur so ist": Narrative des antimuslimischen Rassismus. Unbearb. zugl.: Berlin, Techn. Univ., Diss., 2013 u.d.T.: Shooman, Yasemin: „… weil ihre Kultur so ist": das Zusammenspiel von Kultur, Religion, Ethnizität, Geschlecht und Klasse im antimuslimischen Rassismus. Kultur und soziale Praxis. transcript. https://doi.org/10.1515/transcript.9783839428665

Simel, D. L. (1996). Exclusionary Christian Civil Religion for Jewish and Islamic Students in Bavarian Schools. Comparative Education Review, 40(1), 28–46. https://doi.org/10.1086/447354

Sincer, I., Severiens, S., & Volman, M. (2019). Teaching diversity in citizenship education: Context-related teacher understandings and practices. Teaching and Teacher Education, 78, 183–192. https://doi.org/10.1016/j.tate.2018.11.015

Skrentny, J. D. (2004). Minority Rights Revolution. Belknap Press. http://gbv.eblib.com/patron/FullRecord.aspx?p=3300032

Slavkin, M. L. (2012). The Holocaust and education: What impact did educators have on the implementation of anti-Judaic policies in 1930s Germany? Paedagogica Historica, 48(3), 431–449. https://doi.org/10.1080/00309230.2011.603345

Soysal, Y. N. (2011). Die "Kosmopolitisierung" von Staat und Bürgern: Ein europäisches Dilemma. In S. Stemmler (Ed.), Multikultur 2.0: Willkommen im Einwanderungsland Deutschland (pp. 131–141). Wallstein Verlag.

Soysal, Y. N., & Szakács, S. (2010). Reconceptualizing the Republic: Diversity and Education in France, 1945–2008. The Journal of Interdisciplinary History, 41(1), 97–115. https://doi.org/10.1162/jinh.2010.41.1.97

Soysal, Y. N., & Wong, S.-Y. (2007). Educating Future Citizens in Europe and Asia. In A. Benavot & C. Braslavsky (Eds.), CERC studies in comparative education: Vol. 18. School knowledge in comparative and historical perspective: Changing curricula in primary and secondary education (pp. 73–88). Comparative Education research Centre The University of Hong Kong; Springer. https://doi.org/10.1007/978-1-4020-5736-6_5

Spielhaus, R. (2014). Ein Muslim ist ein Muslim, ist ein Muslim … oder? Jugendliche zwischen Zuschreibung und Selbstbild. In W. e. Gayar & K. Strunk (Eds.), Integration versus Salafismus: Identitätsfindung muslimischer Jugendlicher in Deutschland; Analysen; Methoden der Prävention; Praxisbeispiele (pp. 20–37). Wochenschau Verlag.

Sponholz, L., Meuth, A.-M., Weiberg, M., Zajak, S., & Berger, S. (Eds.). (2025). Radicalizing the Mainstream in Western Europe: The Far Right and Narratives of Islam in Contemporary and Historical Perspective. Palgrave Macmillan Cham.

Statistisches Bundesamt. (2017). Statistisches Jahrbuch: Deutschland und Internationales. https://www.statistischebibliothek.de/mir/servlets/MCRFileNodeServlet/DEAusgabe_derivate_00001629/StatistischesJahrbuch2017.pdf

Stenzel, K. (2019, March 3). Kritik nach Karnevalssitzung: Kramp-Karrenbauer witzelt über Intersexuelle. Berliner Zeitung.

Stevens, M. L., Miller-Idriss, C., & Shami, S. K. (2018). Seeing the world: How US universities make knowledge in a global era. Princeton studies in cultural sociology. Princeton University Press.

Štimac, Z. (2014). Wir, die Anderen und die Fremden. Konstruktion von Religion in ausgewählten Ethikbüchern. In Non Fiktion. Schulbuch. Arsenal der anderen Gattungen.

Štimac, Z. (2015). Religiöse Pluralität in Ethikschulbüchern. Analyse ausgewählter Ethikbücher in östlichen und westlichen Bundesländern. In C. Bultmann & A. Linkenbach (Eds.), Vorlesungen des Interdisziplinären Forums Religion der Universität Erfurt: Vol. 11. Religionen übersetzen: Klischees und Vorurteile im Religionsdiskurs. Aschendorff.

Štimac, Z., & Spielhaus, R. (Eds.). (2018). Eckert: Band 143. Schulbuch und religiöse Vielfalt: Interdisziplinäre Perspektiven (1st ed.). V & R unipress.

Stringfellow, E. (2012). Trade unions and discourses of diversity management: A comparison of Sweden and Germany. European Journal of Industrial Relations, 18(4), 329–345. https://doi.org/10.1177/0959680112461094

Suárez-Orozco, C., Suárez-Orozco, M. M., & Todorova, I. (2008). Learning a New Land. Harvard University Press. https://doi.org/10.2307/j.ctv1m0kjvp

Suárez-Orozco, M. M. (Ed.). (2007). Learning in the global era: International perspectives on globalization and education. Univ. of California Press. http://www.loc.gov/catdir/enhancements/fy0806/2007018638-b.html

Suárez-Orozco, M. M., & Suárez-Orozco, C. (2009). Globalization, immigration, and schooling. In J. A. Banks (Ed.), Routledge international handbook series. The Routledge international companion to multicultural education (pp. 62–76). Routledge.

Sunier, T. (2013). Schooling and New Religious Diversity across Four European Countries. In J. R. Bowen (Ed.), Cambridge studies in law and society. European states and their Muslim citizens: The impact of institutions on perceptions and boundaries (1. pbk. ed.). Cambridge Univ. Press.

Süssmuth, R. (2007). On the Need of Teaching Intercultural Skills: Challenges for Education in a Globalized World. In M. M. Suárez-Orozco (Ed.), Learning in the global era: International perspectives on globalization and education (pp. 195–212). Univ. of California Press.

Swidler, A. (1986). Culture in Action: Symbols and Strategies. American Sociological Review, 51(2), 273. https://doi.org/10.2307/2095521

Szelei, N., & Alves, I. (2018). The missing link: Teacher learning for diversity in an area-based initiative in Portugal. CEPS Journal, 8(3), 79–98.

https://doi.org/10.25656/01:16006
Tarrow, S. (2012) Power in Movement: Social Movements and Contentious Politics. Cambridge University Press.
Taylor, C. (2007). A secular age (First Harvard University Press paperback edition). The Belknap Press of Harvard University Press.
Terkessidis, M. (2010). Interkultur. Lizenzausgabe für die Bundezentrale für politische Bildung.
Thomas, G. (2011). How to do your case study: A guide for students and researchers (Reprinted.). SAGE.
Thomsen Vierra, S. (2018). Turkish Germans in the Federal Republic of Germany: Immigration, space, and belonging, 1961-1990. Publications of the German Historical Institute. Cambridge University Press; German Historical Institute. https://doi.org/10.1017/9781108691475
Thornton, P. H., & Ocasio, W. (1999). Institutional Logics and the Historical Contingency of Power in Organizations: Executive Succession in the Higher Education Publishing Industry, 1958–1990. American Journal of Sociology, 105(3), 801–843. https://doi.org/10.1086/210361
Thornton, P. H., & Ocasio, W. (2008). Institutional Logics. In R. Greenwood, C. Oliver, T. B. Lawrence, & R. E. Meyer (Eds.), The SAGE handbook of organizational institutionalism (Second edition, pp. 99–129). SAGE.
Thornton, P. H., Ocasio, W., & Lounsbury, M. (2012). The institutional logics perspective: A new approach to culture, structure, and process. OUP Oxford. https://doi.org/10.1093/acprof:oso/9780199601936.001.0001
Tight, M. (2017). Case Study Research. In D. Wyse, N. Selwyn, E. Smith, & L. E. Suter (Eds.), The BERA/SAGE handbook of educational research. SAGE reference; BERA British educational research association.
Uitermark, J., Mepschen, P., & Duyvendak, J. W. (2013). Populism, Sexual Politics, and the Exclusion of Muslims in the Netherlands. In J. R. Bowen (Ed.), Cambridge studies in law and society. European states and their Muslim citizens: The impact of institutions on perceptions and boundaries (1. pbk. ed., pp. 235–255). Cambridge Univ. Press.
UNESCO. (2017). Making textbook content inclusive: A focus on religion, gender, and culture. https://unesdoc.unesco.org/ark:/48223/pf0000247337.locale=fr
United Nations. (n. d.). Equality and Non-Discrimination. https://www.un.org/ruleoflaw/thematic-areas/human-rights/equality-and-non-discrimination/
Urt. V. 23.02.2000, Az.: BVerwG 6 C 5/99 (Bundesverwaltungsgericht). https://www.judicialis.de/Bundesverwaltungsgericht_BVerwG-6-C-5-99_Urteil_23.02.2000.html
van Middelkoop, D., Ballafkih, H., & Meerman, M. (2017). Understanding diversity: a Dutch case study on teachers' attitudes towards their diverse student population. Empirical Research in Vocational Education and Training, 9(1). https://doi.org/10.1186/s40461-016-0045-9
Vavrus, F. K., & Bartlett, L. (2006). Comparatively Knowing: Making a Case for the Vertical Case Study. Current Issues in Comparative Education, 8(2). https://doi.org/10.52214/cice.v8i2.11410
Vavrus, F. K., & Bartlett, L. (Eds.). (2009). International & development education. Critical approaches to comparative education: Vertical case studies from Africa, Europe,

the Middle East, and the Americas (1st ed.). Palgrave Macmillan US. https://doi.org/10.1057/9780230101760

Vertovec, S. (2007). Super-diversity and its implications. Ethnic and Racial Studies, 30(6), 1024–1054. https://doi.org/10.1080/01419870701599465

Vertovec, S. (2011). Migration and new diversities in global cities: comparatively conceiving, observing and visualizing diversification in urban public spaces (MMG Working Paper 11-08). https://pure.mpg.de/pubman/faces/ViewItemOverviewPage.jsp?itemId=item_1388649

Vertovec, S. (2015). Introduction: Formulating Diversity Studies. In S. Vertovec (Ed.), Routledge international handbooks. Routledge international handbook of diversity studies (pp. 1–20). Routledge Taylor & Francis Group.

Vertovec, S. (2019). Diversifications (MMG Working Paper 19-03). https://www.mmg.mpg.de/339075/wp-19-03

Vertovec, S., & Wessendorf, S. (2010). Introduction: Assessing the backlash against multiculturalism in Europe. In S. Vertovec & S. Wessendorf (Eds.), The multiculturalism backlash: European discourses, policies and practices (pp. 1–31). Routledge.

Vieth-Entus, S. (2016, November 15). Zehn Jahre Ethik-Unterricht in Berlin: Das Thema „Ehrenmord" steht nicht im Lehrplan. Der Tagesspiegel. https://www.tagesspiegel.de/berlin/schule/das-thema-ehrenmord-steht-nicht-im-lehrplan-3773773.html

Vieth-Entus, S. (2018, January 24). Erfolg für Berlins Schülervertreter: Politik kommt aufs Zeugnis. Der Tagesspiegel. https://www.tagesspiegel.de/berlin/politik-kommt-aufs-zeugnis-3918721.html

Virchow, F., Häusler, A., & Döring, M. (2020). Pandemie-Leugnung und extreme Rechte in Nordrhein-Westfalen (CoRE-NRW Kurzgutachten, 3). https://www.ssoar.info/ssoar/handle/document/88176

Vu, V. (2018, July 11). Kein Witz. Zeit Online. https://www.zeit.de/gesellschaft/zeitgeschehen/2018-07/horst-seehofer-69-abschiebung-afghanistan-69-geburtstag-fluechtlinge

Weaver, M. (2010, October 17). Angela Merkel: German multiculturalism has 'utterly failed'. The Guardian. https://www.theguardian.com/world/2010/oct/17/angela-merkel-german-multiculturalism-failed

Weber, E. (1976). Peasants into Frenchmen: The modernization of rural France; 1870 - 1914 [Nachdr.]. Stanford Univ. Press.

Weber, M. (2003). Heterogenität im Schulalltag.: Konstruktion ethnischer und geschlechtlicher Unterschiede. Gefälligkeitsübersetzung: Heterogeneity in everyday school life. Construction of ethnic and gender differences. Leske und Budrich.

Wenger, E. (1998). Communities of Practice: Learning, Meaning, and Identity. Cambridge University Press.

Wenger, E. (2000). Communities of Practice and Social Learning Systems. Organization, 7(2), 225–246. https://doi.org/10.1177/135050840072002

Will, A.-K. (2019). The German statistical category "migration background". Advance online publication. https://doi.org/10.18452/20626

Willmott, H. (2015). Why Institutional Theory Cannot Be Critical. Journal of Management Inquiry, 24(1), 105–111. https://doi.org/10.1177/1056492614545306

Wilson, B. R. (2016). Religion in Secular Society: Fifty Years On. Oxford University Press; Oxford University Press.

Wilson, F. (2001). In the Name of the State? Schools and Teachers in an Andean Province. In T. B. Hansen & F. Stepputat (Eds.), States of Imagination: Ethnographic Exploration of the Postcolonial State (pp. 313–344). Duke University Press.

Wittmann, C. (2016, June 23). „Für mich war das wie ein Kulturschock!": Studium Islamische Theologie. Bayrischer Rundfunk. https://www.br.de/fernsehen/ard-alpha/sendungen/campus/islamische-theologie-universitaeten-studium-100.html

Wolff, S. (2015). Dokumenten- und Aktenanalyse. In U. Flick, E. von Kardorff, & I. Steinke (Eds.), Rororo Rowohlts Enzyklopädie: Vol. 55628. Qualitative Forschung: Ein Handbuch (11. Auflage). Rowohlt Taschenbuch Verlag.

Worden, E. A. (2011). The "Mock Reform" of History Education in Moldova: Actors versus the Script. Comparative Education Review, 55(2), 231–251. https://doi.org/10.1086/657999

Xifra, J. (2008). Soccer, civil religion, and public relations: Devotional–promotional communication and Barcelona Football Club. Public Relations Review, 34(2), 192–198. https://doi.org/10.1016/j.pubrev.2008.03.005

Ye, J. (2015). Situating diversity in the global city: Emerging challenges and possibilities in Singapore. In S. Vertovec (Ed.), Routledge international handbooks. Routledge international handbook of diversity studies (pp. 173–180). Routledge Taylor & Francis Group.

Yuan, H. (2017). Preparing Teachers for Diversity: A Literature Review and Implications from Community-Based Teacher Education. Higher Education Studies, 8(1), 9. https://doi.org/10.5539/hes.v8n1p9

Yuan, H. (2018). Educating Culturally Responsive Han Teachers: Case Study of a Teacher Education Program in China. International Journal of Multicultural Education, 20(2), 42–57. https://doi.org/10.18251/ijme.v20i2.1609

Yurdakul, G. (2006). Mobilizing Kreuzberg: Political Representation, Immigrant Incorporation and Turkish Associations in Berlin [Dissertation].

Yurdakul, G. (2024). Postmigrant thinking: Definition, critiques and a new offer. International Migration, 62(3), 120–123. https://doi.org/10.1111/imig.13269

Zajak, S., Steinhilper, E., & Sommer, M. (2023). Agenda setting and selective resonance – Black Lives Matter and media debates on racism in Germany. European Journal of Cultural and Political Sociology, 1–25. https://doi.org/10.1080/23254823.2023.2176335

Zawatka-Gerlach, U. (2009, April 18). Ethik und Religion: Zehn Jahre Gezerre um die Werte. Tagesspiegel. https://www.tagesspiegel.de/berlin/zehn-jahre-gezerre-um-die-werte-1753405.html

Zick, A., Küpper, B., & Berghan, W. (2019). Verlorene Mitte - feindselige Zustände: Rechtsextreme Einstellungen in Deutschland 2018/19. Friedrich-Ebert-Stiftung.

Zick, A., Küpper, B., Krause, D., & Berghan, W. (2016). Gespaltene Mitte - feindselige Zustände: Rechtsextreme Einstellungen in Deutschland 2016. Friedrich-Ebert-Stiftung; Verlag J.H.W. Dietz Nachf. http://www.fes-gegen-rechtsextremismus.de/pdf_16/Gespaltene%20Mitte_Feindselige%20Zust%C3%A4nde.pdf

Zick, A., Küpper, B., & Mokros, N. (2023). Die distanzierte Mitte: Rechtsextreme und demokratiegefährdende Einstellungen in Deutschland 2022/23. Verlag J.H.W. Dietz Nachf.

Ziemann, B. (2011). Religion and the Search for Meaning. In H. W. Smith (Ed.), The Oxford handbook of modern German history (1. publ, pp. 690–713). Oxford Univ. Press.

Appendix

Table 1: Overview of Schools in the Sample. Source: This study, and individual school statistics SEYS for the school year 2015/2016

School Number	Track Level	Level of Diversity	SES	Size[47]	Teachers interviewed
1	high	Diverse	Low	700	7
2	high	Diverse	Median	700	3
3	High	Non diverse	High	700	2
4	Low	Non diverse	high	900	2
5	Low	Non diverse	Median	800	1
6	Low	Diverse	Low	400	1
7	High	Non diverse	high	700	2
8	Low	Diverse	Low	1000	5
9	Low	Non diverse	Median	400	1
10	High	Non diverse	High	800	3
11	High	Diverse	median	800	3
12	Low	Diverse	High	1000	1
13	Low	Diverse	High	800	1
14	High	Non diverse	High	700	1
15	High	Non diverse	High	800	1
16	High	Non diverse	Median	800	1
17	High	Non diverse	High	900	4

---

47 Refers to the size of the student population from 7th through 10th or 12th grade. To protect the identity of the schools I provide the closest hundred, where 700 would mean more than 700 students but less than 800.

Table 2: Overview of Participants. Source: this study

Pseudonym/Gender	School	Religion	Career Level	Qualification
Herr Stade	1	n.a.	Late	Additional Training and University
Frau Summers	1	no	early	University
Frau Bern	1	no	Late	Additional Training
Frau Mutombo	1	Protestant	Late	Additional Training
Frau Hase	1	n.a.	Early	Additional Training
Frau Winkel	1	Protestant	Mid	Additional Training
Herr Romansky	1	n.a.	Early	Additional Training
Herr Joschua	2	Buddhist[48]	Mid	University
Herr Jagdmann	2	No	Early	University
Herr Alkim	2	no[49]	Mid	None
Frau Mussel	3	n.a.	Early	University
Frau Janka	3	n.a.	Early	University
Herr Lauda	4	n.a.	Mid	University
Frau Stollen	4	Christian	Mid	Additional Training
Frau Schuhmacher	5	n.a.	Early	University
Frau Singer	6	Catholic[50]	Late	Additional Training
Frau Zimmermann	7	n.a.	Late	Additional Training and University
Frau Wels	7	No	Early	University
Frau Ruediger	8	n.a.	Late	Additional Training
Herr Bock	8	Christian	Mid/late	None
Frau Smith	8	n.a.	Mid	None
Frau Nehls	8	Protestant	Mid	Additional Training
Herr Burkhardt	8	n.a.	Early	None
Herr Klausen	9	Agnostic	Early	None
Herr Alter	10	n.a.	Mid	University
Herr Dorn	10	n.a.	Mid	University
Herr Sawanitz	10	n.a.	Early	University
Herr Vogel	11	n.a.	Late	University
Herr Dachsen	11	no	Early	Additional Training
Frau Paul	11	n.a.	Mid	Additional Training

48   Converted from Protestantism.
49   Has a Christian mother and Muslim father but described himself as "anti-religious".
50   Explained that she left the church and can thus be considered non-practicing.

Pseudonym/Gender	School	Religion	Career Level	Qualification
Frau Boehm	12	n.a.	Mid	Additional Training and University
Herr Lock	13	Protestant[51]	Early	University
Herr Anderson	14	n.a.	Early	University
Frau Mayer	15	Protestant	Mid	University
Frau Muller	16	n.a.	Late	Additional Training
Herr Walter	17	No	Mid	None
Herr Supper	17	n.a.	Mid	University
Frau Bolton	17	Catholic	Mid	Additional Training and University
Herr Stark	17	Christian	Mid	None

---

51 Converted to Protestantism at age 14 from Catholicism.

Table 3: Comprehensive Chronological Order of Events Leading to the Introduction of Ethics Education in Berlin. Source: Compiled from multiple data sources

Date	Event	Level	Importance for the Introduction of Ethics in Berlin
6/11/1945 Reaffirmed 4/4/1946	first formulation of Berlin Modell of religious education (opt-in solution)	Federal State Berlin	The Russian occupation exercises their influence to demote RE from mandatory (opt out) subject to elective (opt in)
6/26/1948	adoption of school law for Berlin	Federal State Berlin	Justifies Berlin's claim on article 141 of the Constitution
5/23/1949	(West) German constitution takes effect	National Level	The German constitution took effect after Berlin's school law was passed
1951	CDU motions to make RE mandatory	Federal State Berlin	CDU tries to make RE a mandatory subject according to the GG – opt-out Model (cf. Häusler, 2007, p. 27) However, the Christian churches block this project as they fear to lose their right to determine the curriculum (cf. Gräb and Thieme, 2011, p. 32)
8/5/1952	School law for West Berlin	Federal State Berlin	West Berlin enacts its school law, keeping religious education as opt-in elective subject in full responsibility of the faith communities.
1970s	Multiple school reforms	Federal State Berlin	Change in the way the faith communities were compensated by the state (75% of salaries for RE teachers, 90% in 1986) and religious education can be taught in vocational colleges, however, it is no longer counted as subject for those in grades 11 and 12 and thus loses participants (cf. Gräb and Thieme, 2011, p. 33)
1988	CDU motions to make RE subject with grades	Federal State Berlin	Religious education is taught without grades and not relevant to move into the next grade level, the CDU tried to change this but failed due to opposition from its coalition partner FDP (Laurien, 1989, p. 5)
11/28/1988	Six Theses of Protestant Church	Federal State Berlin	The Protestant church publicly advocates for the opt-out solution for the first time. (cf. Gräb and Thieme, 2011, p. 34
11/9/1989, 10/3/1990	Fall of the Berlin Wall and German Reunification	National Level	Influx of former East Berlin into West Berlin's governing structure
12/2/1990	Election	Federal State Berlin	Big coalition of SPD and CDU; PDS and Green party move into opposition
School year 1991/92	West-Berlin education law is effective for all East-Berlin districts	Federal State Berlin	East Berlin districts are now also subject to paragraph 141 GG, Berlin has a unified school law (Häusler, 2007, p. 29)
August 1992	Start of LER Modell trial	Federal State Brandenburg	Berlin anticipated the merger of Berlin and Brandenburg and thus watched this trial run closely; a model that could easily reconciled with Brandenburg's model was to be found
November 1992	"Conception for the introduction of a subject combination Religion – Ethics"	Federal State Berlin	Presented by members of the CDU to the senate, this document establishes the CDUs support of a two-subject solution (cf. Beschorner, 2006, p. 71)
September 1994	Start of Ethics/ Philosophy Trial in Berlin	Federal State Berlin	First trial run to test an opt-out model for Berlin, started with eleven schools in 1994/1995 with a total of 684 participating students which was 45.4% of the student body eligible to participate at these schools (30.6% participated in Christian religious education, and 24% chose neither), and would eventually expand to 37 schools total
10/22/1995	Election	Federal State Berlin	Governing coalition of CDU and SPD; PDS and Green Party move into the opposition

Date	Event	Level	Importance for the Introduction of Ethics in Berlin
July 1996	Constitutional complaint against LER in Brandenburg	Federal State Brandenburg	The catholic and protestant church of Berlin and Brandenburg file a constitutional complaint against LER in Brandenburg, claiming it restricts students' and parents' constitutionally granted right of religious freedom; Berlin's government closely watches the legal trial to evaluate possible legal opposition to new solutions in Berlin
8/24/1998 Struck down in the subcommittees on 5/10/1999, 5/27/1999, 6/16/1999	motion to change school law by CDU	Federal State Berlin	This motion proposed the introduction of the opt-out model in Berlin for the school year 1999/2000, this model would abandon Berlin's claim on article 141 of the German constitution
11/4/1998	Islamic Federation accepted as faith community in Berlin	Federal State Berlin	The high administrative court of Berlin accepts the Islamic Federation as a legitimate faith community able to provide RE according to Berlin's school law. Berlin's government files an appeal with the federal administrative court.
10/10/1999	Election	Federal State Berlin	Governing coalition with CDU and SPD, PDS and Green Party move into the opposition
December 1999	Klaus Böger positions himself in favor of out-out model	Federal State Berlin	Against his own party's position, the new senator for education publicly advocates for an opt-out solution (Zawatka-Gerlach, 2009)
2/23/2000	Verdict of the federal administrative court about IRE in Berlin	National Level and Federal State Berlin	The federal administrative court decides that the Islamic Federation is allowed to teach IRE in Berlin (*Urt. V. 23.02.2000, Az.: BVerwG 6 C 5/99*, 2000)
6/18/2001 Struck down in the subcommittees on 9/20/2001, 9/27/2001	Motion to change school law	Federal State Berlin	The CDU again motions to change Berlin's school law to introduce an out-out solution for moral, values and religious education.
10/21/2001	Election	Federal State Berlin	After a corruption scandal that cost the state millions, the big coalition breaks, and new elections take place. SPD and PDS become the new governing parties, CDU, FDP and Green Party move into the opposition.
12/11/2001	Consensual compromise in LER case	National Level and Federal State Brandenburg	The Federal Constitutional Court reaches a compromise that mandates that LER is no longer mandatory. Instead, parents and students may choose whether to participate in either LER or religious education (opt-out of LER for religious education).
6/24/2003 Enacted 1/15/2004 Effective 2/1/2004	Draft of new school law (D297)	Federal State Berlin	New regulation of religious education in paragraph 13 (was §23 and 24): addition of clause speaking to the eligibility of faith communities, and the education of those teaching religious education for the faith communities
11/22/2004	Böger speaks about introduction of LER in Berlin in newspaper interview	Federal State Berlin	Senator for education Klaus Böger speaks about the introduction of a mandatory subject (LER) in Berlin and the finished draft of a corresponding new law (Nowakowski et al., 2004)
2/7/2005	Murder Hatan Sürücü	Federal State Berlin	A young woman of Kurdish descent is murdered by her youngest brother in Berlin; students of a nearby lower secondary school (Hauptschule) endorse the murder which leads to an intensification of the discussions about value education in Berlin and adds significant public and political pressure to the matter (Miller et al., 2005)

Date	Event	Level	Importance for the Introduction of Ethics in Berlin
3/15/2005, 4/9/2005	Party conventions of PDS and SPD about education	Federal State Berlin	Both governing parties hold conventions and decide to move forward a mandatory subject to teach values and morals in Berlin.
4/13/2005	Federal government discusses Berlin's plans for value education	National Level	Discussion of the issue in the Bundestag, many leaders of the federal SPD speak out against the plans of Berlin's SPD to implement a mandatory subject. This is especially remarkable since education policy is regulated at the Länder level, and the federal government has no jurisdiction in the matter.
6/2/2005	Protest by catholic and protestant church and Jewish community	Federal State Berlin	Christian churches hand over a list of 50,000 signatures against a mandatory subject (Gräb and Thieme, 2011, p. 49)
6/10-11/ 2005	Angela Merkel speech	National Level	Chancellor Merkel speaks in front of the protestant wing of the CDU/CSU against mandatory ethics and in favor of RE as the only way to teach values and morals (Merkel, 2005)
2/6/2006	Committee hearing	Federal State Berlin	Committee for education hears stakeholders on the issue: present are representatives of protestant and catholic churches, teacher union, action coalition for value education, Alevite community, Islamic federation, humanistic association, and Berlin's commissioner for integration[52]
3/23/2006	Senate votes for change of school law	Federal State Berlin	Against CDU and FDP, Ethics as a new mandatory subject for Berlin is confirmed in §12.6. It is to be implemented in steps starting with grade 7 in 2006/2007, adding grade 8 in 2007/2008, 9 in 2008/2009 and 10 in 2009/2010.
11/23/2006 Later rejected on federal level 3/15/2007	Lawsuit against mandatory participation in ethics	Federal State Berlin	A student and her parents sued Berlin over the mandatory participation in Ethics in Berlin's high administrative court, arguing that Ethics is not neutral and thus violates her right of religious freedom. The court decided against her. The suit was later rejected by the Federal Constitutional court. (cf. Gräb and Thieme, 2011, p. 50)
March 2007	Pro Reli e. V. is founded	Federal State Berlin	Association with the goal to start a referendum and change the school law in favor of the two-subject solution.
November 2007	Signatures for referendum	Federal State Berlin	Pro Reli has collected enough signatures to move to the second phase of a referendum
5/20/2008	Pro Ethics is founded	Federal State Berlin	The association was founded from various previous associations that had fought in favor of mandatory ethics instruction in Berlin.
9/22/2008 To 1/9/2009	Second Phase of signature collection starts	Federal State Berlin	Pro Reli had to collect at least 140,000 (7% of the voting population) signatures for the referendum to take place. By the end they were able to present 265,823 (10.9%) signatures and thus the referendum had to take place.
4/26/2009	Referendum	Federal State Berlin	51.4% of the votes were against a law change and thus the implementation of the two-subject solution (voter turnout at 29.2%). Thus, mandatory Ethics stayed in Berlin's schools. RE remained an elective.[53]

52 A representative of the Jewish community was invited but was unable to attend the hearing. However, the Jewish community had previously sided with the Christian churches on the issue (cf. Beschorner, 2006, p. 83; Gräb and Thieme, 2011, p. 49).

53 The votes were distributed clearly across old East and West Berlin borders. Voters in the former East wanted ethics to remain. Voters in the former West were predominately in favor of a two-subject solution with religious education as mandatory and an opt-out option and Ethics as the place for students who did not want to participate in religious education.

Index

belonging 16, 30, 41, 47, 50, 56, 80, 94, 98, 100, 108, 109, 110, 131, 143, 144

community 5, 19, 34, 36, 38, 42, 44, 47, 48, 51, 64, 69, 71, 74, 78, 79, 80, 82, 83, 87, 88, 89, 92, 94, 102, 107, 114, 121, 125, 137, 140, 142, 144, 172, 173, 174

conviviality 24, 132, 133, 136, 144

culture 24, 26, 27, 30, 35, 41, 42, 43, 45, 46, 69, 72, 82, 84, 87, 88, 91, 95, 96, 97, 98, 99, 100, 102, 103, 104, 120, 121, 132, 134, 135, 138

discrimination 18, 23, 30, 46, 48, 49, 106, 112, 113, 124, 133, 137, 140, 141, 142

ethnicity 24, 45, 59

exclusion 19, 20, 23, 28, 32, 37, 47, 48, 49, 101, 111, 112, 127, 133, 137, 138, 140

extremism 23, 24, 26, 79, 80, 141

far-right 20, 32, 139, 141

imagination 19, 20, 43, 44, 48, 50, 51, 52, 62, 85, 89, 90, 92, 109, 112, 114, 121, 122, 126, 127, 128, 129, 130, 131, 135, 137, 141, 142, 143

immigration 15, 20, 24, 27, 28, 29, 30, 31, 32, 34, 43, 80, 91, 112, 133, 134, 138, 144

inclusion 14, 20, 23, 25, 26, 28, 30, 32, 34, 37, 47, 49, 51, 56, 104, 111, 137

institutional logics 19, 35, 38, 39, 42, 43, 45, 47, 52, 56, 57, 94, 112, 113, 114, 130

integration 17, 21, 22, 23, 24, 26, 28, 29, 30, 31, 32, 34, 35, 37, 38, 46, 55, 70, 73, 78, 82, 83, 85, 87, 90, 91, 92, 106, 107, 110, 111, 130, 133, 137, 139, 141, 143, 144, 174

Islam 16, 24, 30, 33, 68, 73, 79, 80, 89, 91, 97, 98, 99, 132, 133, 136

legitimacy 19, 36, 40, 43, 46, 74, 86, 90, 112, 113, 114, 115, 116, 118, 119, 120, 122, 125, 126, 127, 128, 129, 130, 131, 135, 136, 137

migration 14, 15, 16, 17, 18, 21, 22, 28, 29, 31, 34, 45, 46, 47, 59, 66, 67, 96, 100, 133, 140

multiculturalism 26, 31, 44, 80, 132

neo-institutional 39, 40, 44, 47, 52, 130

policymaking 29, 32, 35, 36, 38, 40, 41, 43, 47, 50, 52, 53, 56, 78, 91, 128, 129, 131, 143

post-migration 28

sense-making 43, 44, 46, 53, 92, 94, 95, 107, 108, 109, 110, 117, 131

vertical case study 18, 35, 38, 52, 53, 55, 56, 70, 128

Claudia Equit (ed.)

Participation in Residential Childcare

Safeguarding children's rights through participation and complaint procedures

2024 • 255 pp. • Pb. • 54,90 € (D) • 56,50 € (A)
ISBN 978-3-8474-2709-4 • available as e-book in open access

Article 12 of the UN Convention on the Rights of the Child establishes the right to participation: children and adolescents are entitled to participate and to have their views taken into account in all issues affecting them in accordance to their age and maturity.

The volume explores this right to participation in residential care. The impact of participation and complaint procedures in residential care facilities are evaluated by means of crucial results from an empirical study. How do these participation and complaints procedures work? The authors discuss crucial facilitators and barriers with regard to the implementation of children's rights to participate.

www.shop.budrich.de